GLOBALIZATION AND THE DECLINE OF SOCIAL REFORM:

Into the Twenty-first Century

Other works by Gary Teeple

Capitalism and the National Question in Canada (ed.)
Marx's Critique of Politics

GLOBALIZATION AND THE

DECLINE OF SOCIAL REFORM:

Into the Twenty-first Century

Gary Teeple

Department of Sociology and Anthropology

Simon Fraser University

Garamond Press
Aurora, Ontario

Humanity
Books

an imprint of Prometheus Books
59 John Glenn Drive, Amherst, New York 14228-2197

Printed and bound in Canada

A publication of Garamond Press

Editor: Robert Clarke
Typesetting and Layout: Robin Brass Studio/Gerda Rowlands
Publisher: Peter R. Saunders

Cover photo courtesy C.I.D.A.

Garamond Press,
63 Mahogany Court
Aurora ON L4G 6M8

Canadian Cataloguing in Publication Data

Teeple, Gary, 1945–
    Globalization and the decline of social reform : into the 21ˢᵗ century

2ⁿᵈ ed.

Includes bibliographical references and index.
ISBN 1-55193-026-9

1. International economic relations - Social aspects.   2. Welfare state.
3. Capitalism   I. Title.

HX44.5.T44 2000   909.82'9   C99-932444-6

Published 2000 by Humanity Books, an imprint of
Prometheus Books

First published in the United States of America in 1995 by
Humanities Press International Inc.
Atlantic Highlands, NJ

Library of Congress Cataloging-in-Publication Data

A catalog record for this book is available from the Library of Congress

ISBN 1-57392-873-9

To my daughters, Anna and Emma

Contents

Acknowledgements

As always there are many contributors in one way or another to published works. I would like again to thank Peter Saunders, who was continuously encouraging and critically perceptive; and Robert Clarke, whose reading and editing of the argument were as always incisive, clear, and thoughtful. I must also thank in particular Trevor Anderson, Steve McBride, and Cyril Smith, for their comments or discussions on various parts of this second edition. And a special thanks to Monica Escudero for her encouragement and patience, among many other things.

Acknowledgements for the 1995 Edition

I am very grateful to a number of people who helped to clarify the ideas in this book and who through their comments and criticism encouraged its completion.

Foremost among these was my good friend and colleague Hamish Dickie-Clark at Simon Fraser University, who read two drafts of the manuscript and gave his time generously for any discussions of it I wished to have. Chris Pickvance at the University of Kent graciously found the time to read the first draft and give his suggestions, which were very helpful. Also at the University of Kent, I presented parts of the argument to a graduate seminar in the Department of Politics and to a faculty seminar in Social Sciences, both of which provided me with valuable criticisms and forced clarification of several ideas. Comments from David McLellan were especially useful.

Ron Brown and Leonard McCannon made constructive suggestions that made me rethink parts of the argument. In an external review, Professor John Holmes at Queen's University made several salutary points that aided my revisions for this final version. Peter Saunders of Garamond Press was an enthusiastic publisher from the beginning, and his encouragement was always welcome during the long period of writing and revising. Thanks also to Robert Clarke, who not only did a thoughtful job of copy-editing, but also made many helpful substantive suggestions.

No work, however modest, is ever completed without the assistance of a great many people along the way, and I thank all who helped or encouraged this small book to its conclusion.

Preface

Following its publication in 1995, *Globalization and the Decline of Social Reform* became a relatively popular text in universities, community colleges, and various non-government organizations and agencies. Given the continuing interest in the subject and the many global changes since the book appeared, the publisher proposed a second edition.

About seven years separate the completion of the writing of the book and this second edition, and the intervening period has made the reality of globalization more apparent and, I think, affirmed the arguments made in the text. During this time there have been no empirical developments, or reviews of the book, to suggest that the central argument did not broadly, albeit briefly, capture the meaning and implications of globalization. For this reason, I have restricted changes to the existing text to an expansion of chapter IV and minor, mostly stylistic, revisions elsewhere.

To complement and update the text, however, it was thought useful to elaborate on and add some key points in additional chapters. Given the rapid growth of a body of literature on globalization but the persistent lack of consensus and continuing debate on its meaning, further clarification of the definition seemed appropriate, and this I have tried to do in three ways.

First, to understand any phenomenon properly we must have an account of its origins. For this reason I have expanded the discussion of the preconditions of globalization in chapter IV, with a focus on the reciprocal relation between the rise of transnational corporations and the creation of a global "enabling framework." Amongst the preconditions is the technological basis of this new stage in capitalist development, and so I try to make a more convincing case that the impetus behind globalization has been the transformation in the means of production, distribution, and communication.

Second, given the difficulties of conceptualizing the phenomenon of globalization, a new chapter, "Globalization as the Second Bourgeois Revolution," takes up a definition by analogy. This new chapter VII makes an analogy to the transformations that took place with the coming of the first bourgeois revolutions, most of which occurred in the eighteenth and nineteenth centuries. Too often we assume implicitly the continuous existence of a world of capitalist nation-states, without recognizing that those states came into existence at a certain point in history; and like the social, political, and economic structures that they displaced, they too will necessarily be displaced or transformed. This, we suggest, is the meaning of the process of globalization.

Third, a sobering way to clarify a concept is to examine critically the arguments made by those with sceptical views. With this in mind, a new chapter VIII, "A Critique of the Sceptics," continues with a critical review of some current objections to the idea of globalization. By addressing counterarguments, we can analyse and assess the shortcomings of the concept and the nature of the reality conceptualized.

Some criticisms of the first edition pointed to a certain sense of despair that it seemed to engender. This was hardly my intention, but it was perhaps a byproduct of the focus on the nature of globalization and its implications rather than on the global responses. I have tried to address this problem in a final note, chapter IX, "The Question of Resistance and Alternatives," by examining the new contradictions that globalization brings and the consequent necessity for new forms of resistance and alternatives. For a least two decades a wide variety of attempts at opposition have been carried out; some of them were doomed at the outset by their sheer spontaneity or lack of understanding of the issues involved, but more of them have increasingly been carried out with a clear sense of what it is that has to be defeated and why and what is needed in the future. There can be no successful opposition without knowledge of what it is that is opposed or without knowledge of the principles of the future that is desired.

Introduction

The 1980s was a watershed decade, a turning point in the history of capitalism. It was a period that witnessed the beginning of the end of a vast system of collective or state property in the so-called socialist countries, the establishment of computer-aided modes of production and distribution, the arrival of the global economy, and the adoption around the world of neo-liberal policies whose principle was the unrestrained economic power of private property. The decade signified the beginning of what has been called the triumph of capitalism.

For every triumph, there is a defeat. Visible in this decade was the apparent end of the achievements of the preceding decades, in which rebellion, revolution, and reform had sought to rectify injustices inherent in capitalism. The dismantling of the social and economic reforms to the laissez-faire economy, which had brought degrees of "distributive justice" and class "harmony" and had assisted in the consolidation and expansion of national capital formations over many decades, began in earnest.

These reforms, which culminated in the post-World War II period as the Keynesian welfare state (KWS), rested on certain economic and political conditions that had made their continued improvement possible. By the end of the 1970s the erosion of these conditions, a consequence of the internationalization of capital, new means of production, and declining national growth, had undermined the continuing expansion of reforms. Economic stagnation and inflation appeared in most of the industrial countries as the continuing expectations of the Keynesian era clashed with the new imperatives of the coming global economy. In the 1980s capital moved decisively beyond its historic political shell, the nation-state and its associated mitigating forces and influences.

The conditions allowing for social and economic reforms from the late nineteenth century to the 1970s also produced a corresponding political phenomenon in the shape of *social democracy*. Parties of this persuasion gave political voice to social strata within the working class whose immediate interests, while not those of capital, were tied to the success of capitalism and were embodied in reforms. By the 1980s, as these strata began to be levelled and the economic and political conditions permitting reforms went into decline, social democracy began to lose its social base and political purpose, and everywhere adopted policies and programs similar to those of parties representing the corporate sector. From a choice of more or less reform to the system, politics became mainly a choice of style.

By the 1970s this same economic transformation had called forth neo-liberal political and economic theories and public policies, directly challenging the social and economic reforms of the postwar era. Now introduced into almost every country of the world, neo-liberal policies are the *hallmark of the transition between two eras.* They are the policy changes that will "harmonize" the world of national capitals and nation-states, creating a global system of internationalized capital and supranational institutions. Such global organization represents the coming demise of long-established social and political institutions in the industrial nation-states.

Neo-liberalism as economic theory had a long period of gestation in the works of Ludwig von Mises, Friedrich Hayek, and Milton Friedman, among others. It was in 1973, however, that the theory received its first opportunity to be applied, to become the subject of an experiment in a given nation. In that year, the military coup d'état in Chile put an end to democracy, to the reforms of the welfare state, to the trade union movement, and to civil liberties. For several years after, the regime tortured and put to death many thousands of people. Into this Washington-inspired dictatorship came the "Chicago Boys," "free marketeer" economists hired to restructure Chilean society, attempting to place it on a foundation of "market forces" with a minimal state.[1] The coup d'état, as well as the subsequent military-police state and the abrogation of all aspects of democracy and reform, made for optimal conditions for this first attempt to create a resolutely market society, for this experiment to minimize the role of the state in social and economic life.

By the mid-1970s, neo-liberalism had become a distinctive influence in most existing conservative parties around the world; and it soon became, though not without internal struggle, the mainstay of party policy. Yet overall it appeared as only one party platform among others. As Thatcherism or Reaganism or monetarism or neo-conservatism, moreover, it seemed then to be a form of anomalous political extremism, a modern caricature of pre-nineteenth-century social contract theory. By the early 1980s its proponents had taken over most conservative parties and then increasingly won political power.

The opposition parties – liberal or social-democratic – at first decried the "free market" vision and the attack on social reforms. Yet, within a short time they gradually began to adopt similar policies or openly to declare no intention of reversing legislation designed to implement the vision of the "new right." Even where the electorate replaced conservative parties in power with liberal or social-democratic parties with a certain expectation of maintaining or protecting the reformist gains of the postwar period, the new governments proved eventually to be at least as committed to neo-liberalism as their political opposites. Such has been the case more or less around the world: in New Zealand, Australia, France, Portugal, Spain, the United Kingdom, and in the Canadian provinces of Ontario, British Columbia, and Saskatchewan. Even where social-democratic parties have been in power for long periods, as in the Scandinavian countries, they have had little choice in recent years, given their commitment to capitalism, but to adopt such policies.[2]

Neo-liberalism has increasingly come to appear as a set of ideas "whose time has come," while social democracy, trade unionism, and the Keynesian welfare state have begun to appear more and more anachronistic. As the conditions for the postwar expansion of capital gradually waned, and as the great compromise between labour and capital in the industrial world began to come apart, the state was portrayed as a behemoth strangling the efforts and initiatives of the market, and the reforms of the welfare state came under attack in theory and practice. The vaunted "reformed capitalism" of the postwar period appeared to be increasingly "unworkable," its political proponents naive, and its costs "unaffordable."

At the same time the political options for government seemingly narrowed, with a corresponding growth in political apathy and cynicism about politics and politicians. The idea that politics determines national policies has gradually dissipated, and in its place has come the open assertion that economics is the deciding factor in more and more aspects of society. As two business commentators put it, "Economics is, *au fond*, the driving force behind politics in the modern world."[3] The social and political possibilities and illusions built on postwar economic prosperity within the industrialized nation-state had begun to disintegrate.

Although the new right agenda reflects the interests of internationalized capital and goes far to advance the possibilities for accumulation on a global scale, it also accelerates the consequences of this consolidation of the rule of capital. The general trends of capitalist development in the industrial nations are hindered less and less by national social and economic reform. As a result, there is a progressive increase in economic inequality, with structural unemployment and poverty growing continuously; the trends in planetary pollution and environmental destruction continue to deepen; there is a decline in national sovereignty, with autocratic rule and coercive social control gradually becoming more common and alternations of the party in power increasingly meaningless; and there are widespread legislative assaults on wages, trade union rights, and labour standards. The victory of capital hastens its own very visible limitations.

These consequences have not gone unchallenged, for at the same time countermovements, opposition, and challenges of all sorts have been expanding, both outside and inside the mainstream economic and political systems. While these alternatives and resistance are growing, the odds they face are enormous. The continuing legitimacy of the system, the persistent national "mind-set," hegemonic corporate control over the mass media, the conservatism of the trade unions, the concerted counterattacks by the state and representatives of capital, the paucity of financial resources, the growing sense of disillusionment, cynicism, and impotence, and the inadequate analysis of the present situation have all conspired to limit the growth of resistance and alternatives. The opposition, however, is far from moribund or non-existent, and much of it remains latent.

The profound and dramatic changes of the past decade or so raise many questions about all aspects of the post-World War II status quo. What is the nature of reforms, and why has social change in the industrial nations taken the shape of reform and not revolution? Why has the political voice of the organized working class taken the form of social democracy and not more radical political parties? Why do reforms and social democracy no longer seem viable as solutions to a host of growing problems? Why is the "reformed capitalism" we have taken for granted coming undone, and a new set of principles in the form of neo-liberalism gaining currency in theory and practice? What will a system of reproduction based primarily on the principles of the market mean for the future?

The pivotal point of the following argument is that we have entered a transitional era between two phases in the development of capitalism. In this period there has been a profound shift from a mode of production based on semi-automated processes, sometimes referred to as advanced Fordism, to a more automated mode based on microelectronics and computer applications. In this transition, in which nationally based economic development has been more or less transfigured into a self-generating global economy, all the social and political institutions associated with the national economy come into question and indeed begin to undergo a commensurate transformation.

Central to this transition are the neo-liberal policies and programs now being introduced around the world. These current changes in public policy are no mere ideological impositions, able to be reversed with the election of different political parties; they are, rather, the political reflection of the present transformation in the mode of production and the decline of nationally based economic development. They reflect the demands of new forms of production and the global market, accompanied by the undermining of modes of resistance to national capital by working classes and the change of conditions that once allowed for national compromises between capital and labour. In short, they represent the conscious retrenchment of national state intervention in the spheres of social reproduction. The neo-liberal agenda is the social and political counterpart to the globalization of production, distribution, and exchange.

To understand these neo-liberal changes, it is necessary first to have a grasp of what it is that is being changed. The argument begins, in chapter I, with an examination of the general reasons for the rise of the welfare state in industrial societies, of the complex rationale for the existence of social reform given the structure of national capitalism. If the welfare state arises over decades and comes to its "full" development only in a certain era, then, it can be defined as a product of a historical period in the development of capitalism, as resting on a certain national and international configuration of social forces, ideas, and political and economic institutions. Given this, we can also attempt to uncover the meaning implicit in social reform, to see the nature of its limitations. In general, the chapter is intended to address the question of what it is that neo-liberal policies are designed to undo.

If the welfare state arose out of certain conditions in a particular stage in the evolution of capitalism, the political structures, parties, and ideals in which it was represented have rested on similar foundations. Chapter II makes a case against the notion that the Keynesian welfare state was anything more than the political manifestation of a common phase in the national development of capitalism. It follows that the class basis of social democracy, the main political expression of the principles of social reform, must be grasped if we are to understand why the road to reform and not revolution was taken. A brief exploration of the nature of social-democratic policies helps to show their consistency with the demands of national capitalist classes in a particular era.

Similarly, an examination of the impact of social reform and social democracy on social inequality and of the nature of social redistribution, in chapter III, complements the arguments that neither the KWS nor social democracy has ever implied a fundamental transformation of capitalism and that they have both rested on historical preconditions that are now passing away.

The coming of the global economy and the nature and implications of the transition that began after World War II, culminating in the 1970s, are the focus of chapter IV. Several qualitative changes distinguish the arrival of the global economy from the preceding era of international economic relations. It is the consequences of globalization for social reform and social democracy that are pertinent here; the same changes wrought by globalization are the rationale for neo-liberalism.

For analytical purposes the main policies of neo-liberalism can be grouped into several categories, according to their meaning and implications. There is, to be sure, a common element to them all, namely, the principle of corporate private property, and its defence and advancement; this fundamental factor embodies the attack on the welfare state represented by neo-liberalism. Chapter V focuses on the many sides of this attack.

Chapter VI considers the implications of the global economy and neo-liberalism and briefly addresses several key questions: the multifaceted meaning of the triumph of capitalism at the global level; the immediate dilemmas that confront the existing political parties; the possibilities of developing alternatives and resistance to the international economy; and, last, the import of a global economy without resistance or reforms.

In an attempt to clarify the phenomenon of globalization, chapter VII draws an analogy between the current transformation and the historical rise of capitalism to national economic and political pre-eminence. Chapter VIII examines the many sceptical views put forward about the concept and its implications. A final chapter points to some of the new contradictions engendered by globalization – contradictions that must be grasped and analysed in order to mount effective opposition and pose alternatives to this world in transition.

The triumph of capitalism, or the unmitigated rule of corporate private property, is unlikely to be benign, as attested by the example of Chile, among other nations, by the structural adjustment policies of the International Monetary Fund and the World Bank, and by growing disparities in wealth everywhere. It is now apparent that the social and political consequences of a single world market ruled by the coercive force of "economic justice" will be marked by increasing fear, poverty, and unfreedom. For that reason, resistance and alternatives to it should not be left merely to evolve. They must be made the subject of another conscious but counter agenda that is international in scope.

I

Social Reform
and Capitalism

Since the 1970s enormous changes have taken place in social policy and economic regulation in the industrial nations. A transformation is well under way, and the neo-liberal policies of governments around the world provide numerous examples of conscious efforts to undermine, retrench, or eliminate long-standing social welfare programs and regulatory agencies.[1] Regardless of the social and economic insecurity they engender, these policies appear to be the main items on government agendas everywhere.

Contrary to the images cast by the mass media, however, the majority of citizens in most industrial countries remain in favour of the reforms that have come to be known as the welfare state. Despite more than a decade of concerted attempts to undermine these reforms, and despite repetitious declarations, even by left-wing writers, that "welfarism" has lost its public favour, that "big government" is a major if not the central problem, that state intervention in the economy inhibits growth, and that neo-liberalism has won the battle for "moral hegemony," the reforms comprising the welfare state have shown a remarkable resilience and continuing popular support.[2]

That most citizens are in favour of the social and economic reforms that have been achieved since World War II should not be surprising. Capitalist society is characterized by contradictory interests, divided fundamentally between those who own the means of production and distribution and those who do not. By virtue of this ownership, the business sector possesses enormous power over a highly stratified working-class majority. *Without reforms* such a society would be marked by extreme fear and unalloyed exploitation stemming from unmitigated differences in wealth, ownership, and power. Given the constant demand by corporations above all to maximize profit, their power would be used to reduce standards to the lowest possible levels; and given a competitive labour market without reforms, wages and conditions of work in general would be driven down to "minimums." Because the reforms achieved have offered a degree of security from the labour market it has now become difficult to imagine such conditions, even though it was not so long ago when reforms were few or non-existent and the effects of "unreformed" capitalism plain to see.[3]

Even in capitalist societies *with reforms*, pervasive fear, although often implicit, remains – particularly of unemployment and of the financial consequences of illness, injury, childbirth, or old age. This is because reforms are still just reforms; that is, they rarely provide more than minimal support and certainly give no guarantee that membership in society will bring employment, decent housing, accessible education, freedom from poverty, a living pension in old age or in sickness, an un-polluted environment, or higher employment standards. For the most part, social reforms provide only limited security or standards for a par-ticular need; and while these "minimums" can be raised, they can also be lowered. Given present widespread budgetary cutbacks, restrictions to reforms, and rising unemployment, these fears have become explicit for growing numbers of people in the labour force. Unemployment rates in most of the industrial nations since the late 1980s continue to be high, yet the statistics do not normally take into account underemployment, part-time work, or those who have given up looking for work. The glo-bal rate of long-term or structural unemployment, moreover, continues to rise despite the continual narrowing of the definition.[4]

Such fears in the industrial nations are at the very least implicit, but there can be little doubt about the consequences of retrenchment and even elimination of social reforms. Examples of capitalist societies with minimal or no reforms are close at hand. Here are found workplaces without standards, child labour, coerced workforces, high rates of illit-eracy, environmental degradation and destruction, and enormous dis-parities in wealth. These are largely the direct or indirect result of corporate activity with few or no restraints. In general the simplest regulations must be imposed upon capital, and even these are often re-sisted by the corporations, at enormous expense. In areas poorly or not regulated by a political state – in the Third World, in the newly in-dustrialized countries (NIC), in free-trade zones (FTZ), and in the high seas or the global atmosphere – the disregard of the well-being of nature and human beings is extreme.[5]

If the future of social reform in the industrial nations appears to be one of continuous retrenchment, it has placed the question of the nature of the welfare state and the reasons for its decline at centre stage. We can, then, begin to understand the present dismantling of welfare systems around the world by examining the origins of the welfare state and the principles and rationale of reforms.

The Origins of the Welfare State

The introduction of social reforms has varied in time and circumstance across nations. If it is not possible to identify all the specific reasons and how in each case they contributed to the welfare state, we can at least isolate a common premise and other factors pivotal to the development of all national reform programs in the nineteenth and twentieth centuries.

The shared premise was the development and rise to pre-eminence of industrial capitalism and the subordination of landed property to capital within the political framework of the nation-state. These changes brought in their wake new forces, class contradictions, and social consequences peculiar to capitalism. In all the nations where industrial capitalism came to prevail, social reforms followed sooner or later as corollaries of the breakdown of the old and the coming of the new mode of production.

The most significant consequences of the destruction of precapitalist modes of production were, first, the creation of a capitalist labour market and working class, or the "freeing" of labour from its means of production and existing forms of bondage, and, second, the breakdown of social institutions, labour processes, and communities that embodied to a considerable degree an integrated social, political, and economic life. As a corollary to these developments, capitalism gave rise to objective "needs" that had previously been coherent aspects of a way of life, such as child care, old age facilities, and schools. It also created new needs and new problems, which arose from and were associated with the capitalist labour market, the "freedom" of the worker, and new labour processes, such as unemployment insurance, workers' compensation, employment standards, and pollution regulation. In itself, capitalism had no answer to these needs and problems aside from the wage relation and the purchase of commodities; the answers were to come as imposed reforms.

The "freed" working class, now possessing no means of production and dependent on employment for its livelihood, found it necessary to defend itself against the depredations of the capitalist class and the vagaries of the labour market. The consequent struggle between labour and capital brought into being trade unions, which became the principal force behind the introduction, defence, and extension of many social reforms. Class conflict of one sort or another, or at least the potential for class conflict, has been the common context for all social reform.

Far from homogeneous, the fragmented working class produced corresponding fractures in its organized representation. As a counterforce to capital, trade unions were perpetually weakened in most countries by the irresolvable sectionalism and narrow interests and cautiousness of unions representing certain strata.[6] In part because of the uneven development of the trade union movement – that is, the absence of a unified, militant, and class-conscious movement – the class conflict intrinsic to the system was increasingly framed in gradualist terms, and the outcome was to be limited to forms of compromise and accommodation.[7]

This same organized resistance also spurred the struggle for universal enfranchisement and gave rise to political parties representative of certain strata of the working population. Such changes broadened the institutional political choices, allowing for a modicum of access to state power and the public purse and for more political leverage for reform legislation. The number and inclusiveness of reforms owe much to these extraparliamentary struggles and to the nature of the political expression for the working class within the nation-state.[8]

Out of the resistance to industrial capitalism came theories of socialist alternatives. The spectre of socialism or communism, a direct consequence of the coming of capitalism and the organized working class, has always been part of the motivation for the introduction of systematic reform programs. All the industrial countries in the late nineteenth and early twentieth centuries had working-class parties and trade unions well versed in socialist theory and aware of the potential for revolution. This is not to mention the actual attempts at revolution – throughout Europe in 1848, in Paris in 1870, Russia in 1905 and 1917, Germany in 1918, and so on – or the numerous examples of general strikes the world over.[9] The success of the Bolshevik revolution was no small inspiration to reforms in the West. Even after much of the political theory of the working class turned from revolution to reform and social democracy, there were still the examples of ongoing wars of liberation and of the

Soviet Union and later China and Cuba as, at least in rhetoric, "workers' states" – in short, certain reminders to the representatives of capital who might resist reforms.[10]

By the late nineteenth century, new technology, increased productivity, and expanded markets had begun to increase the segmentation, stratification, and social mobility of the labour force. The resulting complex hierarchies and numerous strata created a multitude of varying immediate interests within the working class, which actually rested on the continuing expansion of capitalism. Such divisions along many lines, which fractured the working population, and the grounding of the interests of some strata in capitalism itself made substantial sections of the class more amenable to reform than revolution.

With industrial capitalism also came the business cycle – the periodic rise and fall of economic activity and employment. In times of economic slumps, the working population, with no alternative to employment for its livelihood, suffered profoundly. These periodic deprivations created no uncertain amount of social unrest, and at times even piqued the conscience of certain middle-class strata and corporate leaders. Organized and unorganized social disruption (and, to a small degree, charitable sentiments) during recessions or depressions has been the motivation for some reforms.[11]

There is another general aspect to the origin of the welfare state, and that is the concessions made by organized capital, as well as its promotional efforts. The concessions are explained in part by the delimited national labour market and relative immobility of national capital in the relatively closed national economy, prior to the 1970s. The promotional efforts arise from the desire of the corporate sector to "socialize" and thereby limit some of the costs to industry that are incidental to its operations.[12] This desire has led, in different countries, to the introduction of old age pensions, hospital insurance, and even public education. The origin of industrial accident insurance schemes, while not without the component of working-class demand, lies largely in the efforts by corporations to create a system both limiting their liability for industrial accidents *and* "socializing" the costs through industry-wide insurance premiums and chronic inadequate compensation to workers and their families.[13]

Another outcome of industrial capitalism was increased productivity and the consequent growing necessity to expand overseas, producing colonial or imperial systems to "complement" the productivity of the industrial metropoles. This expansion of capitalism brought with it the possibility of ameliorating its inherent conflicts. Among the effects of this export-led growth was the rapid increase in capital accumulation in the metropolitan countries. In turn these developments allowed for a rise in the general standard of living, enhanced and confirmed the legitimacy of the system, and ultimately made it possible to generate sufficient revenues from "high" wages for the creation of a social wage, the fiscal foundation of modern social reforms.[14]

If these have been the principal reasons for and conditions underlying the coming of the welfare state – with national particularities but common to all industrial countries – they must be seen as comprising a multidimensional rationale, in the context of the contradictions of nationally structured capitalism. The empirical analysis of social reforms in a given country will almost certainly reveal the greater relative importance of one or another factor, with a single factor rarely standing alone. Despite the commonality of these conditions, moreover, they do not necessarily translate into the same legislated forms across nations. While reforms throughout the industrial world attempt to address broadly the same needs and problems intrinsic to capitalist society, the specific forms they take as "policy regimes" depend on a host of particular historical and national factors.[15]

A Definition

There is no single historical moment in any country when these social reforms were introduced as a comprehensive system. In fact, they and the various modes of implementation have generally appeared in a piecemeal fashion following the long development of capitalism and the modern state. For the most part, before World War II they were specific and limited responses to trade union pressures, corporate desires to socialize costs, and the destabilizing effects of unemployment and worker unrest. These disparate beginnings and this checkered development have given rise to the question of when a society can be defined as a welfare state or, more briefly, what a welfare state is.[16]

Although there have been several attempts to define the welfare state, there is no generally accepted and coherent concept. Approaches to its analysis and the choice of the defining variables all vary considerably, and a critical review of these variations does not bring us much closer to a viable definition. The brief outline of causal factors, however, leads to a plausible, comprehensive, and workable concept.

Although sometimes used as a generic term for government intervention "on many fronts," the welfare state can also be seen as a capitalist *society* in which the state has intervened in the form of social policies, programs, standards, and regulations in order to mitigate class conflict *and* to provide for, answer, or accommodate certain social needs for which the capitalist mode of production in itself has no solution or makes no provision.

These state interventions are typically made in four key, overlapping arenas of societal reproduction. Perhaps the arena most commonly associated with the welfare state is that of *the physical propagation of the working class and its preparation for the labour market.* This includes the health-care and educational systems, and many of the non-contributory social benefits (the largest recipients of which are women and children), which include subsidized child care, child/family allowance, food stamps, and transfer payments to single mothers.

Another arena is the *labour market,* and here the state has intervened not only to mitigate the extent of leverage that capital has over labour in this market, but also to prepare fresh workers for the market and to ensure an "adequate" labour supply. Typically, this arena includes regulations on the minimum wage, hours of work, child labour, retirement age, education/training, injury insurance, immigration, and so on.

The third arena is the *point of production*: the point of contact between workers and the representatives of capital *and* the point at which labour has submitted to the dictates of capital. Here the state intervenes to provide the institutional framework for class conflict (collective bargaining) and to protect the workers from the worst effects of the exploitation by capital. Collective bargaining rights are central here, but employment and health and safety standards are also important.

The fourth arena is the provision of income assurance for the *"unproductive" and after-productive life.* This includes old age pensions and other pensions and social assistance of all kinds paid out to those who for whatever reason are unable to work in the system.

The most commonly recognized form of implementation of these social reforms is most likely the provision of services, such as education, health care, and child care. But reforms are also realized through income transfers, such as pensions, unemployment or injury insurance, and social security payments. In some countries the supply of goods, for example in the form of public housing, is also an important kind of social reform. Lastly, the state has promulgated a large number of laws, regulations, and standards to institutionalize inherent conflicts and protect the disadvantaged in a system resting on inequalities.

This definition is clearly both broader and narrower than a specification of the general role of the state in a capitalist society. On the one hand, the state in welfare state refers to the body politic, the organized community; in this sense, it is all-inclusive and not a reference merely to government. On the other hand, the welfare in welfare state pertains to certain functions of government, which concern the four arenas of societal reproduction but do not usually include, for instance, the provision of infrastructure, the maintenance of law and order, or subsidies to capital. All of these functions, as well as many of those associated with the welfare state, have been historically part of the definition of the state as government, but to make them inclusive of the definition of the welfare state is to conflate the two and make one or the other redundant.

When does state intervention become "the welfare state"? To maintain the distinction we might ask, when can a society be defined as a welfare state? That is, when do the kind and amount of state intervention in the four arenas give rise to the definable phenomenon of the welfare state?

The general answer is that the welfare state has arrived when class conflict, reduced to the contest between workers and the representatives of capital, presents a chronic threat to the stability of the system and has to be "institutionalized" (placed within a legal framework of industrial relations); and when the majority of social needs pertaining to the reproduction of the working classes are addressed formally (by the state via "public" policies) rather than informally (via the community, family, friends). This definition, of course, leaves aside the question of when exactly in history these conditions occur, but that is a problem that remains specific to each country.

In general, however, the arrival of the welfare state is a post-World War II phenomenon. In light of the conditions in the postwar period, the welfare state became a political and economic "necessity." At that time, with the exception of the United States, the industrial economies lay exhausted or in ruins, and for the working classes the experience of the 1930s and the collective war effort made socialism an attractive alternative to the fears and indignities of the capitalist labour market. To reconstruct national capitalism in Europe and to resist widespread popular support for socialism in the industrial world, the capitalist classes had to employ the state to a degree not seen in earlier decades to socialize the costs of reconstruction and to circumvent a repeat of the Depression and its consequent class struggles.[17] So began almost three decades of unprecedented state intervention.

The modern welfare state is often referred to as the Keynesian welfare state (KWS), the name deriving in part from the economist John Maynard Keynes. The principal assumption in his work was the existence of a national economy in which, he argued, the state could intervene to influence levels of investment and domestic income and thereby partially regulate unemployment through national "demand management" policies. Such intervention represented a certain socialization of the costs of production (with state credits, guarantees, grants, and concessions) and of working-class reproduction (through public works and forms of income support), as part of a political compromise with the working classes in an attempt to moderate the business cycle (to prevent a repeat of the unrest of the 1930s), to help rebuild the war-destroyed economies of Europe (to ensure the reconstruction of capitalism), and to contain or diminish a growing interest in socialism due to the experience of the 1930s and the devastation of the war. In an open letter to Roosevelt about the New Deal, Keynes wrote: "If you fail, rational change will be gravely prejudiced throughout the world, leaving orthodoxy and revolution to fight it out." Donald Winch argues that Keynesian policies were "an effective weapon for use against the Marxists on the one hand and the defenders of old style capitalism on the other; a real third alternative, the absence of which before the *General Theory* had driven many into the Communist camp."[18]

This rationale for state intervention in the economies of the industrial nations was complemented by several other postwar developments that combined to create the general conditions demanding and allowing for the construction of the welfare state in this period. These conditions were multifold and interrelated, but the most significant was the persistence of the national state, the political counterpart to the existence of national corporate enterprise. Here lay the political and operational framework of the welfare state. That is, social reforms have been defined and administered as *national programs*; they have represented the political compromise between a national capitalist class and resistance to its particular forms of exploitation by sections of a national working class or social movements; and they have depended partly on the kind and degree of political alternatives that have evolved in particular nations.

The ability of the state to finance the programs of the KWS rested on several economic prerequisites. One was massive state indebtedness and expenditures during and after World War II (Lend-lease for the war effort, the Marshall Plan for reconstruction, then the Korean and Vietnam wars, for instance). Another was decolonization, which created new markets and an expanded labour supply. A third prerequisite was the "deepening of the domestic market," consumerism by another name, which depended on the vast expansion of ever-cheapening domestic commodities. Under these conditions enormous surplus value was generated, gross national products expanded relatively constantly, and high wages became a possibility, with the tax bases in the industrial nations growing in concert.

Advanced Fordism transformed the capitalist labour market, expanding and consolidating it with dramatic reductions in farm labour and the rapid growth of unproductive sectors.* A relatively consistent high demand for labour and corresponding rises in wages and salaries in these postwar decades formed the basis for the growth in number and size of trade unions. New or more comprehensive institutions of collective bargaining accompanied this increasing union strength. The importance of collective bargaining for maintaining capitalism, in its national form – with the organized working class otherwise presenting a threat to state power and capitalist hegemony – is much underrated.[19]

The concomitant development of huge numbers and many layers of technical, paraprofessional, and administrative workers in both the private and public spheres substantially increased the strata of the working class, with its immediate interests resting on employment hierarchies, a growing state sector, and national economic expansion. Here lay the

---

* As the prevailing mode of production in the industrial world after World War I, Fordism arose out of the cauldron of that war. It is generally seen as a system of mass production employing semi-automated assembly lines and giving rise to rapidly expanding domestic and external markets for "cheapened" consumer goods—that is, mass consumption. These developments are associated with large production units, complex work hierarchies, and national labour markets.

Advanced Fordism arose out of the forced industrial growth of World War II. Here major advances in science and technology were subordinated to capitalist production, which vastly expanded the quantities and qualities of goods and services. As a mode of production, advanced Fordism was characterized by a delimited national labour market, a protected product market, and growth based on extranational and "internal" expansion, planned obsolescence, and the rise of media advertising. The resulting "high standard of living" for the majority of the working class in the industrial nations and continuous capital accumulation allowed for a grand compromise between trade unions, corporations, and governments; the compromise took the form of the Keynesian welfare state.

rationale for the political platform promoted by social democracy and its vision of reformed capitalism.

It is in this postwar period, then, that we find the culmination of social reform in the shape of the KWS. Most of the labour force had become working class, with substantial numbers organized into trade unions. Class conflict now implied a chronic threat to the reproduction of the system and so had to be contained by institutionalized legal means. Moreover, with the transformation of the labour force and demise of precapitalist modes of production, most social needs necessary to the reproduction of the working class (health, education, and social security) could only be met in formal, institutional ways by the state through public policies, programs, and standards, that is, through macroeconomic policies based on state indebtedness and the social wage.

The Meaning of Social Reform

The social reforms that constitute the welfare state represent, then, the attempt by government to contain intractable conflict arising from the contradictory interests of the subordinate and ruling classes, and to implement redistributive or "averaging" mechanisms as a response to resistance by working classes to intolerable conditions surrounding the reproduction of their labour. Social reforms are a compromise response to the outcomes of the contradiction between labour and capital in a system with no inherent mechanisms for addressing such conflicts.

In other words, reforms are an "answer" to class conflict in the form of concessionary state policies, made possible by the potential for party alternations in power, the existence of partially organized dependent classes, an accommodative ruling class, *and* by the ability to secure the necessary revenues from "surplus wages" or state indebtedness. They are the "solutions" to class conflict in a certain period of history when the political and economic preconditions make it possible to construct class compromises.

Given this definition, it can be seen that reforms are not ends in themselves but rather state-mandated "accords." Through these accords the capitalist class can continue to exploit the working classes and natural resources, and the subordinate classes are able to protect themselves and provide reasonable assurances of their reproduction in a manner that maintains or improves health, education, and living standards. The reforms are, in short, compromises that allow corporations to ameliorate social unrest and to socialize various "costs" of production, and that prevent the otherwise unprincipled degradation of the working classes and nature by capital.

It follows from this that implicit in reforms as a product of state legislation is a division of societal power in which some classes and institutions are able to grant concessions, while some are able only to demand and receive. A society with reforms, by definition, is a society in which working people do not possess power over their own lives, but can make changes to their well-being only indirectly, and ultimately can only be recipients of concessions. This point holds true even when social reforms are defined as "social rights," that is, when social assistance appears as "entitlements" and is sufficient to free individuals from complete dependence on the labour market. Such claims, however, do not by any means completely free the working class from the labour market; they do not change fundamental relations of ownership in society; and they are only possible under certain social and economic conditions.[20]

The hitherto apparent permanence of reforms, moreover, stems from their more or less rapid growth after World War II into the welfare state, which gave the mitigated contradictions the appearance of reformed capitalism and strengthened the idea that capitalism was reformable, grounding the notion of reformism. The more the reforms, the stronger and more pervasive the belief.[21] To see beyond reformism has always been very difficult as long as reforms could be conceded or demanded (because the prerequisites made them possible), *or* as long as reforms were a plausible answer to social, economic, or environmental problems. By the late 1970s, however, the erosion of reforms had begun. This erosion continued throughout the 1980s, revealing the nature of reforms as a product of class tension in a period of national capitalist expansion. Although the ideology of reformism has come increasingly under attack by industry and government, it is still harboured by the organized sector of the working class as the only visible alternative to the utter subordination that the class sees for itself within the capitalist system.

Because social reforms are compromises, they embody the contradictions from which they constitute a temporary reprieve. They are mutable concessions designed to ameliorate the worst effects of capitalism and to placate resistance to these effects. But they are *not* resolutions to the contradictions between these classes, between different fractions of the ruling class, *or* between capitalism and nature. They are a sort of respite for unresolved contradictions, which at some point must be resolved; and the degree of reform in a nation-state closely reflects the degree of continuing conflict and the organized strength of the parties involved.

Reforms, furthermore, have only a temporary existence. They have always been provisional or conditional measures, with their limits determined by the particular conjunction of the elements defined as the preconditions of the welfare state. Reforms are a living reminder that the resolution to these conflicts is merely postponed. As long as the possibility of a revolution is not there, the choice becomes reforms or an unchallenged deterioration of the working class and nature into dissolution.

Reforms are, therefore, paradoxical in nature. They are, on one hand, a form of resistance to the capitalist mode of production, necessary for the protection of the working classes and nature. On the other hand, they comprise important elements in maintaining capitalism, the object of their corrective purpose, not to mention in bolstering the legitimacy of the state.[22] Such a paradox inhabits all reforms.

By grasping only one side of the paradoxical nature of reform, a great many writers on the left (cognizant and critical of the nature of capitalism and desirous of its transformation) have been led to dismiss reforms or the welfare state as mere class compromise, as the co-optation and integration of the working class into capitalism, as a counter to "class war," or an "alternative to socialism."[23] These arguments, however, usually assume a great deal.

They overlook, first of all, the possibility that capitalism without reforms might *not* spur a working class into revolution but instead simply reduce it to poverty, destitution, and fear of itself – and thereby break its will to resist. Second, they take for granted that in times other than extreme crisis and social breakdown the working classes could be an effective opposition to a trained and disciplined modern army or police force. The evidence would strongly suggest otherwise.[24] Third, these arguments imply that reforms are adopted at the cost of class consciousness and revolutionary aims, but fail to see the other side, namely, that reforms can raise working-class consciousness and expectations, can lead to demands for more reforms, and even in some cases be legislated at the expense of capital. In short, any dismissal of welfare state policies that does not address these assumptions would appear to come from rather privileged or romantically revolutionary positions.

Also missed by those who dismiss the welfare state as mere compromise is the implicit criticism of capitalism represented by reforms. The very existence of reforms attests to the fact that subordinate classes have had to defend themselves against the depredations of the corporate sector; they reveal that the much vaunted marketplace cannot provide employment or distribute goods and services in a way that ensures a tolerable existence for all; and they are testimony to the fact that the most elementary regulations have had to be imposed upon the corporate sector to prevent the wholesale degradation of water, air, soil, and food – the elements of life itself – not to mention the debasement of human beings and the basic conditions of work. To be sure, a certain fraction of the business class understands this point, hence the phenomenon of corporate "liberalism" in the United States and reform-minded industrialists in Britain and Europe.[25]

To dismiss reforms is also to misunderstand their necessity. No social order, to paraphrase Marx, is ready for transformation until all the possibilities for development within it have been exhausted. If we accept this, then, a transition to a co-operative and human society from industrial capitalism before the latter has completed its possibilities for expansion, while not impossible, is difficult and unlikely. In the meantime, without reforms, both the working class and nature might be exhausted long before a transition would be possible. Here again is the paradox.

To grasp the nature of reforms is to understand the dilemma they embody: they are necessary for the well-being of working classes and for society and nature in general, yet they are compromises that perpetuate the system, bolster its legitimacy, and conceal contradictions that remain unresolved. It is also to understand that because reforms are the product of the historical evolution of certain conditions, they correspond to a certain period in the development of the capitalist mode of production; they are not permanent or immutable. Reforms do not make capitalism other than what it is; they represent the imposed amelioration of the worst effects, but they do not transform or fundamentally change the principles or contradictions in operation. They merely temper them over a period of time.

II

The Socialism of
Social Democracy

The origins of the welfare state, and its most coherent expression as the Keynesian welfare state, have rested on several conditions more or less common to all industrial nations.[1] In other words, social reforms of one sort or another were politically, economically, and socially *necessary* and financially *feasible* with the coming of industrial capitalism, but particularly during the post-World War II reconstruction period. If this argument is defensible, then, at least two points about the welfare state should be drawn out.

If the KWS is understood as a form of socialism, as it frequently has been, then "socialism" in this sense can be seen as the political manifestation of a common phase in the national development of capitalism. The KWS, while "necessary" to capitalism in the postwar period, does not produce any fundamental change in the capitalist mode of production. Furthermore, the political assertion that capitalism is reformable – a position that takes the institutional form of social-democratic parties – has rested, albeit with historical and national peculiarities, on certain common social and economic foundations. The most important of these has been a stratified and segmented national working class whose immediate fortunes have corresponded to the continuous expansion of national capital. Social democracy is less a cause of the KWS than the *political* corollary of the same conditions that made the KWS necessary.

We Are All Socialists, Now[2]

If the general conditions that gave rise to the welfare state have been common to all industrial nations, the welfare state, albeit to different degrees and in different forms, would most likely also be general to all industrial nations. To a greater or lesser degree, moreover, all political parties that have gained political power in the industrial West have enacted similar policies, both before and certainly after World War II, up to the mid-1970s. Social-democratic parties have not by any means been alone in introducing reform programs or in advocating state intervention in the economy. Indeed, it has been argued that the spread of Keynesian policies amongst industrial nations in the postwar period was in part due to U.S. government direction.[3]

It is a common but rather self-serving argument to suggest that it was social-democratic parties that "pressured" non-socialist parties to behave in this "socialist" manner. This ignores the fact that the prerequisites for these interventions were similar in all industrialized countries and comprised an underlying necessity for an expanded state role to counter the extremes of business cycles, to provide unprofitable but necessary economic services, to defend and promote the interests of national capital in domestic and overseas markets, to ensure the reproduction of the working class, to act as guarantor of social order, to mitigate working-class interest in revolutionary socialism, and so on.

Just as all political parties in the West were confronted by the need to address these questions, they were similarly confronted by a limitation: that state policy had to be subordinate to the maintenance of the system and to expanding opportunities for the accumulation of capital. If there has been a contrast between social-democratic and conservative parties, it has been found in the limited region of state autonomy, which allowed for marginal differences in just how these questions should be addressed. If the nature of the response has always been broadly determined by systemic demands – hence the similarity of policies across nations – there has always been a certain political leeway in the degree and form of state intervention.

Social-democratic parties have given a political voice to pressure from certain strata in the working class, but they have done so within the confines of the system, that is, in the form of social reforms that have been both sufficient given the truncated nature of the class struggle and financially feasible given the Fordist mode of production and nationally defined capital and labour markets. For these reasons, social-democratic reforms are fundamentally like the reforms of all other parties in power.[4] Social-democratic parties have neither changed the political and economic power relations nor challenged seriously or for long the private accumulation of capital anywhere in the world.[5]

Social Democracy

Social-democratic parties in the industrial nations (including the United States[6]) have everywhere become one of the two or three main political parties, often alternating with conservative parties in power or, indeed, forming the government for extended periods (as in Norway, Sweden, Britain, Austria, and Australia). They are seen around the world as the party of labour and as the main promulgators of social reform. Indeed, throughout the West in times of economic recession, social-democratic parties, promising protection from the vagaries of the capitalist economy, have typically been favoured by the electorate.

Even so, they have been dismissed by some on the left as a party of opportunism and class collaboration, and by much of the right as promoters of restrictions to the "free" operation of capital. Such rejections rarely address the questions of why social-democratic parties have the power and influence in the West that they have had, or how it is that they have set the agenda for the left as a whole, or why over the decades they have all but eclipsed most other left-wing parties. The dismissal by the left is based on a view of social democracy as mere ideological manipulation, collaboration, and compromise. The right sees social democracy as a "foreign" ideology. Both sides see social democracy as a kind of conspiracy at the level of consciousness and ideology and not a genuine expression of a matrix of real interests existing in society.

If we adopt the view that political parties are not independent or unrelated entities with their own self-derived ideas but rather political expressions of real class interests, it is possible to leave the level of ideological dismissal and to probe the roots of past social-democratic "success." By examining its class base, we can also begin to grasp the reasons for the present abandonment of social-democratic policies and their convergence with those of the new right.

Class basis

The working class, for our purposes, includes all those dependent on a salary or wage for their livelihoods,[7] and has a changing structure largely determined by the changing needs of capital and its level of development. Indeed, the working class comes into existence because of the accumulation of capital and has no meaning outside of this relationship. Although the demands of capital are pre-eminent in this relation, this is not to say that working-class demands do not have a reciprocal effect, which, for the most part, has taken the shape of reform in the industrial countries.

From the late nineteenth century to the post-World War II period, industrial capitalism passed through several stages, spurred by changes in technology and labour processes, trade union organization, greater centralization of capital, and war-induced, forced growth. During this long period, despite periodic economic slumps, the evolving accumulation and centralization of capital generated continuous increases in productivity. This growth produced vast and increasing new commodity values, which had to be realized in an expanding world market, along with an expanding public sector to administer the economic growth.

The effects of this continuously increasing productivity on the structure of the working class were multifold, but included four principal changes. The first was the relative decline of manual workers in the productive sector, even though productivity grew and the sheer volume of commodities increased many times over. At the same time in the same sector, there was a relative and absolute growth in the number of scientists, engineers, technicians, and administrative, managerial, and clerical staff. The second change was the corresponding expansion of the unproductive sectors, those activities making up the sphere of circulation.[8] One part of this sector comprised the growth of capital in the arenas of exchange and distribution. The other part comprised the growth of the public sector, which developed to aid the reproduction of capital by providing infrastructure and to assist the reproduction of the working class by institutionalizing employment standards, public education, and health care. A third changed involved a relative increase in the "surplus population of workers," offset in particular by the expansion of the unproductive sectors, but nevertheless continuing a secular increase from World War II to the present.[9] Fourth, especially after World War II, due to technological and scientific changes there was the decline of that part of the labour force on the land involved in petty-commodity production, creating a large increase in the capitalist labour market.

An intrinsic part of this changing working-class structure was the developing set of "social needs" that arose along with the growing "reserve army" of labour, particularly during economic downturns but also on a permanent basis. In other words, not only were new needs arising, but other needs that were formerly but no longer met within existing social institutions were also increasing as these institutions succumbed to the development of capitalism.

This expansion of the working class was accompanied at the same time by the creation of pervasive divisions within it. The internal cleavages, almost too numerous to mention, did not change the essential position of the working class vis-à-vis capital, but they were and remain objective and experienced and therefore significant factors in dividing the working class within itself.[10] All of these differences, depending on time and place, have played a greater or lesser role in producing a complex fragmentation and stratification of the working class with a corresponding truncated view of itself as a class.

The stratification has even perpetuated itself in several ways. To the degree that it has provided a route of upward mobility towards greater security, each level has been seen and defended as a step away from the bottom. But more importantly, several strata of the working class have actually found their interests resting on the existence of a hierarchically stratified class. Put another way, the proximate interests of some sectors of the working class have stemmed from the domination of labour by capital, from hierarchical systems based on the privileged acquisition of knowledge and skills, unequal distribution of wealth, and differential power. Many professionals, quasi- and paraprofessionals, scientific and technocratic strata, skilled workers, and vast numbers of public servants, all part of the working class, have found a certain interest in maintaining the status quo, if only because their occupational existence has been defined in part by the stratification. The stratified particular interests, in turn, have militated against a perception or experience of common interests; they have created divided loyalties, ambiguous attitudes, individualized perspectives, and constitute existing interests standing in opposition to essential class interests.[11]

This brief schematic description of changes to the structure of the working class does not, of course, address the question of the relation of class to political parties, but it does help to explain the rationale for social democracy. While it can be argued that political parties are the principal means by which civil society as class-divided and stratified is represented in a legislature, it does not follow that there is a singular or direct relation between the two. Generally, because neither classes nor political parties have been characterized by unified or homogeneous interests, a simple linear relation between them is not to be found; yet parties are not completely autonomous entities; that is, they do represent class interests in a divided society because that is their *raison d'être*. The more internally consistent the interests of a class, the more clearly identifiable its relation to a political party as its representative; but the relation has never been free of differing interests between class fractions or social strata or of cross-class ideological views.

With the arrival of industrial capitalism and the gradual reduction in the number of classes of any significance to two, the capitalist and working classes, there was a corresponding reduction in the number of parties, approximating the contradictory interests of the remaining classes and strata under capitalism. Since World War II, there has in fact been in most countries a reduction of politically significant political parties to two, one social-democratic and the other conservative. Although the former is more reform-minded, neither is dramatically dissimilar from the other. The lack of clearly singular class-based parties and policies and the apparent minor differences between them are due in part to the hierarchical structure of the working class *and* to the systemic need for reforms in the capitalist nation-state.

On the one hand, although conservative parties are more clearly representative of a class (of capitalists or fractions thereof) than social-democratic parties, their reflection of these class interests in state policy is mitigated by the reforms demanded through working-class struggles and other contradictions in the system. On the other hand, the lack of a clear-cut single and unified working-class party is a reflection of the fragmentation and stratification of the working class. It is a class in which several fractions have some interest in the status quo and to varying degrees find a real, albeit only immediate, stake in the hierarchies resting on the domination of capital over labour. For this class as a whole, consumerism and a relatively high standard of living in general complete the obfuscation of common, essential interests.

Social-democratic parties have represented that part of the working class, with national variations, that has had an interest not only in maintaining the basis of the stratification but also in representing the whole working class, albeit by way of reforms. This is because the privileged positions of these strata are still positions within the working class; they remain part of that class and are therefore without the security or ultimate power of the owners or managers of capital. It is the "contradictory locations" of these strata that give rise to the phenomena of social democracy, at the centre of which lies the belief that capitalism is reformable.[12] A stratified working class with no coherent sense of itself or its essential relation to capital is in effect destined to make compromises in a system with which it appears to have a stake and a future.[13]

28

In the 1970s the class basis of social democracy began to change. New technology, in particular computer-aided manufacturing and the micro-electronics revolution, introduced a wide-ranging restructuring of the working class. Productivity increases forced large-scale redundancies in the resource and industrial sectors, and computerization allowed for a levelling of hierarchies, which contributed to the dramatic decline of middle-level management. The globalization of the economy brought pressures for international standards and wage structures and destroyed the tacit link wage-earners had to the "success" of national capital; and the erosion of national sovereignty reduced the political leverage held by the working class or trade unions on the national state. Trade unions themselves began to face increased antagonism from both capital and the state, with stagnation or even loss of membership beginning to appear by 1980. With the growing loss of their class foundations and increasing international constraints, social-democratic parties began to shift to the only policies open to national parties in an age of dominant international capital. The era of social-democratic theory and practice, it is now widely held, has passed and has become a subject left mainly to historians.[14]

Brokerage politics and social reform

By the last decades of the nineteenth century, prominent social democrats had already begun to revise the classical Marxist definition of class.[15] They began to redefine the party's role as representing a growing diversity of strata within the working class and, also, its goal as making the benefits of capitalism available to all. Although often dismissed as "revisionism," implying a merely ideological compromise with the class enemy, it would seem more likely that such revisions were an implicit reflection of the increasing heterogeneity of the working class and an attempt to give voice to strata whose *immediate* interests lay with the status quo.

If this were the case, the rise after World War I of two main parties on the left, the social democrats and Marxist or communist parties, would not be the reflection simply of ideological differences.[16] Rather, these parties would reflect real differences in the interests of political constituencies arising from the stratification of the working class, a consequence of the growth of industrial productivity and expansion.

By the early twentieth century, social-democratic parties had abandoned most references to a working-class base and ceased what remained of their class analysis of capitalist society. Instead, they defined themselves as powerbrokers to a broad spectrum of the electorate, and they conceived of society not as being divided by class but as stratified by occupation, income differences, and individual interests. Although they borrowed this pluralist vision from certain socially minded liberal theorists, it was in part consistent with the life experience and therefore consciousness of increasing numbers of working-class people.[17]

The nature of reformist policies was to give political expression to those strata of the working class whose occupational positions appeared out of keeping with their class position or, in fact, stemmed from the unequal relations of capitalist society. Reform as the goal of political activity, which is the heart of social democracy, was not simply an ideological position, but one grounded in the reality of a stratified, non-homogeneous working class.

Because reformism sprang from a reality shared by so many, it made for a political program very difficult to counter by the radical left, which has attempted to represent "essential" class interests. Reformist policies have combined the hegemonic ideology – capitalism as meritocracy, success as individual achievement, goals of wealth and power – with a "human" element, namely, forms of social insurance and a sense of social justice, *and* with a "political" point of view that implies that state interventions to promote economic growth and "full employment" are fully political decisions.

This has been an attractive political position for the whole of the working class because to a large degree workers have been immersed in the ideology of the status quo and have worked in a system that, even if unable to provide a high standard of living for all, at least provided continuous hope of material advancement. Brokerage politics of the reformist ilk, as a consequence, has fit very well with the reality of the structure, consciousness, and material well-being of the working class, especially in post-World War II national industrial capitalism – that is, up to the 1970s.

Although social-democratic programs have reflected the heterogeneity of the working classes, they have also played an important role in perpetuating certain political consequences, that is, in depoliticization. As the dominant voice of the working classes, social democracy has defined their interests in ways compatible with liberal-democratic capitalism and confined their expression to parliamentary modes. It follows that the most conscious and articulate class members – for the most part social-democratic trade union leaders – have found themselves completely preoccupied with keeping the organized working class within the limits of the system, that is, keeping them engrossed in the effect of certain reforms – for instance, absorbed by the legal niceties of collective bargaining, grievance procedures, arbitration, and policing of the contract. Moreover, both trade union leaders and social-democratic politicians have actively resisted extraparliamentary expression of political issues, thus preventing alternative leaders and organizations from rising to prominence. They have fashioned the party into a "vote-getting machine," while leaving untapped the social and political role it could have had in society.[18] The actual operation of welfare state reforms, furthermore, makes the working class into passive recipients of their own wealth via social programs, rather than empowered, active members of society who themselves decide what to do with the surplus-value they have created.

Whereas this accommodation may well have been the product of genuine beliefs in the principles of social democracy, it has also been the consequence of conscious manipulation by political forces intent on undermining radical class consciousness and anti-capitalist political policies and parties. The U.S. State Department, the AFL-CIO, and the CIA have all been influential in social-democratic parties (especially in Europe) since the end of the First World War. After the Second World War their influence in these parties was considerable, and they made systematic and consistent attempts to split labour movements and divide political support for radical parties. In particular, much of their effort in social-democratic parties was directed against communist parties and related trade unions in Europe, both of which enjoyed widespread sympathy after the war.[19] The important point here is the congruence between the principles of social democracy and these U.S. intrusions.

The parliamentary road to socialism

Because the strata represented by social-democratic parties have found their immediate interests resting in the existing national political economy, both progressive change and the route to that change have been conceived as lying within the purview of that system – nationally based capitalism. This historically transitory convergence of certain interests between labour and capital has been the basis for the parliamentarism of social democracy, that is, the uncritical acceptance of the validity of the political institutions of national capital.[20]

Parliamentarism, however, cannot be construed as a benign belief in a people's democracy; it carries within it several implications that are worth spelling out.

First, parliamentarism suggests that political goals are to be achieved through parliamentary "struggle," that is, electoral contests and legislative debate. Implicit here is a vision of the primacy of politics, of the state as independent of economic restrictions, of electoral success as a reflection of popular will and a general mandate to rule, among other notions.[21] Second, it understands parliamentary process as the sole legitimate arena of political activity; and as a corollary, it accepts that parliament should have a monopoly over political power. Third, it connotes that political parties have a monopoly over the definition of political issues.

The fundamental critique to be made of parliamentarism is that the monopoly of power invested in the legislature is the obverse of the lack of power outside of parliament and its agencies. It follows that the extraparliamentary exercise of power has been little short of anathema to social democrats.[22] This is partly because class conflict "in the streets" has threatened their interest in maintaining the status quo, and partly because any real empowerment of the people would make the legislature, as we know it, redundant and expose the inverse relation between parliament's possession of power and the people's deprivation.[23] Social democracy has opposed the idea of a revolutionary transformation of capitalism for the same reasons: revolution has promised, at least theoretically, to result in the empowerment of the people and the end of the exclusive alienation of social power in the legislature.[24] Parliamentarism and reformism bear an intrinsic relation.

Social-democratic criticisms of modern democracy have rarely gone beyond questions about political corruption, the misuse of governing institutions, and the persistence of non-democratic institutions such as the monarchy or unelected second chambers.[25] Without denying the validity of such criticisms, it must be said that the apparent abiding respect for the institutions of liberal democracy appears, more than ever today, rather naive. If the capitalist classes and their conservative parties ever respected these institutions, it could hardly be said that respect is the case today. Wherever the rule of capital in national or international spheres has been challenged by duly elected legislatures, liberal democracy has been paid scant respect. The lessons of Chile and Nicaragua, and many other nations, are more than ample testimony to the lengths to which capital will go to replace elected governments with their own unelected representatives.[26] This is not to mention how the representatives of capital have made extensive fraudulent use of elections around the world for achieving undemocratic ends under the guise of democracy.[27]

Social democracy has typically seen military interventions in politics through legal/political eyes. The interventions are seen as transgressions against due process that must be condemned and rectified. What is missed is the frequent connection between military intervention and the challenge to the rule of capital arising from the empowerment of the people outside of parliament.

In more hidden and usually less bloody ways, other unelected representatives of capital – namely, the IMF and the World Bank – have regularly dictated national policies in both the Third World and industrial nations when governments ("democratic" or not) fail to do what is necessary for capital accumulation.[28] Even the published views of representatives of international capital on democracy have been far less sanguine and more realistic than those of social-democratic parties. The Trilateral Commission's analysis of the "crisis of democracy" concluded in 1975 that there was too much democracy, that curbs on its expansion should be implemented, and that to the degree that democracy "worked" it was largely because of the political apathy of the working classes.[29]

It need hardly be said, moreover, that social-democratic criticisms have never viewed modern liberal democracy as a political phenomenon resting on the same economic and social conditions as social democracy itself. Just as in this particular historical period social democracy is a product of a certain structure of capital and labour and of the uneven accumulation of capital in the metropolitan countries, so too are the state structures of liberal democracy. As these conditions change, so too will political institutions and party forms and platforms.

Uncritical acceptance of the institutions of liberal democracy, or parliamentarism, and the belief in reformism go hand-in-hand. They imply each other, and both imply, indeed rest on, a separation of political power from the people within the capitalist nation-state. As the national state loses its powers with the arrival of the global economy, this separation becomes more evident, just as the nature of the KWS and the institutions of liberal democracy come to be seen for what they are.

The social-democratic critique of capitalism

The social-democratic vision of capitalism has been fundamentally a legal one; capitalism is seen as a system of property rights and not as a mode of production. The significance of this is that the understanding of capitalism remains on the level of commodity exchange and circulation, where everyone is seen as a property owner (if only of their labour power), entering into contractual relations of their "own free will" and exchanging commodities of equivalent value. Society is presumed to be but a set of contractual relations between property owners – a view very similar to classic liberalism.[30] While a radical critique would examine the mode of production, in particular the nature of private property, in search of the source of inequality, class conflict, and the rationale of the state, social-democratic analysis remains on the level of the marketplace and legal rights and sees only individual differences and private relations. The principle of this critique of capitalism has not gone beyond the legal; that is, the perceived shortcomings are of the order of abuse of process, illegality, dishonesty, and monopoly power.

If social democracy had an "economic" critique of capitalism, its focus was the development of monopoly capital, which was seen to restrict the activity of private property owners in the competitive sphere. The promulgation of anti-monopoly laws, however, has had only limited effect in preventing the development of corporate consortiums because state-imposed limitations on the concentration of capital contradict this tendency inherent in the system. In light of the historic difficulty of curbing concentration, and confronted by continuous economic expansion and growth of the unproductive sectors, social democracy accepted certain revised "theories" that made these corporate giants into examples of economic "planning" units, run by a benign "technostructure" with a "social purpose."[31] The Galbraithian apology for modern capitalism, along with other elaborations of Keynesian-regulated capitalism, such as *dirigisme* in France, became the new postwar perspective of many social-democratic parties. Since then, social democracy has not presented a critique of the economics of capitalism.

There has been a sociological critique, however. The social consequences of capitalism have been there for the looking. Unanswered human needs and all members of society except the owners and the employed become social problems: the young and the old, the ill, the poor, the criminal, the uneducated, the unemployed, all become dilemmas and paradoxes perceived as "external" to the system. The origins of these problems are never addressed because the source, the system itself, is difficult to see from "within." The destruction of precapitalist social institutions and ways of life that did accommodate human needs and the "unproductive" is perpetrated by a system that provides no accommodation for those needs and, moreover, creates new "unanswered" needs and dilemmas. Being in principle at one with the system, however, social democracy has defined such problems in depoliticized ways – as causally unrelated to the system, as "naturally occurring," as individual failures, as defects in the operation of the system, but not the system itself – and therefore as unavoidable consequences of human progress. It is therefore necessary to intervene to mitigate the economic cycle, to determine the "extent" of the problems, to document their characteristics, and when this identification is completed, to provide "answers" in the form of "social policies." Hence Keynesian macroeconomics, sociology, and social welfare.[32]

Since the origins of "social problems" are not seen as lying in the system itself, their "solution" is seen to lie in reforms, not of the system but of the individuals and corporations that constitute the "problems." These individuals and corporations are the "difficulties" that must be "reformed," that is, made the subject of social and economic policies, even though they are not the real source of the problem. Reformed capitalism, then, is really capitalism with reforms for individuals who are not productive in the system, for corporations that are corrupt or abusive or have the need to socialize costs, and for its cyclical tendencies.

The expanded state as socialism and solution

Social-democratic solutions to social and economic problems have typically been found in reforms as a means of socializing corporate costs or as palliatives for the worst effects of capitalism, administered by an expanded state sector. For the most part, this has not distinguished them from other political parties that, if not philosophically at least in practice, have promoted the growth of government throughout the postwar decades. Social democracy may have been somewhat different, however, in its open advocacy of economic planning, in its encouragement of tripartism in the formulation of policies, and in its willingness to create state-owned corporations. Still, it is a difficult argument to make when we examine the actual practice of Western governments. We need only cite Andrew Shonfield's well-known *Modern Capitalism* to make the point, for it documents the postwar rise to prominence of "public power" in all Western nations regardless of the political party in power.[33]

The postwar expansion of the state sector and the rise of *planning* in capitalism are really consequences of the experience of wartime planning and the natural evolution of capital and not the imposition of some kind of socialist philosophy. The unprecedented growth of capital accumulation after World War II produced several related effects. As productivity and industrial output increased, there was a concomitant growth in the sheer number of corporations and in the competition between them. In turn there was a corresponding increased need for regulations and their administrative agencies, for infrastructure (power, water, transportation, communication), research and development, and financial guarantees. These needs called for a vast expansion of the public sphere.

Accompanying this capital accumulation, a host of new human needs was created, requiring new policies and programs now subsumed under health, education, social assistance, and labour relations. The accommodation and administration of these new needs also required an enlarged state. Furthermore, to avoid the extremes of the business cycles, to save capitalism from a repetition of its long and severe crisis in the 1930s, state intervention in the marketplace was advocated in the form of Keynesian policies. The growth of the public sector, then, had little to do with socialism. Rather, it was closely tied to assisting capital accumulation or, broadly put, the sustained growth of the GNP.[34]

The planning that has taken place through state regulatory agencies has been simply a form of control of the national market; and despite its diverse specific origins, this planning has generally been intended to maintain or advance the interests of capital.[35] Similarly, the planning that falls under the rubric of Keynesianism was intended to reduce the effects of the business cycle and thereby avoid rates of bankruptcy and unemployment threatening to the system. Keynesian economic policies never challenged market forces; indeed, such policies assumed the primacy of the market. Like the overall expansion of the state, these planning functions were in aid of capital, not a step towards its subversion.[36]

Corporate planning also became part of the social-democratic viewpoint. This form of planning arose as well because of both the size and the nature of capital. All corporations strive to reduce competition in the market, which diminishes both profits and control over investment, product lines, and consumption. But corporations can actually "plan" control over aspects of the market only after they reach a certain size. On this point, Galbraith asserted: "Much of what the firm regards as planning consists in minimizing or getting rid of market influences."[37] He listed three means by which corporations establish control over the market: "vertical integration," whereby market forces in the production of given commodities can be controlled from resource extraction to retailing; the formation of cartels, oligopolies, or monopolies to control supply and demand, geographic markets, and prices; and the growth of the advertising sector, which is in effect an attempt to control and create demand. There are other means as well: interlocking boards of directors, intercorporate ownership of stock, and corporate indebtedness interlock, among others.[38] It is fair to say that what remains of the mythical laissez-faire market is very circumscribed, which is not to say that capitalism has been "transformed." Corporate planning is simply the implicit recognition that the unreliability of the market (not to mention the unreliability of government) cannot be tolerated given the enormity of capital investment.

The postwar necessity of increasing amounts of planning within the corporate sector, the expansion of the state planning functions, and the extensive public construction of infrastructure, among other developments, produced (especially in European countries) the immense layered structure of technocrats who were highly trained and educated. The interests of these technocrats were grounded in the persistence of this expanded role of the state, and their existence in turn rested on expanding national capital.

Here in large measure is the foundation of social-democratic support for planning or, better, the source of continuous pressure for the expansion of planning. In fact, no political party in the West could oppose either form of planning on the effects of the market, because they were essential to a greater or lesser degree to postwar national capital accumulation.[39]

The key to understanding these forms of planning lies in the fact that they have represented attempts to work *with* the "law of value," to even out its operation, to ameliorate its negative social consequences, to limit its unpredictability.[40] Nevertheless, however much of this planning is done, it does not eliminate the private ownership of the means of production. It does not overcome the contradictions between capital and labour or between capital and nature, and it does not end the rise and fall of the business cycle. And this is so because it has been planning for the advance of capital. It has not been planning with a social purpose, which is essentially different in that it replaces the law of value with democratic decisions on societal priorities as the mechanism for determining the apportionment of investment and supply in the productive sector.

Aside from planning, social democrats have been advocates of *tripartism* as a solution to some of the problems of national capitalism. Tripartism refers to all those attempts to bring together representatives from business, labour, and government to make common effort to promote economic growth and its assumed result, the enhancement of the standard of living. Its premise is the requirement of *national capital* to expand, with the alternative being the absorption or subordination by other national capitals; and labour and government are expected to find their own interests combined in this goal. Implicit in tripartism, then, is the recognition that there are contradictory class relations in capitalism, but that the subsumption of the interests of labour to those of capital will have beneficial effects for both capital and labour. It is the acknowledgement that the combined efforts of labour and capital and government are needed to maximize the productivity and therefore competitiveness of national capital. It is a mechanism for marshalling the main social forces in a society in the interests of national capital.

The evidence suggests that in the postwar decades tripartism worked very successfully to place the capitalists of those nations practising it in superior positions and, as a spin-off effect, to create a high standard of living for the working classes. Germany and Sweden are two of the most easily recognized examples, although Japan might also be included. Although tripartism can mitigate aspects of open class contradiction, especially during periods of capital accumulation, it is a temporary measure that holds up only as long as economic growth continues. It cannot fundamentally reconcile the two sides of labour and capital, which becomes clear in periods when the possibilities for national expansion have run out or when the structure of capital has become global. The "experiment" then falters and social democracy loses a central policy in its program.

The third remedy for the economic problems of capitalism lay in the policy of *nationalization* or state ownership of some of the means of production, distribution, and circulation. The constitutions of several of the leading social-democratic parties in the West explicitly called for the creation of public corporations, especially in the "commanding heights" of the economy. For some time, however, for reasons to be explored later, these "offending" constitutional clauses have been ignored or excised, reflecting the changing needs and demands of capital, as well as the immediate interests of those social strata supporting social democracy.

There are, nevertheless, some aspects worth noting about the theory and practice of social-democratic policies of state-ownership in the periods before and after World War II. Nowhere, for instance, was the policy intended to imply nationalization without compensation; even if the capitalists were to lose control and ownership they would be compensated and, in many cases, very generously. Moreover, of all the reasons that public enterprises were created, socialism was not one of them, at least not if socialism implies workers' control and effective benefits for all citizens. It was state, as opposed to private, capitalist corporations that were being created. These policies of the social democrats, furthermore, had diverse company: in France after the war, General de Gaulle carried out a major nationalization program; in Spain during the same period, General Franco's government was responsible for creating numerous public corporations; and in Italy, a conservative Christian party in government was busy reworking the fascist corporatist state. In fact, there were few industrial countries after World War II, with the notable exceptions of the United States and Sweden, in which nationalization, quite extensive in some cases, did not take place.

Social-democratic "solutions" to the problems of capitalism have one other notable facet. In general, they have constituted forms of state intervention, not in the sphere of production in which real economic power lies, but in the realm of distribution. This is because the problem is seen to be an unfair distribution of "wealth," and the goal is a fairer, more equitable distribution. Hence, the solutions become intervention to regulate the supply of resources and labour-power, the "effective demand," the conflict between labour and capital, and capital and nature. What this emphasis misses is the fact that the distribution of the total social product has already occurred in the sphere of production as the outcome of aspects of class struggle, in particular, through collective bargaining and minimum wage laws, among other factors. The most important distribution has already taken place *before* taxes and other deductions are collected for redistribution by the state. If there is intervention into the sphere of production, it is usually to prevent bankruptcies or fill economic gaps. And where state-owned corporations have been created, they are often mandated to operate as if they were in the private sector.

• • •

The socialism of social democracy was simply the making into political principle the political practice that all political parties, with the coming of large-scale industry in the late nineteenth century, were more or less obliged to follow in order to mitigate the inherent conflicts and social lacunae of the system and to advance the interests of national capital. State intervention, the linch-pin of this practice, became especially important in the post-World War II reconstruction period, and it is here that social democracy came into its own. The historically necessarily heightened role of the state as the pragmatic plan by capital to secure its future after the war intersected with the immediate interests of many strata within the working class.

The political expression of certain interests in the working class as social democracy made this pragmatism into political principle: in a word, *reformism*. The principle was a product of a stage in the development of national capitalism, and as such it has represented the convergence of the pragmatic needs of capital and the class aspirations of many strata in the working class with an interest in the maintenance of the system and the expansion of capital. It is for this reason that social democracy has been critical only of the defective operation and not of the system itself. It has never challenged the status quo and has in general been instrumental in placating the militancy of many sectors of the working class to the benefit of capital.

Even if it can be argued that the actions of social democracy made for a more comprehensive welfare state, necessary and valuable for the working classes as a whole, at the same time it cannot be forgotten that the KWS did not constitute a transformed capitalism, and the vaunted "redistribution" of wealth has always been very limited. Capitalism continued to develop and so to outgrow the postwar conditions that made social democracy and the KWS possible and necessary.

III

The Impact of Social Democracy and the Welfare State on Social Inequality

Inequality

Throughout the West, the period from 1945 to the early 1970s – the era of the development of the KWS – saw a certain constancy of income and asset inequality, albeit with national variations.[1] Most of the indicators of inequality point to little significant change in the decades after World War II, at least until the 1980s when trends towards *greater* inequality became apparent.[2] During the same period permanent unemployment showed a long-term secular rise in most industrial countries, with no prospect of diminishing. Poverty in most Western nations has never been eliminated and, along with wage disparities, continues to grow.[3]

Illiteracy in the West, especially in North America, is surprisingly high and on the rise.[4] Rates of morbidity and mortality have remained closely related to class membership; and while some diseases have been eradicated, many are returning in epidemic proportions, and certain new medical problems continue to grow.[5] The social subordination of women remains largely unchanged; and the objective of pay equity for women in the labour force, introduced in the 1980s, is far from realized despite affirmative action programs. Children, moreover, remain by and large the property of their parents or wards of the state, poorly protected by civil rights and largely unseen as embodiments of humanity; but they are increasingly made the objects of consumer marketing.

The persistence of economic inequality has given rise to questions about the general impact of the welfare state, and the issue became the subject of several studies in the 1970s and 1980s. One survey suggested that the effect of the welfare state on unequal economic relationships was at best an ambiguous one. Moreover, social-democratic administrations made little or no difference in impact, when compared to the policy results of other political parties in other nations. The survey concluded that "differences in parliamentary politics have hardly mattered" to the existence of social and economic inequality.[6] This study and others pursuing similar questions reveal little strong or consistent evidence to link social democracy with a more "redistributive" welfare state, or the welfare state with less inequality."[7]

The effect on inequality can be seen most poignantly in the relation of the welfare state to women and children. In the industrial nations, women and children are the largest recipients of non-contributory social benefits; but other than to alleviate the worst effects of poverty, the welfare state has not affected their role or place in society. In fact, it both reflects and reinforces their subordinate and dependent positions.[8] Although women have become economically less dependent on men since the 1970s, because they have entered the labour force in increasing numbers, the continuing reality of their subordination is perpetuated in part by the few and limited rights to social insurance as mothers, housewives, or domestic workers of one sort or another. Social benefits such as pensions, unemployment and disability insurance, and maternity leave generally assume wage contributions from employment. Women as mothers or unpaid workers, however, are assumed to be dependent, and the consequent underdevelopment of family benefits, child care, and other domestic services creates an unspoken pressure to enter into or to rely on a subordinate relationship.

In most countries mothers who are dependent on non-contributory state benefits, that is, not dependent on a male, are often encouraged or even obliged to seek maintenance payments from a father, thereby re-establishing a certain dependency on a male; they are usually not permitted to cohabit without the assumption of dependence; they are often forced into part-time, low-paid employment to supplement state income; and in general they find that the provision of state-subsidized child care and other family services is so limited that it hinders their escape from the trap of low-paid jobs or life on social security. In effect, the institutions of motherhood and the nuclear family bear a strong relation to the form of women's participation in the labour force as low-paid and casual workers; and the welfare state, with some exceptions, has not only done little to change this subordinate social position but also worked to reaffirm it.

42

With the decline of the nuclear family and growth of single parent-hood in the last two decades, most industrial nations have witnessed a corresponding "feminization of poverty." For women in many ways this merely represents a "shift from private to public dependency."[9] The dependency is made worse by an accompanying negative social stigma, and it tends to be based on non-contributory social benefits that have been subject everywhere to more severe cutbacks than those made to contributory or self-funded benefits resting on paid work.

The most compelling touchstone of the impact of the welfare state is found in its attitude towards children. Far from recognizing their quin-tessential humanity or treating them as the precious future of human society, the welfare state leaves children as the property of their parents, to share a similar fate by inheriting their parents' wealth or suffering their poverty. Children as children have no place in the welfare state except as objects of charity or wards of the state, subject to the legalism, professionalism, and bureaucratism of the warders.[10]

Redistribution

Despite welfare programs, social-democratic parties, and the huge state apparatus engaged in redistribution, then, the redistribution that has taken place would appear paradoxically to be very limited. Most aspects of the welfare state were designed to redistribute a portion of wages and salaries, collected by the state in the form of tax revenues, premiums, and deferred income. They were not intended to redistribute social wealth, the accumulated capital assets of society.[11] To do this would contradict the essence of the system, that is, the private accumulation of capital, and thereby challenge the powers vested in such private ownership.

In the redistribution of the social wage, the function of the welfare state has rested on a *prior distribution* of social wealth, determined by existing property relations and by the ongoing struggle between the working class and the corporate sector over their respective shares of the social product. A number of variable factors determine these shares: for instance, historical and current expectations, the legislated mini-mum wage, the supply and demand for labour, the degree of unioniza-tion, the restrictions on collective bargaining, and the business cycle. These factors determine the "initial" distribution of the social product, which takes the form of wages/salaries and profits. It is from an *already* divided pie, then, that the state collects its tax revenues, premiums, and deferred income. How these shares are taxed and how incomes are deferred become the key to grasping what is being redistributed.

Some welfare state programs, such as industrial accident insurance, unemployment benefits, pensions plans, and medical care, are state-run indemnity schemes financed by premiums or deferred income paid by the working class out of wages and salaries. (Although corporations often "share" these costs in part, they calculate their share of the premiums as part of the wage bill or the "incidental expenses" of doing business, like fire and theft insurance.) Other programs, such as public education facilities, mothers' allowance, social assistance, or public housing, are usually paid out of general revenue. The lion's share of general revenue, however, comes from taxes on wages and salaries.

The programs of the welfare state, then, provide two forms of redistribution. One is the general redistribution of deductions from wages and salaries to pay for schemes that assist the working class to reproduce itself, within the confines of the capitalist system. The other is a certain redistribution of revenues upwards in social strata, because the more affluent strata make proportionally greater use of the more costly programs (such as health care and public education), but contribute proportionately less of their income in support because of the structure of the tax regimes.

If we examine the general allocation of tax revenues beyond the social welfare programs, it becomes clear that if all the deductions from wages and salaries (both direct and indirect) constitute the largest share of total government revenue, and if the costs of the welfare state are less than this share, then the working class is in effect paying through taxes, premiums, and deferred income not only for these social programs and most of the activities of the state, but also for a portion of the subsidy to the corporate sector – in grants, loans, subsidies, and concessions.[12]

This argument raises questions about several common notions and even some academic treatises on the meaning of the *social wage*, defined as all the deductions from wages and salaries employed in transfer payments and provision of services to the working class. Many people see these expenditures as "handouts" from the state, whether they are "universal" programs or in one way or another means-related. Indeed, academics have also made a case for "net transfers" taking place from public revenue to the working class.[13] What these positions miss is the fact that there can be a net transfer only if the taxes paid by the working class are less than what is received by way of transfer or services from the state. Given class differences in wealth, power, and access to the public purse, this is unlikely to be the case. A number of studies corroborate the view that taxes on income always exceed the transfers back to the working class.[14]

The argument for the net transfer is made in an article by Samuel Bowles and Herbert Gintis, who suggest that there is "substantial redistribution from capital to labour."[15] But since the total amount of transfers, including expenditures in health, education, and welfare, do not exceed total revenues collected directly and indirectly from income and premiums, their position is difficult to accept. Other studies draw a far more plausible conclusion, showing "net transfer from workers to the state."[16] They provide evidence that the working class receives less from the state than what is extracted from it, and the difference is allocated according to priorities set by the state, including transfers as diverse as those to ballet companies, scientific research, highway maintenance, corporate loans and grants, or military procurement.

The evidence suggests that the redistribution associated with the welfare state has had little effect on economic inequality, and this is mainly because it was never intended to level economic differences. Although a degree of levelling may take place because of the averaging of a portion of labour income, this is an unintended consequence of the principal goal of such programs: to ameliorate the worst effects of economic inequality and to placate resistance to all the political and social implications of such inequality. The intent of the welfare state has been to produce a modicum of social security, certain minimum standards, a degree of class "harmony," and socialized costs of production – but not economic equality. In short, the existence of social policies and programs has not threatened the basis of inequality, that is, the structure of ownership and control, and it has not changed the necessity for workers to sell themselves in a competitive labour market.

Social Citizenship or Decommodification

If the preceding is a negative evaluation of the impact of the welfare state, a positive evaluation must bring into focus the concept of "social citizenship" – the notion that all members of society have a right to certain social services and programs such as health care, education, old age pensions, and unemployment insurance.[17] The degree of universality of these reforms is the degree to which the concept has been put into practice. Social citizenship implies an equality of status in the social realm, just as "citizenship" denotes equality in the political realm: just as there is universal enfranchisement, there is in the welfare state (with many conditions) universal entitlement to certain social guarantees.

Like the historical striving for universal suffrage, driven by the desire of the working population to gain control over their lives, so the demand for universal social security represents the implicit desire of the working classes to be free from the insecurity of the labour market and the bondage of wage-labour. The only recourse that wage and salary workers have had to the instability of the labour market and servility of employment – in a word, to the commodification of labour-power – has been to organize into trade unions to secure concessions from corporations or to obtain through protest state-sponsored social and economic reform. But the reforms and the union rights to bargain collectively, to strike, and to organize are never more than conditional guarantees against the insecurities of the competitive labour market. They represent a qualified "decommodification" of labour power in the labour market. The degree to which workers' reliance on the labour market for their livelihood is mitigated is the degree to which labour law and social benefits are legal rights and have universal and comprehensive application.[18]

Decommodification, whatever its degree, runs counter to the principles of the capitalist labour market. The existence of a "social net" and union/employee rights undermines the negative effects of competition, powerlessness, fear, and poverty, which are part and parcel of the labour market. We can say more: the idea of social citizenship represents the highest development of the principle of welfarism or social reformism. Just as universal enfranchisement marks the completion of politics, the concept and achievement (albeit incomplete) of social citizenship mark the completion of social welfare: the end result of a citizenry striving to have social security and meaning in an alienated society. Within capitalist social relations, the working class can do no more.

Because it contradicts the principle of private property, the progressive expansion of social citizenship became a perceived threat to the system. As the postwar growth of the welfare state reached its high point in the late 1960s and early 1970s, a reaction appeared in business, government, and academic circles around the world. In pointed words, Daniel Bell called these developments in social reform "the revolution of rising entitlements."[19] In part in response to this "revolution" the Trilateral Commission financed a study of the implications and raised the spectres of "excess democracy" and the growing "ungovernability" of the industrial "democracies."[20] Conservative writers worried about the "politicization of society."[21] They focused their attack on what they called "big government," rather than admitting to the conflict between the expansion of popular social and economic reforms through the mechanisms of liberal democracy *and* the demands of the marketplace.

The attack on "big government" has essentially been an attack against any state intervention aimed at ameliorating the conditions of the working class or against a growing politicization of the distribution of the social product. "Big government" as an epithet is aimed at the welfare state but not at state support of corporations. Ignored in this aspersion are the gifts, grants, and favours that have been extended to the business sector in the form of tax expenditures, inflated contracts, control of labour unions, legislated suppression of wages, socialization of production costs, social control, and creation of infrastructure. Despite the popular assumption that business could manage well without government and would do better with less government, the corporate sector is hardly about to abandon these vital roles of the state, which support capital.

Although under attack, the partial and conditional achievement of social citizenship in the Western welfare states has clarified the intrinsic limits of reformism. Even in those countries in which social and union rights have gained wide application, those victories have always remained provisional. First, they often do not apply to certain categories of the population outside the labour force or marginal to it. Second, the "boundaries" of application are continuously subject to conflict, that is, they reflect a balance of class power and compromise. Third, "social citizenship" is still, after all, a question of welfare reform offered as compromise by a state and capitalist class. And fourth, it does not bring economic equality and presents no fundamental challenge to existing power relations. In most countries, moreover, social citizenship is by and large a post-World War II phenomenon, resting on several economic and political preconditions that are rapidly disappearing.

Whatever the degree of social citizenship achieved in the welfare state, the reforms have almost always involved a degree of public/private mix in the programs and their delivery.[22] In other words, government and the private sector (corporate and non-profit) co-exist in one way or another within the welfare state. In most state medicare systems, for instance, doctors have remained self-employed, with their fees for treatment determined in negotiations with government, rather than becoming state employees. Hospitals, while staffed by public employees, have been supplied by the private sector. In this mix the prevailing principle of the system, private property, is always present; reform is always an imposition on private property; and the degree of decommodification achieved is continuously confronted by its opposite, the pressure to commodify.

• • •

This discussion is not intended to disparage legislative attempts at redistribution of income for economic security. Reforms, after all, are positive gains for the working class. They are not "gifts" from anyone, and they should be defended (and will have to be defended) as gains, however paradoxical their nature. The point, rather, is to uncover what "redistribution" is actually redistributing and to question the prevailing myth surrounding welfare state expenditures. In short, these social security programs, from unemployment insurance to state pensions to health care, are financed by deferred or diverted component parts of wage income, not by deductions from the profits of capital, although they do presume wages high enough to allow for deductions. The existing programs are forms of state-controlled redistribution of a portion of working-class income intended to facilitate the reproduction of wage-earners, to provide limited economic security, and to serve as emollients for the lack of economic privilege.

The existence of the welfare state and social democracy has rested on certain historical preconditions, the most important being an expanding national economy (implying a limited labour market and relatively immobile capital), a stratified, heterogeneous working class defined by a Fordist mode of production, and a degree of national sovereignty delimited by the interests of national capital. As long as such factors were obtained, the postwar KWS and social-democratic parties found the basis for their progressive development, and in several countries the changes even appeared as permanent achievements. Before the 1970s, the limits of these prerequisites became visible only during periods of fiscal crisis, when state revenue became insufficient to meet the usual expenditures without excessive indebtedness.[23]

While the specific causes of these crises may have varied in time and place, their "solution" was remarkably similar. Even social-democratic parties in power, despite a proclaimed social conscience, dealt with these fiscal problems in ways that were little different from how they were handled by conservative parties. The shortfalls were addressed variously by cutting government and welfare services, "restraining" public sector wages, raising taxes, and increasing indebtedness, all of which avoided the real causes of the crises and made the solution various forms of retrenchment for the working classes.[24]

By the end of the 1970s the crises appeared to have become chronic. The consequences in North America and most of Europe soon became obvious: the irrevocable dismantling of the national welfare state had begun,[25] and social democracy was losing whatever distinction from other parties it may have had. The reasons were beyond the control of political parties that accepted the primacy of the changing conditions of the economic order.

Despite national variations, the prerequisites to the existence of the welfare state and social democracy were beginning to shift or disappear. National economic growth began to slow, spawning an increase in individual taxation and the use of deficits to finance the welfare state. Fordism began to give way to the microelectronics revolution, restructuring and polarizing the working class with a large expansion of low-wage temporary jobs confronting new strata of high earners. The "contradictory class locations" began to disappear for increasing numbers of workers, with a decrease as well in working-class support for social democracy. High disposable incomes began a secular decline, bringing into question the "affordability" of the welfare state and narrowing the possibilities for social-democratic programs. Trade union membership began to fall, weakening the main source of pressure for social reforms and undermining an important foundation of social-democratic parties. The powers of the national state were increasingly transcended with the emergence of an independent international economic sphere; and the consequent growing loss of national sovereignty over social reform and government policy began to become replaced by the imperatives of global markets.

IV

The Global Economy and the
Decline of Social Reform

Changes in the postwar development of the welfare state became evident during the 1970s, and despite national variations these changes revealed numerous international parallels. In the context of fiscal crises and lower rates of growth, governments introduced shifts in tax structures, caps on public spending, wage and price controls, and "anti-inflation" monetary policies. Further expansion of reforms slowed or stopped, and the principle of the welfare state itself began to come under attack.[1]

The general cause of these shifts was not a changed political vision but rather what has come to be called the "new reality," the byword for the internationalization of capital, the coming of the global economy. In this new world market capital became "denationalized," that is, characterized by such a high degree of productive capacity and interlocking trade and investment that it cannot be said to have a national home. This is not to say that the largest and most industrialized nations no longer act in the interests of their "national" capital or that the national state is no longer an important source and means of capital accumulation. It is, however, to say that, once internationalized, capital: 1) requires "freedom" from national controls or intervention; 2) has ultimately no national allegiance; 3) has interests that span the world and far exceed national jurisdictions; and 4) operates within a world economy and possesses a "global perspective" in which domestic or national markets form only one element and indeed are too small for the productive capacity it possesses. The global economy produces its own demands that are distinct from those of the national economy. It also produces an integrated international arena that is both distinct from and a challenge to bounded and protected national economies, now moribund as such but characteristic of the development of capitalism up to the 1970s.

It follows that the persistence of a national framework in the form of trade barriers, monetary and fiscal regulations and institutions, and a vast number of laws and standards must be overcome. Just as with the formation of the nation-state in the eighteenth and nineteenth centuries, when local and regional barriers to trade had to be eliminated and national standards established in order to provide the possibilities for capital to expand more or less unfettered within a defined geographic territory, so too national standards and barriers to trade now have to be eliminated to allow capital to compete without such restraints in a global economy. We have arrived at the end of the era of the nation-state, and its declining significance is an important factor in the erosion of social reforms. Economic powers are now able to determine the direction of development at the international level, where compromises with national working classes, and indeed national governments, are not so necessary.

The Coming of the Global Economy

Throughout the history of the capitalist mode of production there has been an expanding world market. Capitalist classes have always sought to encompass and capitalize not only their domestic markets but also the "external" market. Such expansion, moreover, has been facilitated by a corresponding growth in the size and power of the state, in the public debt, and in financial mechanisms, that is, in international banking and credit facilities. There have also been correlative developments in the nature of the labour supply: the development of capitalism engendered the forcible "freeing" of farmers or peasants from their land, the enslavement of non-Europeans, the purchase of indentured or bonded workers, the export of convicts, and the use of child labour.

To be sure, a world economic system was evolving, but it was coming about through the expansion of nationally defined corporations that were branching out, in competition with other capital formations, to increase their overseas territorial dominions as markets for their commodities, sources of raw materials, and avenues for investment. It was defined by the increasing interdependence of national capitals, but it was still a system of national capitals whose interests were promoted by a national state, and whose expansion gave rise to the modern colonial system, forms of protectionism, and international wars.

By World War I, the most industrialized national capitals supported by state military power had divided the world into spheres of influence, but they had also spilled over their national foundations in other ways.

They had formed international cartels, trusts, and banking syndicates for the control of world markets; and after the First World War they had attempted to create international organizations and regulatory agreements to mitigate imperial rivalry (League of Nations), to regulate inter-imperial trade, investment, and capital markets (Bank of International Settlements, BIS), and to help guard against the expansion of socialism (the tripartism of the International Labour Organization, ILO).[2]

Despite these transnational beginnings, the world economic order between the two world wars remained dominated by competing national capitals. The Second World War, like the First, represented competition between national capitals raised to the level of the mobilization of the resources of the entire nation. It was, however, to be the last of such wars.

The immediate preconditions of globalization lay in World War II, the last major conflict characterized by the expansion of capital in its national form. Prior to that war, capital was largely national in character, and corporate interests, as "national interests," were jealously guarded at home and abroad by means of standing armed forces, tariff barriers, currency controls, and nationalism and citizenship, among numerous other national laws and policies. The war represented the historical denouement of the contradiction between the continuous impetus of capitalist expansion and its form as the nation-state.

From the point of view of capital, the war's end presented two dilemmas: how to reconstruct capitalism in Europe – but in a way that avoided rebuilding the contradiction between expanding capital and its national political form – and how to contain socialism, a form of property antithetical to the growth of capitalism. The solutions were more often than not combined in the same developments.

For the capitalist nations, the period between World War II and the 1970s constituted an interregnum between the age of competing imperial powers and the coming of the global economy. As the pre-eminent capitalist power at the end of the war, the United States was in a position to restructure the postwar world to reflect its own interests. Those interests, however, were in essence the interests of capital as capital, albeit still in national guise. Given this, the U.S. restructuring of the postwar capitalist world marked the beginning of the resolution of the contradiction that had given rise to both world wars. The world as it was – national governments representing national corporations – could grow no further except to encounter more collisions between national forms and with the obvious outcomes – bilateralisms, commercial warfare, national economic problems, and war. Moreover, given new atomic weaponry, another world war between the industrial nations had become unthinkable.

So began a period in which the boundaries of international relations were largely prescribed by the claims and exigencies of one imperial power. The "international regime" introduced after the war was a reflection of the international demands of U.S. corporate interests. As the dominant postwar power, hitherto limited in its access to the European and Japanese economies and their colonies or spheres of influence, the United States was intent on opening up new markets to itself. Its efforts were to lay the groundwork for a single world economy of competing capitals.

Establishing a global 'enabling framework'

The U.S.-designed postwar rapprochement saw the creation of political and economic structures and policies that remained dominated by the United States throughout the period. Under U.S. auspices in 1944, the future members of the United Nations (UN) held a conference at Bretton Woods and established the basis of an international monetary system.[3] The delegates created an exchange-rate mechanism by setting the parities of national currencies against the U.S. dollar; and they established, among others, two institutions, the International Monetary Fund (IMF) and the World Bank (WB). The IMF was intended to regulate international trade balances, but its general function was described as "a sort of Magna Carta for a future world economic order." The World Bank was designed to manage an international fund for economic development. Alongside these mechanisms, the General Agreement on Tariffs and Trade (GATT, established in 1947) would provide the institutional means for a negotiated removal of all national barriers to world trade and to create universal regulations for increasingly freer commerce.

Although these economic institutions and agencies were of primary importance after the war, the United Nations, dominated by the United States, was formed as the beginning of supranational quasi-government, as the political foundation for the new internationalism. Among other things, the UN took upon itself powers to oversee the long process of decolonization (one of the purposes of peace-keeping operations), which in most instances aided U.S. penetration into the former European colonies and advanced the geographic expansion of the capitalist mode of production and the destruction of remaining precapitalist modes.[4] The

UN was also employed to contain the expansion of socialism (Korea, the Congo, Greece, Indonesia), to promote the principles of liberal democracy and the rights of private property as a political system consistent with the advance of capitalism, and to establish international laws grounded in private rights for the "world community."

Although the United Nations appeared to be the embodiment of a genuinely democratic and multilateral world in the making, it was dominated by an executive (the Security Council), whose members (with the exception of the U.S.S.R.) were largely beholden to the United States. The UN was, moreover, financially dependent on the United States, as were most of its member nations, making it largely an instrument to make the world over in the image of America.[5] This quintessentially capitalist nation and the principles that it stood for were to be the model for the new world in the making, and U.S. dominance in supranational agencies and institutions remains to this day.

The liberal democracy promoted and established in the former Axis regimes and the decolonized world was the Trojan Horse of the new order – it held no intrinsic national character. Its principles were the principles of corporate private property, and the political system would amount to the periodic choice of different policies within this property regime; and as a result those principles would ultimately overreach national barriers. The assertion of national interests was possible, and they were promoted, to be sure, but in the final analysis national goals would prove contrary to the embedded political principles.

Besides liberalized world trade, the containment of socialism, and the furtherance of liberal political and legal principles, another pillar of the new internationalism was the aggregation of national markets. As early as the late 1940s the United States encouraged the European countries to see their future as the "United States of Europe" (a larger market for the postwar expansion of capital), and to this end they entered into the Organization for European Economic Co-operation (OEEC), whose main function was to promote intra-European free trade.[6] The Treaty of Rome (1957) soon followed, establishing the progressive growth of a European economic community. But Europe was not alone; by the 1960s, almost the entire world was part of one or another customs union, common market, or free-trade area.[7]

Although engineered by the United States to suit its economic needs and prevent the imperial conflicts of the past, this rapprochement contained contradictions that were to frame the period of its existence. The most obvious concerned the ascendency of U.S. military and economic power over the industrial nations of Europe and Japan. In effect, the United States represented one configuration of national capital interests, albeit the most powerful, in a postwar world in which other national capitals and their states were far from moribund, and in which their economic reconstruction was necessary to the success of the new world order. A second contradiction involved the persistence of national interests in the face of the developing "international regime." With no realistic alternative to an international future, national capitals were confronted with the dilemma of defending national interests while embracing the internationalism necessary for expansion.[8] Another contradiction came with the struggle between capitalism and socialism as the two main postwar roads to the future.

Throughout Europe the spread of socialism after the war as a promise of workers' power and a form of property antithetical to capitalism was pervasive. To ensure the future of capitalism, socialism had to be contained, and to this end the U.S. administration took up several initiatives. One comprised a massive financing of capitalist reconstruction on strictly U.S. terms (UNRRA – the United Nations Relief and Rehabilitation Administration, set up in 1943 to provide material relief for liberated nations – and the European Recovery Programme, or Marshall Plan, initiated in 1947), which involved a substantial degree of state intervention in both capital and working-class reproduction. Another involved the U.S. promotion of Keynesianism as a means of reconstruction that gave the working class varying degrees of protection from the effects of capitalism and involvement in its reconstruction. To affirm the U.S. commitment to this reconstruction of capitalism, a military alliance, NATO, was created in 1949 with a permanent U.S. commander-in-chief ensuring that country's military dominance over Europe. In addition the postwar period saw interference in European elections, political parties, government policies, and trade union movements.[9]

Although socialism as state capitalism was ultimately abandoned in the 1980s and 1990s, the postwar period saw the consolidation of Soviet hegemony over Eastern Europe, the victory of the Chinese People's Liberation Army, and numerous wars of liberation in former colonial countries. All of these events suggested that the socialist road might indeed succeed, a possibility that was always implied in the co-operative military and economic arrangements of the interregnum.

The same problems of rebuilding and consolidating capitalism, containing socialism, and ending national barriers to accumulation also presented themselves in the European colonial empires and spheres of influence. Within one decade of the end of World War II, struggles of national liberation arose in most of the colonial world: in Vietnam, China, Malaysia, Dutch East Indies, Korea, the Philippines, and India; in Algeria, Egypt, and Kenya; and in the Middle East. For U.S. capital, and capital in general, the socialist and nationalist movements of liberation had to be fought or co-opted, and the colonial systems had to be dismantled and opened to international trade. While military means were employed in many of these cases, greatly supported by the United States, the chief means of disengaging the colonial link and establishing the foundations of a capitalist economy were United Nations peacekeeping (both military and diplomatic operations) and the installation in the colonies of liberal-democratic or dictatorial regimes as required. The colonial systems could no longer be tolerated because their very nature favoured restricted trade relations with the metropole, while liberal democracy (or, in many cases, authoritarian systems) opened the door to foreign investment and embraced the principles that would ultimately supersede the structure of the nation-state.

To bring an end to colonialism and to ensure that the newly independent countries remained within the orbit of international capital accumulation, the preferred solution appeared to be a form of political independence embracing the formalities of liberal democracy and constitutionally entrenched principles of private property. Neo-colonialism – the subordination of former colonial countries mainly by economic means and principles – was established as the new relation between the industrial metropoles and the "lesser developed" nations. Transformed from colony *to* nominally independent nation-state, from subordination to one industrial metropole *to* compliance with the new international regime of corporate private property, most of the former colonies were, under the guise of political freedom, opened to international trade. A political shell of independence without the "content" of an indigenous capital formation obscured the real content, which was in essence the multinational corporation of the industrial world.

From the point of view of capital, both the war and its aftermath represented the restoration of the conditions for renewed accumulation. The war brought an end to economic depression, with state intervention in labour supply (regulated wages, restricted union activity, and even slave-labour in Germany and Japan) and in corporate assistance (super-profits and tax concessions for war production); government mobilization of public and private capital; and the destruction of inventories and new products in the war effort. After the war, the basis for renewed accumulation became the reconstruction of the devastated economies, again promoted by state-levered capital for the corporate sector by means of deficit financing, increased taxes, debased money, and, very importantly, U.S. "aid," particularly in the form of UNRRA and the Marshall Plan. Moreover, new markets and sources of raw materials emerged as many of the former colonial territories were opened to international capital.

Within a decade after 1945, the main elements of a framework of a supranational regime of accumulation, albeit dominated by the United States, had been established. There were the principles of liberal democracy ensconced in the United Nations, Marshall Aid for reconstruction, the IMF, World Bank, and GATT to regulate and liberalize world trade, incipient common markets promoted everywhere, and U.S. military control and influence throughout the world. All these facets of the postwar world order were progressively realized and operative by the end of the 1960s. A foundation had been laid for the regulation of multinational corporations that in principle transcended bilateral or multilateral relations between nation-states. This global regulatory regime was an essential precondition, a necessary and complementary part of the rise of the transnational corporation and the process of globalization.

Advanced Fordism and postwar economic expansion

The war not only restored conditions of profitability, but also dramatically advanced the means of production. The world's most powerful industrial nations had marshalled their national capital, drafted their scientists and engineers, and placed all these resources at the service of the industrialists for war production. World War II saw many scientific and technological races, which to a greater or lesser degree influenced its outcome.[10] After the war these developments became the basis for transformations in labour processes, communications and transportation, and agricultural and industrial products. Such changes, together with the mechanisms for liberalizing trade and renewed conditions for accumulation, laid the basis of the postwar interregnum.

Well before the war, the capacity of the factories of the industrial nations had exceeded the world's markets, resulting in product gluts, international corporate mergers and joint ventures, and considerable foreign direct investment. These markets, moreover, had expanded to encompass the non-socialist world, albeit divided into colonial systems and spheres of influence, increasing the competition of the national industrial production that continued to expand. Although indirectly a product of Fordism, the postwar framework now became the policy infrastructure for the realization of new developments within Fordism – an advanced Fordism.

Economic expansion in the period between the war and the early 1970s was qualitatively different from all previous periods. The growth in world trade was unprecedented: the increase in commodity exchange over this period grew by over 800 per cent – vastly greater than in any similar previous period and greater than the global growth in GNP.[11] A growing world market in commodities gradually superseded national markets, and global commodity production was established.

In the past foreign investment had principally taken the form of portfolio capital, implying the powers of the creditor. Now it took the shape of direct investment, possessing the powers of control. Foreign direct investment by the United States alone grew over tenfold between 1950 and 1975, and the returns from abroad increased from 7 per cent to more than 25 per cent over the same period.[12] For the corporation, this overseas equity investment had several consequences: the development of international vertical integration, the increase in multinational production, and, it followed, the beginning of the "denationalization" of the corporate perspective and, very importantly, the rise of extraterritorial control over national capital.

The rapid expansion in commodity trade and direct investment had far-reaching implications, which in turn added to the qualitative changes taking place. As multinational corporations grew, gradually becoming the dominant force in economic relations between nations, there arose a concomitant demand for international markets in capital and foreign exchange. Somewhat misleadingly called the Eurocurrency markets, they soon comprised world-wide financial markets trading in currencies outside the nation that had issued the currency. Their growth and size can only be described in hyperbole: from a market of two to three billion dollars in 1960, the Eurocurrency markets by the end of the 1970s commanded volumes of currencies several times greater than the domestic money supply of some nations. By the late 1970s it could be said that "to a very great extent the growth of the Eurocurrency market

[had] integrated the world's money and credit markets."[13] More or less beyond the control of national central banks, the growing global financial markets established themselves as in effect the final arbiter over national investment possibilities and policies. Due to Euromarket foreign exchange speculation, moreover, national interest and exchange rates were similarly restricted by what this market would allow. National monetary policies and direct controls were similarly offset, circumvented, or broadly determined by the action of the markets.

Just as these financial markets grew in accord with the rapid expansion of foreign trade, growing competition at the international level, and the internationalization of productive capital, so too did an international banking system. Between 1950 and 1974, the number of international branches of the large national banks grew from a handful of U.S. and Commonwealth banks with small assets and representing a small percentage of the parent's earnings to a far-flung international branch system with assets and earnings often approaching or exceeding the domestic operations.[14] Because much of the activity of the branches by the early 1970s was in the Eurocurrency markets, a supranational banking system was in effect created – a system that was and remains largely beyond the control of national central bank regulation.[15]

Although this postwar period was marked by an unprecedented expansion of national capitals beyond their national boundaries, most of this rapid growth in production, trade, and finance took place between the industrial nations of North America, Europe, and Japan. In other words, much of the expansion into international interdependence was carried out by national capitals whose dominant strength remained in a domestic market in the industrial countries under the aegis of a national state. The "national" form of this expansion during the interregnum had significant consequences for the structure of the national working classes and the outcome of the national struggle between labour and capital.

Because economic growth and reconstruction during the interregnum took place as national capital within a nation-state, the labour supply was similarly defined by the boundaries of the nation. This national delimitation of the labour force, the relative shortage of "man"-power due to the war, the persistent spectre of socialism, the sustained economic growth rates, and consequent high demand for labour power allowed the working classes in the industrial nations to achieve a relatively high standard of living and degree of social security between the late 1940s and early 1970s. For its part during this period, capital needed an expanded role for the state to aid in reconstruction and to lend support in the heightened competition of the liberalizing world economy. At the same time, the progress of alternative socialist economic systems in Eastern Europe and Asia presented a continuing risk, and the memory of the social unrest of the 1930s remained strong. Capital therefore was relatively open to accommodative arrangements with labour, and as a result the Keynesian welfare state became the compromise product of the period.

Although the KWS in the industrial nations represented the highest achievement by a national working class under a national capitalist regime, it was an achievement made possible by the particular elements of the postwar historical juncture. It was the *national* compromise between an organized working class and an expanding capitalist class in the context of restored conditions of accumulation, a tight labour market, high wages, sustained growth, the socialist challenge, and national capital's need for an increased role for the state.

The decline of national sovereignty

While these conditions allowed for the growth of the KWS, however, the extranational economic expansion was eroding the power and influence of the national state. Corporate trade and investment overseas were growing dramatically as a percentage of total operations, and the multinational corporations (MNCs) had begun shifting profits and operations to places where the advantages in taxation, wages, or state support were greatest. Increasingly, they assumed the powers of sovereign entities, ignoring and interfering in the interests of nation-states.[16] This expansion of the MNCs added international pressure to remove national barriers and level the costs of corporate activities. The rise of foreign currency and international capital markets, moreover, meant not only that these economic functions were increasingly outside the control of national regulation, but also that they increasingly set the limits, as independent markets, on national policies with respect to credit systems, money supply, exchange and interest rates, debt-management, investment policies, and taxation.[17]

The growing erosion of the role and powers of the national state was also visible in the rise of supranational accords or treaties, multilateral agreements and organizations that all in their own way began to restrict national sovereignty. Between 1945 and the early 1970s, international government organizations (IGOs) and international non-governmental organizations (INGOs) broadened their powers and increased by about threefold in number, such that by the end of the 1970s there was hardly an aspect of national life in industrial countries that was not addressed in some way by a supranational body. Military multilateralism in the shape of NATO, the Warsaw Pact, the United Nations, and other regional pacts took the place of the independent national exercise of armed force outside national borders. National policies on international trade, scientific and technical standards for goods and services, transportation and communication, employment and health standards, and pollution were all increasingly subject to modification and reformulation to bring them into accord with internationally set rules and regulations.[18]

The decline in powers of the national state was also reflected in the worldwide increase in preferential trading groups. Although the most important and earliest was the European Economic Community (EEC) in 1958, there was not a single region in the world, including the centrally planned economies, that had not attempted to create a common market, customs union or free-trade area between the 1950s and the mid-1970s. Despite certain political resistance and at times faltering success, economic interdependence at the global and regional levels had everywhere profoundly circumscribed national sovereignty.

The two-tiered development of the interregnum

From 1945 to the early 1970s, capitalism developed in a two-tiered manner that reflected the nature of the postwar rapprochement: the state-managed reconstruction of capitalism took place within the nation-state, while at the same time the framework for international free trade was undermining the national economy, the rationale of the nation-state. The contradiction between the national form of capital and the intrinsic drive of capital to overcome this shell was moving towards its resolution with the erosion of this rationale. Given the expanding supranational economic framework, the size and power of MNCs, and the actual global development of capitalism, the only resolution remaining to the contradiction was the dismantling of the national shell. By the early 1970s, the national relations of production were increasingly seen by transnational corporations (TNCs) as mere fetters to intercorporate relations at the global level.

Throughout this postwar period, and corresponding to the growth of MNCs and international government organizations, there arose international strata of bureaucrats, technocrats, academics, and corporate managers, owners, and advisors. They managed the agencies and organs of supranational governance, and the highest placed also met regularly in certain forums for the express purpose of discussing global trends and policies for the advance of certain interests.[19] Besides the more "public" venues, such as UN agencies, the Organization for Economic Co-operation and Development (OECD), and GATT, private venues such as the Trilateral Commission, the Bilderberg conferences, the Club of Rome, and the so-called think-tanks such as the Mont Pelerin Society and the Heritage Foundation were all employed for these purposes. While not coherent as a national government, here nevertheless was a growing matrix of "public" and private organizations for decision-making and policy-formation at the global level that became increasingly influential as the demands for a global economy increased, and that formed the meeting-ground for transnational strata occupied with the advancement of a global economy.

It is perhaps not possible to say when the global economy became a reality as distinct from interrelated national economies, but certainly by the mid-1970s the end of the interregnum could be seen in two significant developments. One was the extensive reduction in barriers to world trade and production: the productivity of the advanced Fordist mode of production possessed the capacity for world supply, and the postwar "enabling framework" had gone far to erode national restrictions. The other was the loss of U.S. national paramountcy, signalled by several events. Perhaps the most important was the suspension of the convertibility of the dollar into gold in 1971, which ended the fixed exchange rate mechanism that had so benefited U.S. expansion. Another was the waning of the rate of U.S. direct investment and exports to Europe by the early 1970s, while European and Japanese products and capital began to claim ever greater shares of the U.S. market. Also about this time the United States had begun to lose some of its edge in technological superiority to Germany and Japan. On the surface, the United States appeared to be yielding to these rival economic powers; in effect, it was succumbing to the internationalization of capital – built on a foundation that Washington itself had forced on the world. Americanization was becoming tempered by internationalization; the premise was becoming absorbed by its conclusion.

There were other harbingers of the end of the interregnum or the approaching global economy, and all were consequences of two decades of unprecedented capital accumulation. One was the near completion of decolonization and the consequent "opening up" of the entire globe (with the exception of the "socialist" countries) to capitalization. The world was now in effect subjected to the capitalist mode of production.[20] Another precursor was the transformation of increasing numbers of multinational corporations into TNCs, defined by the expanding internationalization of their production and decline of a meaningful home base or domestic market.[21] Related to this development was the rising importance of international foreign exchange and capital markets and of supranational agreements and organizations, and the consequent increasingly obvious erosion of national identity and sovereignty, not to mention the globalization of culture.[22]

Ironically, at the culmination of this interregnum, and before the transformation of the nation-state was about to begin in earnest, the voice of the non-corporate sector began to be heard. In the industrialized nations, a citizenry that had come to believe that their right to vote gave them power over policy began to demand and expect a progressive extension of the welfare state – demands characterized by the corporate sector as the "ungovernability of democracy."[23] In the decolonized nations, leaders labouring under the belief that independence would bring freedom, democracy, and material betterment and not a new form of colonization made demands for an end to unequal exchange, a new international economic order.[24] More successfully, a group of oil-producing nations formed a loose coalition (OPEC) and began to exact a somewhat fairer share of oil revenues, albeit mainly for their own elites, from the oil cartel. By the end of the 1970s, as the "new reality" began to set in, these voices were silenced or compromised, or had found other forms of expression.

By about 1970, the key institutional preconditions for a global economy were in place; they had become a force of production in the encouragement of global economic interdependence and helped foster new means of production. Nevertheless, production was still largely national, although much trade and commerce had turned international. The movement to a global economy in which the circuit of capital itself was global and national integrity weak and in decline had not yet become manifest. About this time a dramatic change in the technology of production, distribution, and circulation began to be realized. These were changes that could not possibly be contained within the framework of the nation-state.

Revolution in the Means of Production

The catalyst that moved the world from one era to the other grew out of the advanced Fordist mode of production. A revolution in technology grounded in the development of computers, in the shift from transistors to solid circuitry or integrated circuits, took place about 1970-71. This miniaturization of electronic circuits vastly reduced the size of computers, exponentially increased their speed and capacity, and enormously decreased costs. With the central processing unit (CPU) on a chip by 1971, a radical transformation in computing began; and with an associated growth in software, the number of potential users and applications of computers multiplied by manyfold in a very short period during the 1970s. Early in the decade it became clear that little in the entire range of the production of goods and services could not be "computerized."[25]

Essentially different from Fordism, computer-aided production made science and technology pre-eminent in the production process, and the resulting highly capital-intensive systems greatly raised productivity and reduced the amount of necessary labour. This led to the growth of "levelled" low-wage jobs confronting relatively fewer highly paid jobs.[26] It ushered in, moreover, an era of permanent revolution in science and technology as applied to the mode of production. In turn, productivity gains over advanced Fordism were not only very large, but also became continuous as the highly competitive global economy forced the introduction of ever more automated processes.[27] If the economies of scale of postwar Fordist production demanded and supplied a global market, the productivity and flexibility of computer-integrated production and distribution reinforced and extended this globalism.[28]

The revolutionary nature of these changes in computing hardware and the development of software rested in the qualitative turn they brought to the pursuit of knowledge, the objectification of science, the transmission of information, and the production process.[29] The amplified speed of access to information, the magnified ability to manipulate data and problem-solve, the vast storage capacity, and the unfathomable number of applications all began to make their impact. No arena of human endeavour was left untouched. Not only could knowledge and information now be completely objectified, stored outside human carriers, but they could also be accessed through and employed by machines. In short order an era began, characterized by continuous rapid growth in knowledge, a relentless compression in time and space, and an "information"-based mode of production. The structure and dimensions of markets changed, the organization and location of the firm were transformed, and the importance of political geography diminished. The possibility and necessity for international co-operation grew because the physical constraints on production and distribution were rapidly declining and no single country possessed the expertise or capital required for the larger Research and Development (R&D) projects. Throughout the late 1970s and early 1980s these applications in manufacturing were extended to all aspects of the circuit of capital: production (the primary and secondary sectors), distribution (transportation and communication), and circulation (finance, administration, and government).

In the realm of production, the computer transformed the entire labour process, including machinery, warehousing, quality control, engineering, and design, and it also paved the way for biotechnology, which had begun to make an impact by the end of the 1970s. In the early 1970s, computer-aided production and continuous processes were already in operation; they raised productivity, lowered costs, increased quality, created new synthetic products, and eliminated jobs. Their application brought into being "lean production," "just-in-time" assembly, and "flexible manufacturing," developments that immensely facilitated global production in multiple sites and from multiple sources and also demanded a global market. Such computer-aided production was in wide use in Japan even before the end of the decade.[30]

As globalized production grew so too did changes in the means of distribution; the reciprocal relation between the two spheres meant that the costs of distribution had to decrease. To make the process of global production possible – that is, to expedite the global conjoining of raw materials, labour power, and instruments – there had to be a corresponding shrinking of time and space. The enormous growth in commodity trade in the 1960s had already brought technical, political, and organizational changes to the means of distribution. These changes were being realized by 1970. Technological innovations had major effects on shipping, including the construction of supertankers, bulk carriers, and new harbour facilities, and the increasing use of containerization. Political changes for the shipping companies involved the shift from national incorporation to so-called "flags of convenience," a form of global deregulation; international air traffic became increasingly facilitated by national deregulation and increasing supranational oversight. Organizationally, as transportation became global it became "intermodal," that is, cargo could move in two or more different modes of transport under one rate to reach its final destination. The computer formed the basis of these changes – in design, construction, operation, scheduling, and navigation. Given global production, distribution had to be similarly organized.

The increase in global activity in these spheres demanded changes in the means of communication. The technology of telecommunications was revolutionized in the second half of the 1970s, when computers and telecommunication systems converged and satellite relays were introduced. New services and products emerged, and the speed and volume of communications increased. The technology for a global system of communications that was reliable, fast, and relatively inexpensive was in place. National systems, where they were not bypassed, would thereafter only be a link in an otherwise global system.

It was this connection of telecommunications and computers in the 1970s that laid the basis for what was referred to even then as the "information society." Information was knowledge and skill objectified outside human carriers in the computer. This knowledge and skill could now be stored and disseminated, used as product, service, or instruction, at speeds and across distances that changed much of the physical basis of economic activity. This was the technological revolution that shifted human activity from being energy-intensive to information-intensive.

The transformation in the technology of telecommunications had significant effects in the sphere of circulation: on the supply and demand, on the movement, of money. In a capitalist system, all production, distribution, and consumption require money as a measure of value and means of circulation. The greater the increase in the kinds and number and quantity of commodities put to market and the broader the market, the larger the amount of money required and the faster its velocity. Telecommunications linked with computers increased the velocity of money in global circulation, greatly assisting the push to a globally integrated economy and affirming the global accumulation process. Transnational banks, stock and capital markets, and associated capital flows all became integrated into a global system resting on this technology.

The globalization of finance means that enormous sums of capital can be shifted around the world with unprecedented speed, reaching out to investments with the highest rates of return and entering activities of a purely speculative nature. It means that goods and services can be produced and distributed globally, independent of national sources of, or restrictions on, capital; national markets can be profoundly influenced by movements of capital free of national interest. With the power and enormity of global financial resources, these goods, services, and capital break through all nationally bounded markets, forcing nations to harmonize policies with the demands of global movement of commodities and capital. The decline of national jurisdiction over monetary and fiscal policies renders the national state into a local minister of global affairs.

All these changes in the means of production represent the subordination of both inanimate and animate nature to the human will in an unparalleled, indeed transformative, way. The implicit power, productivity, flexibility, mobility, and relative inexpensiveness of these new "instruments" make all that is bound up with the historical development of the nation-state seem anachronistic. To be more specific, there are a few key implications of this computer-based mode of production that can be drawn out to show its essential incompatibility with the political structures and property relations belonging to earlier stages in the capitalist mode of production.

First, these new instruments of production possess the potential for minimizing and even eliminating human beings at the points of production, distribution, and communication. The most obvious consequence, and a growing reality, is widespread structural unemployment or underemployment around the world, co-existent with a productive capacity that has never been greater and grows continuously. The computerized mode of production contains no potential for an absolute increase in employment, and by the 1990s the question of the future of work and welfare had become a current if not pressing issue.[31] The estimated one billion unemployed and underemployed in the world cannot but grow.[32] With production dispersed globally, the problem cannot be addressed at the national level. National employment, investment, and social security policies cannot be maintained with rising unemployment and underemployment; they are now global issues that require global answers.

Second, computerization has allowed scientific and technical change to develop into what can only be deemed a permanent technological revolution. Given the introduction of microprocessors into every stage and aspect of the circuit of capital, this revolution means that the grounds for whatever temporal constancy there was in our social structures is disappearing. In the past, all eras were characterized by a given mode of production that remained relatively stable; and in the particular mode of production was grounded the peculiarities of the period in the class structure, the labour process, careers, family and social relations, and political practice and policy. The attributes of the entire social structure rested more or less on the nature of the mode of production and lasted roughly as long. We have now entered an age in which a foundation for such relative social and political stability no longer exists. From relative stability as foundation we now increasingly experience continuous change as the foundation. It is possible to argue that never again will there be an era characterized by a given mode of production. It follows that the national peculiarities of a mode of production and all that rests on that mode are now more or less a question of history.

Third, computer-based production and biotechnology have shifted the focus of production from the "analytic" to the synthetic. While the first synthetic products were produced late in the nineteenth century, most of the world's goods and services remained "analytic" in their production; that is, nature was exploited to serve human needs, and however divided or manipulated in its employment it was still nature in its elemental form. The shift to the synthetic entails a radical change of focus; after nature is reduced to its molecular or genetic foundation certain components are reconstituted to create "man-made" products to address a range of human needs. This power to reconstitute at will the component elements of inanimate or animate nature for human purposes was rather limited until the 1970s. It is now increasingly central to the production for the entire range of human needs. Historically, this change is a watershed; it allows humans to manipulate nature according to will and gives them command over the future of all life forms. In practice, it is the coming to pre-eminence of the overarching principle of conscious engineering and design. Its implications embrace the end of evolution. Yet, it is not humans as such who will wield this power; it exists almost exclusively in the hands of corporations; its use will therefore be circumscribed by private interest and business motives.

The fourth implication of the computer-based mode of production has to do with communications and the creation of the so-called "information society." What this comprises is a network of computers and transmission systems and the objectification (the storage, dissemination, and productive use) of knowledge and skill outside human carriers. Put another way, it means that the labour process shifts from a foundation in human carriers of knowledge and skill to a base in computers or biotechnology in which knowledge and skill are objectified to an unprecedented degree. Under capitalism, this knowledge and skill more than ever become commodified as product or service.

To the degree that the "information society" has arrived, there are certain consequences. The most obvious is the coming of the "virtual" institution.[33] Banks, corporate head offices, government administration, universities and schools, and factories can all be reduced to computer systems storing, distributing, and applying information; and the problem of geographic location approaches irrelevancy. The globalizing implications are immediately evident and indisputable.

There is, moreover, an enormous impact on all the professions in medicine, law, engineering, architecture, and teaching. They represent specialized accumulated knowledge in the form of human repositories, disseminators, and users. But the computer can do much of what they do now and increasingly more, and in principle it represents the demise of the expert, defined by knowledge as a monopoly of the professions. "Come into my parlour," said the computer to the expert – an insight expressed very early on, at the beginning of the computer era. Professional as well as national monopolies over knowledge become less and less significant, while corporate monopoly in the form of patents and intellectual property rights rapidly increases.

Aside from these implications, the "information society" has meant an enormous compression of global time and space. Interconnected via nearly instantaneous communications and rapid transit, global business no longer needs to recognize anything but the non-stop production, distribution, and circulation of capital. Corporate activity goes far beyond the reach of the national state, and the nation increasingly becomes a local or regional market in the process of corporate central planning. With labour value increasingly being levelled across the globe with computerization and the globalization of production and distribution, the fiscal foundation of the KWS in the industrial countries erodes and the decline of the welfare state as it was known in the postwar period becomes apparent. All the conditions for unceasing global economic activity, ever larger corporate monopolies, cartels, and more global corporate central planning are coming into place. It is no small irony of globalization that Hayek will have to pay a visit to Marx to find out what is happening.

There are paradoxes to this objectification of knowledge and skill outside the human carrier. On the one hand, it represents the possibility of the democratization and universal dissemination of knowledge, and all the potential benefits and advances there entailed; unfortunately, this remains by and large an abstract possibility. On the other hand, it increases the corporate monopoly of ownership over information and its transmission. Corporate power over the world's population has never been greater. Despite this power, the increasing capitalization of the production processes leads to an end of the capital-labour relation. The minimization or even elimination of labour as the source of value implies an end to the relations of capital. In other words, the future of computerization and all its implications imply an end to commodity production.[34]

The Global Era

The trends towards the internationalization of capital during the interregnum continued and intensified in the 1970s and thereafter. Commodity trade expanded, though it was now in the shape of world commodities in a world market: by 1980 the sales of many TNCs in "foreign markets" increased to more than one-half of total sales; and the imports and exports of all the industrial nations, except Japan, increased as a percentage of the GNP.[35] A system of highly integrated world trade was an irreversible fact by the end of the 1970s, confirmed and hastened by the new means of transportation and communications, whose increased productivity were transforming the worldwide distribution of products and hence the global conditions for valorization.[36] Also, with the coming of computer-based systems, capitalist production became less constrained by large-scale, long-term investments; and with the continuing diminution of national barriers it could increasingly be "sited" in regions or countries with the most favourable conditions for accumulation (for instance, proximity to markets, types of labour force, and state concessions). This locational flexibility of productive capital became an important factor in the development of a changing international division of labour, and the 1970s saw a geographic restructuring of production leading to a rapid rise in the world share of manufactured exports from developing countries.[37] Along with this came a growth in the Eurocurrency markets, to such a degree that by the end of the 1970s the world's financial markets were close to becoming a single integrated market.[38]

71

Global labour market

All these changes worked towards the establishment of a global labour market. The decolonization and capitalist penetration of the non-industrialized countries after World War II gradually created an enormous potential, internationally available labour supply, previously "locked up" in precapitalist modes of production or restricted to the needs of the capital of the colonial "mother country." During the interregnum, an unprecedented international migration from former colonies to the metropolitan countries and enormous internal immigration in the industrial countries from transformed sectors of the labour market had provided a continuous supply of new labour power.[39] Yet given the sustained national growth rates and limited entry, the supply was more or less readily absorbed until the early 1970s. By this time, Europe and the United States had many millions of ex-colonials and/or illegal immigrants forming a large "underclass" of poor and unorganized workers, condemned to menial work, ineligible for citizenship, restricted in legal rights, and limited in access to the welfare state. The national working classes were to a large degree insulated from the effects of these reservoirs of labour as long as their position in an advanced Fordist mode of production and growing public and unproductive sectors was maintained, and as long as national laws controlled immigration and prevented the integration of the underclass.[40] Even so, these labour pools produced a drag on minimum wages and therefore on the whole wage structure; and despite their limited access to social security, they reduced the redistribution of social surplus to the national working class.

Just as national capital in the eighteenth and nineteenth centuries had created national labour markets, so too had the processes of trade liberalization, changes in the means of production, and increasing international production begun to create an international labour market by the mid-1970s. At this stage it was made up of three main components: the "underclass" of displaced and immigrant labour in the metropolitan countries, the labour force in centres of cheap labour (Puerto Rico, Hong Kong, Singapore, Dominican Republic), and workers in "free-enterprise zones" or elsewhere, wherever commodities for the world market were produced. The more that products from all the less-industrialized countries entered the global market, the more that the value of the labour power in these countries, and embedded in these products, became a part of the internationalization of labour value.

The effects of this emerging global labour market began to become visible from the early 1970s on with a general downward pressure on wages in the industrial world. The incipient international levelling of the value of labour power encouraged the rise of female participation in the labour force, a growth in forms of coerced or unfree labour, and the gradual reintroduction of child labour.[41] Union bargaining rights began to confront increasing legal restrictions, and union membership in the industrial nations started to fall as the establishment of a growing surplus of low-wage workers in the international labour market began to reduce both the high demand for labour and upward pressure on wages. As permanent unemployment climbed in the second half of the 1970s, high wages declined, as did the social wage, and so began the deterioration of the fiscal foundation of the KWS. The contemporary movement towards world wages also commenced.[42]

The making of a global capitalist labour market that will encompass all the world's labour-power is far from complete. It continues, as in the past, by the same legal, illegal, and coercive means. The brutalities continue no less now than in the past, with land clearances, forced emigration and transmigration, war, slaughter, disease, and habitat destruction. The more or less forceful proletarianization of that substantial part of humanity that has not yet entered the capitalist labour market proceeds apace. It is the creation of a labour market that is without protection from either the national state or global agency. The supranational framework that has developed exists by and large for capital alone; no such labour-capital compromise as developed in the form of the KWS in the industrial nations after World War II has appeared at the global level.

Capital as 'self-supporting' at global level

By the mid-1970s all the elements were in place for the existence of a "self-supporting system" of capitalist accumulation at the international level.[43] The relations between capitals, and between capital and labour, had evolved into a system of "self-expansion" increasingly independent of national considerations. International trade in commodities and overseas production both began to exceed national production and distribution in economic importance. The capital and foreign exchange markets had established themselves as largely independent of national regulation. A labour market that in effect embraced the world's labour force (outside the centrally planned economies) had also made its appearance.[44]

With the coming of a self-supporting system of capital self-expansion, a supranational law of value also came into independent operation.[45] The international exchange of commodities increasingly became determined by the world average of socially necessary labour time, which in turn was regulated by factors such as the global supply and demand of labour power, the outcome of the global struggle between the capitalist and working classes, and the productivity rates of the most advanced technology, wherever located. The consequences of the law of value operating on the global level are the same as the previous consequences on the national level: a pressure to equalize the conditions of production and exchange and rates of profit, but now on the world level; and a movement towards world prices and world wages.[46]

For the state the consequences of economic globalization are above all those of erosion of its functions and redefinition at the international level. Under the capitalist mode of production, the role and functions of the state are defined largely by the particular formation and character of national capital and the various conflicts and class struggle that accompany its realization. As long as this capital remained national, even though influenced by its extension outside its home territory, "its" state sought to defend its interests at home and abroad. If capital forged the modern nation-state and made over the administrative-political state in its own image, it was only for as long as capital in its self-expansion remained nationally based in its development. Once capital had expanded such that it required a larger domestic market and increasing sources of raw materials and labour supplies, it entered the age of imperialism and imperial wars, culminating in the two world wars of the twentieth century.

The postwar rapprochement, however, was directed precisely at national barriers and therefore at the national delimitation of capital. The gradual removal of national restrictions and support created the conditions allowing capital to grow beyond national borders as simply capital. The facts that after the war capital still had a national stamp and that U.S. capital had and continued to have a position of dominance are immaterial to the fact that an international regulatory regime, however biased and incomplete, had been imposed on the world of national capitals, making their "nationality" increasingly less important to competitive success.

Capital has been outgrowing the very geographic and political forms it had made for itself. By the end of the interregnum it was superseding its own political framework, and the functions of the state and meaning of nationality were being eroded and becoming redefined at the supranational level. After the 1970s, all the earlier trends towards internationalization continued, beset by all the problems attendant on such a profound transformation. TNCs increasingly assumed the powers of sovereign entities; the markets in capital, commodities, and foreign exchange consolidated their transnational existence; customs unions, common markets, and free-trade areas embraced most of the countries of Europe and the less developed world. Multilateral treaties and agreements, military pacts, and the formation of numerous IGOs and INGOs covered almost every aspect of economic activity, as well as significant aspects of social and political life, placing constraints on national independence. The authority of international laws increasingly asserted itself over all national states. Even general policies and programs for the globalization of the economy became subject to transnational formulation in several venues, namely, in right-wing think-tanks such as the Mont Pelerin Society and the Heritage Foundation, in the Trilateral Commission, and in the annual economic summits of the world's most advanced industrialized nations, known as the Group of Seven (G7).[47]

Without fear of exaggeration, it can be said that the national state has lost and continues to lose much of its sovereignty, although the degrees of independence vary with the degree of remaining integrity to national economic and military formations. It is not so much that a political state cannot act independently because of the erosion or usurpation of its powers, but that its *raison d'être* – the existence of a nationally defined capitalist class – has been waning. Taking its place has been the rise of an international capitalist class with global interests.[48] The idea of national considerations is increasingly becoming an anachronism, as capital has by and large lost its national character and seeks worldwide for advantages for itself in the conditions of accumulation. The present role of national states becomes the task of developing the international mechanisms and agencies to facilitate and regulate the accumulation of capital on a global scale. The more these are developed, the more the functions of the national state themselves will be subverted.[49]

The Decline of Social Reform

One of the central effects of this internationalization of capital has been the shift of the key or core economic policies informing government practice in the industrial world from Keynesianism to monetarism. By the 1980s Keynesianism had in effect been "abandoned."[50] Keynesian policies, reflective of the interests of national capital in an age of late industrialization or Fordism, the last stage of the integrated national economy, had lost their meaning as a philosophy of national economic management when the internationalization of capital began to undermine the economic policies of the nation-state. The stimulation of national demand would no longer necessarily increase national investment, now more and more dependent on international conditions. National or local demand that was stimulated by Keynesian policies might well be met by existing capacity or new investment elsewhere in the world.

The coming of monetarism did not represent a failure of Keynesianism, as some would argue, so much as a change of circumstances.[51] As the global economy emerged, Keynesianism was increasingly at variance with the new conditions, while monetarism conformed to the developments and was promoted as the appropriate form of economic policy. Monetarism represented the policies required by internationalized capital in a global economy, an arena in which political compromise with national working classes was a declining issue, and in which the costs of production became pre-eminent and the costs of reproduction of the working class completely subordinate. It represented the abandonment of national policies designed to maintain national bourgeoisies in positions of national hegemony, and the introduction of laissez-faire policies conducive to international capital, to competition at the international level, and to the levelling of conditions of national economies to standards of a common denominator.[52]

The achievement of these goals was to be pursued not just through the primary policy of monetarism – the war against inflation, intended to bring price stability.[53] The goals were to be met also in the displacement of *politically* controlled economic policies, such as those found in the Keynesian welfare state. Monetarism embodies the depoliticization of economic policy because its adoption moves control over the economy away from state intervention to the attempts of a central bank to regulate money supply. Such an approach to economic policies requires no large public sector with enormous state investments and consumption to effect national compromises between labour and capital. The central bank can control monetary policies without the public sector as it exists; it is no accident, then, that monetarism brings with it numerous associated policies designed to dismantle the Keynesian welfare state.

As macroeconomic policy, monetarism has little need for the state or its bureaucracy, but instead requires a mechanism independent of government, of national and political programs – a mechanism found in the relatively autonomous central banks.[54] The degree of autonomy varies considerably from nation to nation, but the coming of the global economy and the adoption of monetarism have brought with them distinct efforts to increase the constitutional autonomy of central banks. This autonomy becomes a way of securing a mechanism for the promulgation of monetarist policies free of political interference, and it represents an attempt to make monetarism more or less "irreversible" as a single global economic policy.

There have been worldwide efforts to secure the independence of central banks. The Maastricht treaty setting out the terms of European economic union promotes the idea of an independent European central bank; in 1989 Chile amended its constitution to make the central bank independent; in subsequent years Venezuela, Colombia, and Argentina followed suit; and in 1993 Mexican president Carlos Salinas de Gortari proposed a constitutional amendment to give political independence to his country's central bank. This independence serves as a powerful counter to national programs or partisan political policies that might interfere with globalization.[55]

A second major effect of the "new reality" that began to become evident by the late 1970s was the decline of social reform everywhere in the industrialized nations. This retrenchment began with the erosion of the conditions calling and allowing for social reform.

Those conditions, multifold and interrelated, had begun to change even before the 1970s. National capitals, as such, with distinct national interests had begun to decline. The new agencies and definers of policy and action were gradually becoming the terms of membership in trading blocs, the world market, international monetary agreements and institutions, and supranational political and military organizations. The purpose and function of the national state were becoming increasingly usurped by this "higher" level, and its role began to shift more and more to merely "regional" administration and security, and the facilitation of local capital accumulation.

The ability of the state in the West to finance reform programs went into decline, largely because of the falling rates of national economic growth. But whether the rate was rising or falling, economic growth no longer maintained the "positive" relation it once had to "national" wealth in the form of corporate tax revenues and high wages. Since the 1970s, corporations have been more able than ever to play off nation against nation and have taxes reduced while maintaining or increasing concessions. Wage controls and inflation, moreover, have led to a decline in real wages in many countries, while new technology has increased the levels of long-term structural unemployment.[56] An increased tax burden on the working class has been the main factor offsetting declining revenues. The future possibility of syphoning increasing surpluses out of the Third World for the benefit of the industrial countries would appear to be at an end.[57] And the developing global labour market has undermined the delimited national labour market and thereby weakened the main condition allowing for the social wage.

In addition to this declining ability to finance the welfare state, increasing social needs, a depressed or shifting corporate sector, decaying infrastructure, and approaching limits to taxation on falling real incomes have placed increasing demands on state expenditures. Together these pending limits, rising needs, corporate blackmail, and falling potential for national economic expansion have produced the chronic and growing state indebtedness that further limits the resources needed to fund the KWS.

The existence of trade unions has been fundamental to the achievement of social reform because they have been the main organized force arising from the working class, and its only authentic voice. With the introduction of computer-aided production in every sphere of the economy, however, the nature of work and the structure of the working class have changed. New strata have begun to arise, but fewer overall; and structural, long-term unemployment grows while most job creation is at the lower income levels. The global labour market has begun to undermine wages and conditions of work in the industrial nations. As a consequence of these developments, the trade union movement has steadily been losing its members and political and economic importance and has become more quiescent and defensive.[58] The national jurisdictions in which it grew and was defined have become less and less relevant to business decisions. In short, unions are left as national organizations in an era of international forces. They begin to appear as anachronisms because they have not for various reasons followed capital into the international arena.

The conditions that gave rise to the welfare state are being eroded or transformed. The nation-state is losing its *raison d'être*, that is, capital with a national identity; there is a decline in "returns" from the Third World; a continuous revolutionary restructuring of industry is creating weakened trade union movements, a levelling of social strata, and a growth in long-term unemployment; and the consequent changes in the tax-base and growing social needs are increasing state indebtedness. Since the 1970s, when the People's Republic of China shifted to the "capitalist road," and since the early 1990s, when the U.S.S.R. collapsed from its own bureaucratic weight, the threat of socialism in the world, let alone in the West, has been minimized. If part of the rationale of the KWS was to counter working-class attraction to socialism, this concern has dissipated.

If the conditions of the postwar era – capital in its national clothes with a nationally delimited labour market – led to the creation of the KWS as the national mechanism for the reproduction of labour and capital, it cannot be said that these conditions obtain any longer. In the global market, capital can reproduce itself with abundant cheap and unorganized labour from around the world and with few and often no associated "external" costs.

Another factor in this present transformation can no longer be ignored. If the decline of social reform is increasingly leaving social needs unanswered, there has never been much by way of environmental reform, national or international, to confront the consequences of planetary pollution caused by decades of industrial production and consumption. "Nature" now appears as plundered and polluted and in many places apparently unable to regenerate itself in the short term. Several areas of the world's oceans have been badly contaminated or fished out, huge expanses of forest have been depleted, soil exhaustion and erosion are appearing everywhere, fresh water sources are increasingly used up or poisoned, and air in urban and industrial areas is polluted. The impact of this destruction, which economists once considered as mere "externalities," is having a limiting effect on production itself.[59] While critics agree that these effects can no longer be ignored, governments seek to minimize their import, mouthing concern but doing little to clean up or prevent further destruction; and corporations resist the idea of accepting responsibility for the external costs of their industrial processes.

The decline of the conditions allowing for social reform means that no matter which party assumes power, the possibility of continuing those reforms associated with the KWS has been diminished. Such policies were the product of the politics of the age of maturing national capital, that is, capital in the imperialist era, which implied international relations between nation-states, but not global relations between organized capitals.[60]

In this period of transition to a world economy, all political parties in the industrial nations, including those whose tendency is social-democratic, are confronted with the tasks of managing a capitalist economy, now no longer national, with only the tools of the moribund national state. Given this predicament, most parties in the West coming into power since the mid-1970s have pursued more or less similar policies – policies reflecting the demands of internationalized capital, yet at the same time spelling out the conditional end of the nation-state and its associated political alternatives and social reforms.[61]

V

Neo-liberal Policies and Their Rationale

Neo-liberal policies, variously labelled as Thatcherism, Reaganism, neo-conservatism, and the New Right Agenda, were discernible by the mid-1970s and had become formal government policy in many countries by the end of that decade. They are the policy side of the "new reality;" they represent the political requirements of capital internationalized, highly centralized, and global in perspective. They also represent the last national policies to be promulgated, the final act of the independent nation-state, because with their acceptance the economic and political barriers to production and distribution around the world will have been minimized. With their adoption they will have in effect harmonized the national with the global economy.

The possibility of national management of national economies will increasingly be abridged, and national forms of the welfare state will be more and more difficult to maintain. All the industrial nations and almost all of the developing nations are in the process of legislating these neo-liberal policies, and their promulgation will transform social reform as we have known it. Social democracy will rapidly lose its meaning and purpose, if it has not already, as all political parties find themselves increasingly obliged, with greater or lesser resistance, to carry out this "agenda."[1]

In the postwar period capital completed its conquest of domestic markets (commodifying almost every aspect of life within the nation-state) and the international markets (opening up the world for business). In the 1970s, with the coming of a self-generating system on the global level, it began to confront the last terrain into which it could expand, namely, the formidable state sector – the legacy of postwar reconstruction and expansion.[2] While GATT (now the World Trade Organization – WTO), the World Bank, the IMF, and other UN agencies and representatives of capital apply pressure from "without," national governments legislate neo-liberal policies intended to privatize state property, to "free" capital from social forms in which it is under or open to political control and thereby turn those forms into corporate private property. In the end the demands of capital will have few if any official or authoritative national restraints.

Promotion of the Primacy of Private Property Rights

Underlying all the items on this agenda is the principle of private property and the policy of advancing private property rights. At issue here is the very basis of inequity and class definition in capitalist society. The rights of private property are the foundation of differences in material wealth and associated differential power. Their promotion in the political sphere since the 1970s has simply been the open advocacy of the principle on which the attack on all other forms of property rests.

Private property in this sense does not refer to tangible objects. Rather, it is a relationship that members of a social unit have towards each other in regard to the use and disposal of socially necessary objects. To put it another way, property consists of socially defined rights, that is, enforceable claims or entitlements to the goods and services produced or used in a society. This definition of property as rights, as forms of ownership, points to the fact that property is an expression of control or regulation. It implies the exercise of power over things produced, and even over the means of producing things. Such power attached to private property is hardly benign or in the interests of society as a whole. Even at the dawn of industrialization Adam Smith could write that merchants and manufacturers were "an order of men, whose interest is never exactly the same with that of the public, who have generally an interest to deceive and even to oppress the public, and who accordingly have, upon many occasions, both deceived and oppressed it."[3]

In a capitalist society, the prevailing property form is private property, which defines an exclusive "individual" relation to things. On the surface, capitalist private property is presented as the individual ownership of the "conditions of production," as ownership of things as if they were the products of ones own labour. The image created is rather like a Jeffersonian democracy of small landholders. In fact, capitalist private property implies the opposite relationship; it assumes the divestment of workers' own means of production and is a defined set of entitlements in which workers have the right only to sell or not to sell their labour power, while the capitalist who purchases that labour power has not only the right to use it, but also the right to the product of that labour. In other words, the actual producer has no right to the use or disposal of the labour power once sold, or to the product of that labour.[4]

Two points follow from this definition. First, the new right defends and promotes capitalist private property as if it were simple individual private property; and this it does because such individual ownership implies fairness and equality before the law and in the marketplace, and so confirms and justifies economic inequalities as if they were the result of individual achievement. It is a vision that conceals the reality. Capitalist private property, the actuality, not only implies inequality but also can only exist by negating individual private property if it persists on any sizeable scale.[5] Second, because capitalist private property entails exclusive corporate ownership and control over the means of production, which in turn denotes neither ownership nor control by those who must work for another to live, such property rights are the very basis of economic inequality and its continual increase.

Such is nature of the prevailing property rights fundamental to capitalism. Because they are fundamental they are defended by laws and the courts and police, and the military if need be, in order to maintain their inviolability in the system.

These are the rights that comprise the main principles that inform the legal framework institutionalized by the state. As principles, they do not give the particular existing form to the structure of law; they merely define the fundamental basis on which relations between real, material contending interests are played out. What the state sets forth as a particular legal framework is the outcome of a complex configuration of conflicting forces, needs, classes, ideas, and possibilities in a given era. The state, in legislating the particular form of the principles of capitalist property, reflects the rough balance of power among these many competing forces, without allowing a fundamental challenge to the principles.

In defining the particularities of law in a given age, then, and in order to maintain and advance the system as a whole, the state must take into account conflicting claims to property rights. In the conflict between corporations, for instance, the state introduces a host of agencies, regulations, and joint ventures, which define or establish a framework for these rights in some form of law.[6] Where corporate needs cannot be fulfilled by the private sector, the state can define a property role for itself in the shape of a public corporation, for example. When those in civil society without capitalist property rights threaten the social order by demanding countervailing rights, the state can legalize or institutional-ize limited oppositional rights, trade union or tenant rights, for exam-ple. Similarly, many of the entitlements in law that make up the welfare state are a reflection of rights introduced to ameliorate the unmitigated assertion of the rights of capital in the labour market and place of work. Environmental standards and consumer protection regulations also reflect social forces opposed to unqualified rights of capitalist private property. The state can also promulgate anti-trust or anti-monopoly laws, which implies a contradiction between the very existence of the state and its rights on one hand and the growing concentration of the rights of capital on the other.

Given the internationalization of capital and rapid technological change – that is, as capital has outgrown its own need for national regu-lation and developed a productive capacity befitting world markets – the corporate sector has faced increasingly limited avenues for further accu-mulation. All of these different claims and entitlements ensconced in law as so many circumscriptions to the assertion of the primacy of capi-talist private property, then, begin to represent increasingly significant restrictions to private accumulation. In addition to these circumscrip-tions, there are also different levels of government creating different or even conflicting property rights between levels. Moreover, there are internal contradictions between different sectors of the state apparatus due to overlapping responsibilities, not to mention the issue of the state as an actor, a potentially independent variable. Property rights in their various forms, other than those of capitalist private property, have now become fetters to the continued expansion of capital.

The imperatives of the global economy have made it necessary to overcome local and national barriers to accumulation. Fundamental to these barriers is this complex set of property forms other than capi-talist property, along with semi-autonomous state structures with the political power to define and establish such alternative rights. To have all property in the form of private property is to make it open to capitalist accumulation or to remove its opposition to capitalist pri-vate property, so that the processes of concentration and centraliza-tion can proceed worldwide.

The promotion of private property rights is a way of gaining access to all forms of property that are not now private property *and* to make pri-vate property pre-eminent in relation to other rights that might fetter its operation. State-owned land, services, and corporations could all in theory become reduced to private property; and government regulations, including employment standards and workers' rights, could be subordinated to the rights of capitalist private property. Even the undefined and non-legislated "common rights" to clean air and water or, in general, to a healthy environment can be negated by the legislating of private property rights regarding their use, such as the corporate right to pollute. In effect, those without ownership of the means of production are increasingly denied their rights if those rights are not attached to some such forms of proprietorship.

The rights of capitalist private property are the legal basis for ensuring the unequal distribution of wealth *and* for expanding the possibilities for private accumulation. These results are achieved by circumventing countervailing rights, by undermining claims for the existence and fulfilment of public or state responsibilities, and by eliminating the property forms through which the state accomplished what has been seen as its social obligations.

The Market as Panacea

Fundamental to the neo-liberal agenda is the idea of a "free market." The "market" refers to the mode of exchange in which the needs of society are met through the buying and selling of goods and services in the form of private property. It constitutes a mode of social distribution of labour power and capital, of income and wealth, and of production and consumption, resting on competitive supply and demand in the process of exchange. In short, it is the social allocation of goods and services by means of the price mechanism.

The proponents of the free market argue that it has positive political and economic implications. They say it is the source of capitalism's purported political liberties and freedom of opportunity and is the most neutral, or non-political, way to provide for the needs of society.[7] The argument that it forms the basis of economic efficiency is too tiresome to be repeated here.[8] The market is also presented as an alternative to government ownership and regulation of the economy, an alternative that is "successful" and that "delivers." It is touted as the very reality of society itself; that is, humans are mere exchangers of goods and services, and not products of socialization. "There is no such thing as 'society,'" Margaret Thatcher reportedly said.[9]

A market can be said to exist only where numerous firms, none of them dominant, compete in the production of certain goods or services.

Only then does a market as a distinct force operate over and above the competing corporations. Given the degree of cartelization, monopolization, and oligopolization, the reality of the market is to a very large degree an illusion and has been for some time.[10] Its proselytizers might well admit this, but in turn they argue that there are "lesser" forms of the pure market or that what we need is a return to the free market. There is, in fact, no free market; the lesser forms (monopoly markets) are but a transition to ever greater cartelization or oligopolization; and there is no possibility of a "return." Indeed, the promotion of such an idea has other motives.

Some of the restrictions placed by industry itself on the free operation of the market include: vertical integration; business cartels, oligopolies, and monopolies at the national and international levels; corporate planning intent on controlling prices, dividing up markets, and allocating production shares; the advertising industry as intended to control and create demand; interlocking directorships, share ownership, and indebtedness; joint ventures and technical link-ups; and intrafirm trade or transfer pricing.[11] To these can be added: corporate alliances to share the increasing costs of research and development; industry-wide corporate associations, both national and international, which represent attempts at self-regulation and control over particular markets; and international and national associations of certain sectors of capital, which seek to influence government policy and promote opposing views to the trade union movement, consumer advocates, and environmentalists. All of these restrictions suggest that the last thing that capital wants for itself is competition or the "free" market, except perhaps as a means of gaining access to the state sector or "closed markets" or non-market economies. The corporate sector strives continuously to overcome competition in whatever way possible, fair or foul.[12]

The market is also controlled by governments. At the national level, regulations, state expenditures, taxation policies, public corporations, and subsidies all constitute infringements on the freedom of the market. By creating state resource cartels (in oil or uranium, for instance), national governments limit competition on the international level. Moreover, massive state involvement in the economy also occurs through government departments as typified by the Ministry of International Trade and Industry (MITI) in Japan and the Pentagon in the United States. For the most part these are interventions in the interests of corporate welfare.[13]

At the international level there are also many mechanisms for controlling the global market in the interests of business.[14] These include organizations that attempt to determine broad boundaries for national and international policy; for example, the World Bank and the IMF, GATT (or WTO), the Bank for International Settlements (BIS), the OECD and its agencies, and various United Nations organizations (such as the United Nations Industrial Development Organization and the United Nations Conference on Trade and Development).

Even without these restrictions, as we have already seen, competition by its very nature leads to its own demise. Over time, fewer and fewer "winners" control more and more. When competition has persisted, moreover, in many instances combined corporate and government action has been taken to control it by enforcing the creation of cartels or associations to circumvent its deleterious effects.[15] The success of Japanese industry in the global market has much to do with the conscious suppression of competition in Japan's home market.

None of this is to say that competition does not exist, but it is highly circumscribed to say the least. It exists in limited degrees between a trading bloc such as the European Union (EU) and the United States; between the last nations with relatively significant independent political and economic powers, such as Japan and the United States; between certain giant corporations, cartels, or oligopolies over world market share – in automobiles or pharmaceuticals, for example; and between small capitals in the non-monopoly/cartel sector in most countries.

There can, however, be no "return" to the "free" market. The direction of movement is towards the minimization of competition and maximization of control over all markets, and these trends are the natural outcome of capitalist development. World capital is a long way down this road, and a "reversion" to unfettered competition among many smaller capitals has become unthinkable, indeed impossible.

Why then does the neo-liberal agenda promote so loudly the virtues of the free market when it neither exists nor is ever likely to exist? The answer lies in its use: it is the philosophical rationale for the advancement of the interests of private property and for undoing much of the postwar KWS. It is the rationale for privatizing public corporations and for deregulating the operation of the economy, for relieving the state of any functions that restrict private accumulation. It is also the rationale for countering the principle of trade unionism, which is to limit or eliminate competition amongst workers in the labour market.

The idea of the free market, furthermore, offers a counter-ideological view to *reformism*, the idea that reformed capitalism is beneficial to the working class and society and nature; that is, to oppose the notion that capital needs to have reforms imposed upon it to maintain minimal standards for health and safety and protection of the environment. In place of reforms the idea of the market suggests that capital can operate more effectively if left unregulated, that capital can provide more jobs if allowed to expand and that, indeed, it can "regulate" itself.

Here is the theory of self-regulating capital: the chief economist of the World Bank, Lawrence Summers, wrote in an internal memo, "I think the economic logic behind dumping a load of toxic waste in the lowest-wage country is impeccable and we should face up to that." In defence of cost-benefit analyses, Summers also wrote: "The argument that moral obligation to future generations demands special treatment of environmental investments is fatuous."[16]

Here is the practice: in 1991-92, privatized water companies in England cut off water supply to over 21,000 households to force payment of bills. Health officials said the disconnections led to a "dramatic" rise in the incidence of infectious diseases. According to a newspaper report, "Hepatitis and dysentery, diseases of Victorian slums, are spreading in Britain's inner cities as a direct result of privatised water companies disconnecting supplies."[17]

The free-market ideal also becomes the rationale for promoting competition when it can serve the interests of capital.[18] The idea that competition is desirable, healthy, rigorous, and necessary for the advance of the system becomes the unexamined premise or excuse for undermining any concerted collective efforts to counter the effects of the development of capital, where these efforts come from trade unions, consumer groups, environmentalists, or government. Moreover, the power resting on and vested in the colossal degree of monopoly and cartelization on one side is, of course, enhanced by competition on the other – to wit, all those forces opposing capital in one way or another. The argument for competition, it hardly need be said, ignores the power of monopoly over the means of production on the side of capital. In short, the idea of the free market provides the ideological rationale for the agenda that follows.

Free Economic Zones: Model for the Global Economy

In recent years there has been an increasing number of examples of the attempted implementation of this ideal of the free market, albeit in the restricted form of "free economic zones" (FEZ). Despite a variety of different names given to these zones, and variations in kind from country to country, they have certain common characteristics. In general, they are designated territorial enclaves in which special incentives, privileges, and laws are established for the corporations, usually foreign, that invest there. Chief among the special arrangements are duty-free importing, income tax concessions, reduced administrative red tape, circumscription of trade unions, few employment or environmental regulations, and generous state provision of infrastructure.

As early as the 1960s, two UN agencies, the United Nations Industrial Development Organization (UNIDO) and the United Nations Conference on Trade and Development (UNCTAD), promoted the zones as beneficial to economic growth in the Third World. It was held that the zones would attract foreign investment, create employment, and promote technical training and foreign exchange, among other things. Ireland, Mexico, Brazil, the Philippines, and India were all early adoptees of the zones. Since the late 1970s the creation of FEZs has grown rapidly. In the United States there are over 170 zones and over 200 "sub-zones;" worldwide there are over 400 "freeports," many associated with over 200 export-processing zones, accounting for a substantial and growing percentage of world trade.[19] They exist widely in Asia and are considered to have been a significant influence in the rise of the so-called newly industrializing countries, or NICs (Taiwan, Hong Kong, Singapore, and South Korea). China introduced them in 1979 and saw them as contributing to the country's "modernization" program and its "reintegration into the world economy."[20] More recently, in 1990, the Russian parliament passed legislation establishing eleven "free economic zones," some encompassing whole regions, presenting them as "laboratories for the market economy" from which market principles would gradually be extended "to the rest of the country."[21]

The increasing numbers of FEZs are a consequence of the internationalization of capital. No longer for the most part national in character, capital is able to move to wherever the advantages are greatest, and the FEZ represents an attempt by various national governments to provide advantageous conditions for capital accumulation by minimizing the costs of and regulatory fetters to "doing business." An advocate of their introduction to Britain waxed enthusiastically: "Small, selected areas of inner cities would be simply thrown open to all kinds of initiative with minimal control. In other words, we would aim to recreate the Hong Kong of the 1950's and 1960's inside inner Liverpool or Glasgow."[22]

For the "lesser developed countries" (LDCs), the FEZs were adopted, among other reasons, with the intention of increasing their foreign exchange earnings and employment opportunities and "modernizing" their economies through technology transfer and new management skills. In some instances these things have happened; for the most part, the hopes have not materialized.

Since taxes on the corporations have been minimal, the investments often small, and the profits "repatriated," the foreign exchange earnings, such as they have been, have come mainly from wages. The zones attract primarily processing and assembly operations needing largely unskilled or semi-skilled labour, so the wages paid are low and the numbers employed not very significant in relation to the country's total labour force. In general, the zones have not produced the foreign exchange promised for the host country.

They have not, moreover, created the hoped-for employment, and even the jobs created are of questionable net benefit to the country or the workers. On average they pay about the same wage as jobs outside the zone, but when the costs to the state of generating the jobs are taken into account, the zones rarely represent a gain for the host nation.

Although "modernization" through technology transfer was one of the avowed purposes for creating the FEZ, the zones have produced little or no such transfer.[23] From the point of view of capital, of course, this was not the purpose of investment. The investment has been generally made in search of cheap labour. The technology employed has usually not been advanced, and the linkages to the host economy outside the zone have in general been minimal.

All in all, the benefits of the FEZs have been limited, to say the least.[24] The costs, which can include the construction of factory buildings, the provision of utilities (roads, railways, harbours, telephone, and telex), worker housing, and health care, environmental cleanups, or policing the zone, can be and often are far greater than the projected benefits. The zones can also become centres for importing foreign commodities rather than centres for exporting, and in this way actually increase the host country's foreign exchange deficit. Even the UNIDO and UNCTAD now agree that FEZs have been of little use for modernization in the LDCs.[25]

The workers in these zones usually find minimal employment and pollution standards – and even these are often not enforced – and laws barring trade unions. As a consequence, they tend to work long hours, frequently in unsafe or toxic conditions, and without the benefits assumed by workers in the industrial nations, such as sick leave, holidays, pensions, and degrees of employment protection.[26]

If the social and financial costs outweigh the hoped-for benefits, it might well be asked why these zones are expanding in number and size around the world. The answer lies in the nature of the global economy. A country wanting to remain part of the capitalist system, or to join it (as in Eastern Europe, the former U.S.S.R., China, or Vietnam), has few alternatives but to accept the demands made by international capital because the age of national interests and strategies for capitalist or working classes is over. As transnational entities, corporations can play one nation off against another by moving to where the concessions and incentives are greatest, the relative labour costs lowest, infrastructure support the most complete and advanced, and environmental and employment standards the most limited. As national entities, corporations make demands that can always be tempered by resistance from trade unions or social movements and restricted by legislated regulations and reforms. As transnationals, they can minimize such resistance and restrictions by threatening to invest elsewhere should their operations be constrained.

A former president of the Adam Smith Institute in London expressed the ideological view of these zones in a defence of "freeports":

> The job of governments is . . . to step aside from the regulations and duties and burdens which prevent business actively developing. The freeport is not something to be thought of as an island of subsidy where government helps ailing businesses or fledgling industries which would not survive without support. It is an area of freedom where unfettered enterprise shows what it can do without government.[27]

The irony is self-evident: the creation of a freeport or FEZ requires the legislative and coercive power of the state to override the established regulations, standards, trade union rights, and even democratic principles and practice; to enforce these restrictions to civil liberties and human and environmental well-being; and to offer enormous subsidies in the form of infrastructure and tax concessions, usually in excess of the net gain from employment through the increased trade and commerce.

The FEZ is an "area of freedom" for corporations only because the freedom for workers to resist, to protest, and to unionize is circumscribed or forbidden. The record of what "unfettered enterprise" does with this freedom is appalling: human health, employment standards, environmental protection, and civil rights are more or less ignored; and the corruption of the government officials responsible is widespread. In general, the FEZ provides testimony to the amorality of capital and the consequences for workers and the environment when corporations are able to make the world over in their own image while the powers of the state are employed to prevent and undermine opposition or resistance.

Deregulation of the Economy

Economic regulation by government is the imposition of constraints and rules, backed by sanctions, which are intended to modify the activities of corporations in the private sector.[28] In industrial nations there are many, many hundreds of such regulations and scores of regulatory agencies. These regulations can be categorized very generally into three groups: 1) framework regulations, such as collective bargaining law, competition policy, and corporate law, which set out broad guidelines within which certain economic activities must take place; 2) direct regulation, which is usually industry-specific and places constraints on prices, production, profits, and standards of service; and 3) social regulation, which seeks to protect society, the working class, and the environment from the operations of capital. With the partial exception of the third category, these pervasive regulations have all operated largely in the general interests of capital.

This is not surprising, considering the main reason for most of the regulation. There is a strong relationship, with some exceptions, between the development and application of new technology and the emergence of government intervention. New technology may lead to competition between producers with the same technology; it may bring on competition between capitalists with different technology; it may produce monopolies over certain technology, placing other capitals at a severe disadvantage; or it may place human beings or nature at risk. All of these situations necessitate government regulation in the interest of maintaining conditions that allow for the survival of competing capitals of a certain size that have significance for the system as a whole; the regulation is to prevent market failure. Aside from these reasons, regulations are also introduced when the effects of new technologies on workers, society in general, or on nature give rise to extraparliamentary political protest.

The growth of government regulations and associated agencies, then, corresponds more or less to the pace of development and application of new technology. Hence, in the postwar age of expanding technology, the degree of government intervention expanded accordingly. With the present stage of permanent technological revolution beginning in the 1970s, the imposition of government regulations can no longer keep up with industrial innovation and its implications for society and nature.

As a result, government regulation has come under serious questioning since the 1970s. From the point of view of capital, regulations have become a positive hindrance to new developments, in a way that they were not in past, less technologically revolutionary, eras because the government's ability to regulate cannot meet the pace of new applications of new technology. Many existing regulations, furthermore, reflect the technological needs of a fading Fordist mode of production and require restructuring to reflect the new computer-aided production processes.

As well, every sector of the economy has become increasingly dominated by monopolies, oligopolies, or cartels of one sort or another, and if one of the reasons for regulation has been to control national competition between corporations, that reason is beginning to disappear. Furthermore, as competition increases at supranational levels, as profit rates decline, and as corporations search for ways and means to reduce costs, the "costs" of regulation to corporations begin to be questioned, because they are not inconsiderable.

National regulations of all sorts, moreover, vary widely from nation to nation, and the variations themselves constitute barriers to international trade and commerce, to the globalization of markets. Transnational corporations require international standards and regulations, which can be accomplished by the downgrading or elimination of national regulations allowing capital to compete "freely" *and* by the imposition of international standards and regulations, which has already taken place in many sectors. Most international economic organizations, such as the GATT (WTO), OECD, IMF, and World Bank, insist on deregulation or the acceptance of international regulations and standards as a condition of membership or use of "facilities."

Some of the consequences of deregulation in the 1980s have been evident for some time.[29] First, national competition amongst national capitals in the spheres affected became noticeably diminished. Deregulation in the U.S. airline industry, for instance, increased competition for a short time before producing numerous bankruptcies and enormous dislocation of plant and personnel, and then there arose a more powerful oligopoly of very large companies. Second, the lifting of regulations in certain instances opened the doors to an expansion of illegal activity, leaving the state, ultimately the taxpayers, with colossal financial liabilities. The U.S. Savings and Loan companies fiasco and the City of London finance crisis are good examples. Lax enforcement of regulations, to the point of non-intervention, is another problem; see, for example, the Bank of Credit and Commerce International and the Maxwell pension fund scandals.[30] Third, the process of deregulation has not necessarily meant freedom from regulation, because in many instances new regulations have appeared in the deregulated sphere in order "to remedy market failure," or to "force market behaviour" on the monopolies emerging as a consequence of the deregulation. There can be, moreover, a shift in the nature of regulations, from "macro to micro" intervention, or from the maintenance of self-sufficient national economies to promotion of "flexible responses" in global markets, or from national to international regulations.[31]

In sum, the permanent revolution in modern technology, the drive to reduce costs, the attempt to minimize state regulations as forms of property contradictory to private property, and the centralization and internationalization of capital all comprise the demands for deregulating the *national* economy. The consequences of this process, however, have not conformed to the prophesies contained in the visions of the new right.[32] Competition succumbs to monopolies, duopolies, and oligopolies; regulated dishonesty becomes unrestrained fraud; and new regulations have appeared that correspond to post-Fordist processes of production and global markets.

Throughout the industrial nations no political party in power can resist these trends and at the same time maintain a capitalist economy. Here is the rub in particular for social-democratic parties, because regulation has been such a central part of their advocated state intervention.

The Privatization of Public Corporations

"Privatization" – or the "transfer" of state assets and production of goods and services to the private sector – has been carried out in a number of ways.[33] The most obvious is an outright sale to a private corporation, or the offering of stock market shares to the "public." But state assets can also be leased or liquidated and government services can be contracted out or simply terminated. Where the process is politically problematic the preferred route has been "privatization by attrition," the gradual reduction of services.[34]

During the 1980s such "selling off" took place in every industrial country and in many "lesser developed" nations, and the rapid worldwide application of this policy shows little sign of abatement.[35] It is not, however, a popular movement but rather a policy promoted by government elites; that is, the motives come from outside the nation-state. The political hue of the governments enacting these policies seems, on the whole, to be unimportant; from a military dictatorship in Chile, to right-wing conservatives in Britain, to social democrats in New Zealand, Spain, and France, to "communists" in China and Cuba, the policy and practice of privatization have been remarkably similar. Where governments have not promoted the policy, as in a few Third World countries, privatization has been forced upon them in the terms of international loans.

Such a "reform" movement is a curious thing given that public corporations were for the most part created in the first place to aid in capital accumulation. One of the more important reasons for their creation was the need to reduce costs to the private sector by means of government provision of infrastructure. State-financed construction and ownership of canals, harbours, power-generating plants, water-supply systems, and railways and airports have been – and in some cases remain – of enormous benefit to capital. They eliminate the need for a market-related profit, they spread the costs of infrastructure for commercial use over the whole of society, and they allow for an ongoing subsidy for business users from state coffers and/or other users.

Many public corporations were and still are created to protect capitalists from themselves or from the business cycle. In cases of poor management, corruption, or fraud, none of them uncommon in the business sector, or when a recession or depression threatens bankruptcy, the state sometimes steps in with financing to save the corporation by way of bailout or buy-out. Generally this happens only when the possible failure would have economic ramifications too great to permit. Other situations include financially risky exploratory or experimental development, when the state accepts the risk instead of the private sector; legacies of war production, when the state finances production in areas not developed by private corporations; the provision of financial services with the backing of the state, when the risk for the private sector is too great; and the creation or maintenance of a "national" presence in some sectors.

If, in general, the state introduces nationalization in the interests of capital, why then the current wave of privatization? If the motive for nationalization was largely to further the interests of the corporate sector, it is indeed paradoxical that the same motive would appear to underlie the "denationalization" or privatization of public corporations. The answer is that what may have been useful or necessary for capital at one time is not necessarily useful all the time.

The qualitative changes in the world economy since the 1970s are largely responsible for this shift. Massive technological changes in the mode of production have made it possible for ever fewer productive units to supply a single world market. At the same time the possibilities for further increasing capital accumulation are narrowing with the indebtedness of the Third World, rising unemployment in the industrial nations, intensified international competition, and the destruction of nature. Growth in the private sector began to slow down, but growth in the public sector, while varying across nations, generally showed a relative increase by the early 1980s – mainly to counter the recessions and meet increased needs on the side of the reproduction of capital and labour. By that time most industrial countries were spending more than a third of their Gross National Expenditures in the public sector.

Given the internationalization of capital and increasing productivity, however, the corporate sector pursues all possibilities for increasing private accumulation. It sees in state ownership and control the diversion of a large part of the national product away from the "productive" economy; for capital, public ownership represents industries or services that are "unproductive," that is, outside the realm of private exploitation.[36] Worse, it knows them to be paid for by revenues from wages and profits, the "social surplus" *uncapitalized*. The state sector also provides the means for maintaining *national* aspects of the nation-state. From these reasons come the motivation for privatizing the public sector.[37]

While the main public justifications for privatization tend to be the increase in efficiency, productivity, or competition, the elimination of sources of state deficit, or less government intervention in the economy, it has not been shown that privatization has effectively contributed to any of these factors. On the contrary, in many cases it has done just the opposite. It can lead to increased government expenditures because private operations in health care, welfare agencies, highway maintenance, or prisons must produce a profit, whereas public corporations generally do not unless profit is specifically required. Moreover, because competition is far from desirable for capital, privatization might well simply substitute a private monopoly for a public one without producing any of the benefits that supposedly come from the "rigour" of competition. Privatization can also increase the need for government regulation to oversee private corporations operating in their self-interest, whereas public corporations with a mandate to operate in the public interest do not increase this need.[38]

Rationalizations for political policies do not necessarily reflect the reality of their consequences. If the stated reasons for privatization do not match the results, it is because the real reasons may simply not be understood, or, more likely, they may be part of hidden agendas.

"Popular Capitalism" and Support for Privatization

Given the political and economic prerequisites, the KWS in different forms and to different degrees was adopted in all the industrial states after World War II. With the painful experience of the Great Depression of the 1930s, the order and purpose of the "command" economy of the war period, and the need to rebuild the war-shattered economies after the war, the population *and* the ruling elites of the industrial nations easily accepted the Keynesian policies of economic management and other forms of expanded state intervention. This acceptance of the KWS produced an international policy culture, a general acceptance and political consensus about the need for and proper role of expanded government.[39] Now, however, in an era in which capital sees the KWS as a barrier to its expanded reproduction and in which privatization in the broad sense of "unburdening" the state of its KWS functions has been placed at the top of the agenda, a new international policy culture must be created.

"Popular capitalism" is simply the most obvious method of building support and a public consensus for the policies of privatization. In Britain and elsewhere, for instance, the state has made a "public" offering of shares in the corporation to be privatized, often at knock-down prices – a successful manoeuvre in the sense that the opportunity to make an immediate personal gain overshadows the meaning of the act of privatization and obscures the almost certain long-term result of increased economic iniquities or growing monopoly. Another similar mechanism is the public distribution of shares to all citizens over whom the state has jurisdiction. In this process, everyone becomes part of the "people's capitalism" so created, and they find themselves "owners" of a minute fraction of what used to be a state-owned corporation.[40] These "owners," however, have no power because of the wide dispersal of shares; while the representatives of capital usually have it from the outset because of their positions in the executive or board of directors; or they can gain control in short order through the purchase of blocks of shares offered for sale.

Governments promote another form of "popular capitalism" in the many variations of employee stock ownership plans (ESOPs), mechanisms for making the employees or some portion of them into ostensible owners. Here again the intention is to place state assets of one sort or another into the private sector, to make them part of the process of private accumulation.

In a country such as Britain, with a large percentage of the housing "stock" owned publicly, the government was able to gain a considerable measure of support by offering houses to tenants at prices well below market value. Indeed, the British Conservative government managed to privatize much of the United Kingdom's huge amount of council housing.[41] The reality of "home ownership," with its negative effects on the coherency of working-class consciousness, goes far to create a "commitment" to the present economic order.

A less obvious mechanism is the use of tax incentives that make the privatization of certain government services and programs acceptable by allowing tax deductions for those who make use of the private rather than public sector. The privatization of government pension plans provides a good example. Instead of being encouraged to contribute to, and strengthen, a universal state-run pension plan, individuals are encouraged through tax allowances to set aside personal funds as a pension. Because such schemes are theoretically open to all, it is not so obvious that only a small portion of the population can afford to take advantage of the tax incentive. The program, apparently fair and materially advantageous, gains acceptability, and no one questions the annual tax loss, the future of a two-tiered pension system, or the potential loss of a universal pension plan. The mechanism does become somewhat more obvious when the government provides low-interest and inter-est-free loans to people who purchase shares in privatized public cor-porations – with even the repayments made tax-deductible, as in Chile in the mid-1980s.[42]

While helping to make the broad privatization program acceptable, these forms of "popular capitalism" have at least two related objectives. They are intended, first, to go a considerable way to undermining the policy culture, the rather pervasive mind-set, of the KWS and to blunt-ing criticism of privatization by making a simple appeal to immediate material gain and by building a population with an apparently increased stake in the capitalist system. One of the greatest bulwarks of the sys-tem, it has been said, is the ownership of a home; in a lesser way, the ownership of stocks, bonds, or personal pension funds performs the same function.

The other objective of the "new participatory capitalist system" is the undermining of sentiments in favour of trade unions and, where privati-zation has taken place, the outright decertification of unions or at least the weakening of the trade union movement. With the promise of join-ing the system, the working class is being turned against the very mechanism that protects it from the system.

Popular capitalism represents a conscious attempt by the new right to provide a "cultural" alternative to the widespread acceptance of an extended role for the state. It is meant to undermine popular expecta-tions of public or state responsibilities.[43] It is also a set of mechanisms for "shedding" the state of its assets and responsibilities and, at the same time, a means for attempting to create a foundation for providing for social needs in the private sector. It is a ruse: popular capitalism is an ideological and practical counterbalance to state intervention for the provision of social needs – state intervention that was for the most part the product of class struggle over many decades, the product of a con-flict that arose because capitalism could not provide a tolerable, stable, or secure existence for a substantial part of the population.

Transformation of the Tax Structure

The tax system is being restructured in all the industrial nations. Tax regimes vary considerably from country to country, but at least two trends are common to all nations in the West. One is the shift to an in-creasingly larger percentage of total tax revenue being drawn from indi-vidual rather than corporate income. The other is the growing regressiveness of taxes on the side of wages and salaries, in the form of two sub-trends: the lowering of higher rates on high income and the reduction of the number of tax bands; and the increased reliance on indirect taxes, including consumption taxes, social security levies, lotteries, and state-run gambling.[44] How to understand what is happening and what these changes mean?

Taxes are the "economic expression of the state"; wherever the state has existed, so too have taxes. But the state arises only in class-divided societies, in which the interests of one class prevail and those of other classes are subordinate. The central role of the state as the embodiment of these conflicts has been to perpetuate these relations. In the name of "society" the state ensures subordination and advances domination by means of reform, coercion, "bread and circuses," and other means at its disposal. All its functions are financed principally by taxes.

In capitalist societies the state similarly perpetuates the unequal relations between the owners and managers of capital and subordinate classes, and it also finances its activities mainly by taxes. But here, several factors such as an organized working class, the possibility of alternating political access to state power, and a long period of national economic expansion have produced a certain limited "sharing" of the tax burden between corporations and individuals. After World War II this sharing began to decline as taxes on individuals increased and taxes on profits fell relatively, especially with the coming of the 1980s.

The trend closely follows the rise of transnational corporations, or the progressive denationalization of capital. As long as capital remained distinctly national, it had an interest in allowing a part of its revenue to be collected as taxes for the purposes of maintaining the national state or, more precisely, the general conditions of production. When capital began to lose its character as a national existence, it began to find fewer advantages in contributing tax revenues to the "nation" *and* to perceive state ownership and production as restrictions to its own private accumulation. Their enormous size, economic power, and increased mobility have allowed companies to reduce taxation by playing nations off against nations. Everywhere the result has been the restructuring of tax regimes in which the working class bears the larger and rising share of tax with capital responsible for a smaller and declining share.

The accompanying trend, the growing regressiveness of taxation on wages and salaries, is forcing a greater tax burden on middle and lower incomes and producing a decreasing burden on upper incomes. In the

1980s the rationale for this tax policy – the "trickle-down" theory – may well have drawn its content from an earlier work by Hayek, in which he made several points that regularly appeared in print as standard arguments against a progressive income tax. His recommended alternative was a single tax rate of 25 per cent for all.[45] But arguments against a progressive income tax generally overlook a key point: that the existing possibilities for tax avoidance (legal, illegal, and "creative") for the rich have always been numerous and have generally gone a long way to minimize the limited progressiveness. The move towards less progressive taxation in a capitalist society means that the subordinate classes will increasingly be the source of revenue for maintaining the state, which in turn maintains the continuing domination of the economically powerful.

These trends have several implications. For one thing, they mean that the expansion or simply maintenance of the public sector is being disproportionately financed as a tax burden on the working classes rather than on the corporate sector or the rich. If a portion of state revenue, moreover, goes to corporations in the form of grants, loans, guarantees, tax expenditures, and allowances, the trends also mean that some of the "disposable" part of wages and salaries that goes into taxes is benefiting the business sector. This amounts to a state-mediated shift in income from the working class to the capitalist class. In short, the changes in tax structure are obliging the working class to finance increasingly all the functions of a state that in the final analysis acts mainly in the interests of another class.

As the tax burden on the working class grows, the trend reinforces certain negative ideological views about the state: that government is too "big," wasteful, unnecessary; that excessive taxes are a contributing cause to a recessionary economy; and that the social reforms representing a large portion of the state's expenditures are "unaffordable." That there are elements of truth to these views makes them all the more compelling, even though the immediate burden of taxation is far from being the source of these problems.

An increasing tax burden can be used, then, as a rationale to build pressure for the dismantling of the welfare state and for the reduction in the size of the state. The trends allow the capitalist classes and the party in power to promote a social consensus around a negative view of the state, to exploit a disenchantment over high taxes by advancing explanations that point to the inefficiencies of government, to welfare or unemployment insurance abuse, or to the high cost of public health care, and contrast these supposed problems to the "efficiencies" of the market and a minimal state. These pressures can be used to turn around the widespread sentiments in favour of a certain "distributive justice" and work to justify more easily the attacks on the welfare state.

The increasing tax burden also means a reduction of the purchasing power of the working class, which can help generate economic crises and also lead to pressure for wage increases as labour struggles to maintain its accustomed standard of living. Attempts to place a cap on or roll back increasing personal taxes can create additional pressure to decrease the size of the state and its services (because of falling revenue), as well as reduce pressure for wage and salary increases, temporarily easing the secular drop in real income.

The trends are in part a product of the worldwide harmonization of national tax regimes. They comprise an approaching conformity of tax policy around the world to accommodate the needs of internationalized capital.[46] The point is more obvious within free-trade areas or customs unions, where "the maintenance of fiscal frontiers among members . . . is regarded as inconsistent" with an "integrated market,"[47] and the more integrated the world market becomes the more there must be a harmonization of tax policy at the global level. For one reason, transnational corporations are able to demand from national or local governments not only tax concessions but also a variety of other incentives to invest. For another, national "tax wedges" out of step with other nation-states constitute disincentives to invest or reasons for the reallocation of internationalized capital.[48]

The trends not only result in a growing tax burden on the working population and particularly its middle and lower strata, but also create an "empirical" rationale for the dismantling of the welfare state and the minimization of the nation-state itself. They show the fiscal limits to reformism; that is, when the redistribution implied in reforms rests on tax revenue, fiscal crises or changes in tax policy intensify the contradiction between corporate profitability and market incentives *and* the tax-assisted reproduction of the working class.

In the neo-liberal agenda, tax revenues must be at least sufficient to provide for the maintenance of infrastructure, "local" assistance to capitalist accumulation, and security, that is, the protection of private property. Beyond these functions, they represent a diversion of revenue from capital accumulation.

Reduction of the National Debt

Although the need to reduce the national debt has become one of the *causes célèbres* of the new right, it is not a mere irony that an increased indebtedness in many states has been indirectly a consequence of its agenda, although more so a result of the "new reality." The ratio of debt to total government revenues in the Western nations tended to remain relatively stable up to the early 1970s, but thereafter steadily increased.

This growth of debt is the product of several developments. It is partially a response to a cyclical or chronic decline in national economic growth and the greater demands on the side of working-class reproduction due to this decline. In part, it represents an increase in state support to the corporate sector via deferred taxes and various forms of grants and loans. In part, it is a result of a changing tax structure in which corporations pay a decreasing share of the total revenues, forcing an increasing share onto the working classes. It is also partly due to corporate investment abroad, which reduces the social wage. All of these factors create a growing need to expand the debt to meet expected public expenditures.[49]

Accompanying the calls for a reduction of debt is the widespread illusion that "balanced books" or a debt-free state is a goal worth achieving.[50] Despite wide promotion of the goal, the corporate sector necessarily has a second position on the issue. At present, just as throughout the history of the state, the public debt has been a tremendous lever for corporate capital accumulation. Going into debt has been the chief means by which the state has marshalled enormous sums of money to "complement" its revenues for use in territories under its jurisdiction: the capital the state borrows becomes part of the public funds transferred to the private sector through state expenditures of one sort or another. The state's ability to go into debt has, in fact, been a source of enormous enrichment for private enterprise. In most countries the most prominent and powerful corporations have had a direct interest in the indebtedness of the state – at all levels.

Employing indebtedness as an instrument of capital accumulation, the state plays the role of financial intermediary in a three-part relationship. The *creditors* provide the funds borrowed by the state; the most significant among them are the private banks and other financial institutions. The *debtors*, are, for the most part, private corporations; the state distributes funds in return for goods or services, makes loans or grants, or extends tax concessions to them. In turn, this borrowing and lending rest on the state's right and ability to tax all classes in the name of the "public interest," in other words, to spread the costs of state-levered capital borrowing for the few over the whole of society. Although corporate taxes still make up a portion of these revenues, this is a declining portion; *the individual taxpayer* has long provided the majority of tax revenues.

Throughout most of the industrial countries during the 1980s, national indebtedness grew steadily, and it has been allowed to grow because of who benefits from it.[51] Only when the degree of indebtedness has threatened the creditworthiness of the state, created strong inflationary pressures, dampened capital liquidity, or reduced the possibilities for private capital accumulation has there been concern to cut it back. In an attempt to "solve" the problems associated with high indebtedness, national governments have passed legislation or adopted policies variously intended to expand the tax base or increase taxes, reduce social expenditures, and restrict borrowing.

As for the first solution, there have been many changes in the last few years to increase the taxes on individuals. Governments have increased, in number and amount, indirect taxes in the form of excise and sales taxes. They have also adopted lotteries and state-run gambling as taxes on the working classes. They have increased direct taxes in amount and added various new forms, such as surcharges and poll taxes. There is, however, a limit beyond which more tax noticeably depresses living standards (a basis for social unrest) or dampens consumer demand (a contributor to economic decline) or creates inflationary pressure on wages and salaries.

As for the second solution – the reduction of social spending – the welfare state is easily made to appear as responsible for much of the debt because it involves highly visible and significant government expenditures in health, education, and social security. People do not so readily see the real reasons for the debt, namely, the reduction of corporate taxes, national economic decline, increased social demands, and corporate needs.

The third solution – the attempts to restrict borrowing – has been problematic because these attempts must be balanced against the degree of political and social unrest that they engender, the creditworthiness of the state, and the need to maintain social, economic, and military expenditures. Nevertheless, restrictions to borrowing represent another means to shift "unproductive" government consumption of goods and services to the private sector.

Public debt represents, however, not just a source of accumulation, but also the willingness of the state to be indebted to large corporate bondholders. For capitalists this willingness has always been the guarantee that the state has accepted capital accumulation as its *raison d'être*; the state's openness to indebtedness bolsters the chief principles of capitalism. Furthermore, this indebtedness contains much of the secret of capital's control over the state, as creditor over debtor. Since banks and other financial institutions finance government borrowing, these institutions gain, through the public debt, a powerful lever over state policy.[52] The financial markets can refrain from purchasing government debt, the IMF can and does withhold credit facilities, and bond-rating agencies (such as Standard and Poor in the United States) can set higher interest rates, all by way of reflecting the confidence of capital in government programs and policies.[53] In short, the last thing that the corporations want or can afford is a debt-free state. As present or future tax revenues become insufficient to manage the debt, however, the repayment will be squeezed from reduced expenditures in health, education, and social security, or higher taxes on the working class. The lowering of personal income taxes simply increases the pressure to retrench or privatize the welfare state.

Despite the historical significance of indebtedness, as well as its signal importance to the present world economy, the current dominance of monetarism as economic policy has made the idea of a balanced budget a seemingly unchallengeable objective for governments. The main implication of such a goal would seem to be as a counter to the role of the state in Keynesianism. The balanced budget, or the striving to achieve it, acts as a means to reduce or even neutralize the tasks of the state in the economy; it becomes an excuse to dismantle the welfare state; it helps to create the grounds where "economic justice" can prevail over "distributive justice."

The Downsizing of Government

The definition of government used here includes the functions of the state *and* the bureaucracy – the salaried workers in the public sector at all levels employed to carry out these manifold functions. Although the reduction of both of these elements has been an important aspect of neo-liberal policy, there are several other reasons for the declining need for government administration.

Some of these reasons have already been touched upon. The policies of deregulation and corporate self-regulation, for instance, can translate into fewer regulations and fewer people required to oversee them; increased monopolies and oligopolies or fewer corporations mean less intercorporate competition and so fewer commissions and agencies to manage associated problems; the computerization of administrative tasks directly limits the number of administrative personnel required to process information; the coming of world standards and agencies progressively reduces the need to create or enforce national standards; and a growing tax burden on wages and salaries creates political limits to the expansion of tax revenues; all of these make it increasingly difficult to maintain the existing size of bureaucracy.

Perhaps the most important reason for the pressure to reduce the functions and size of government is that the modern bureaucratic model of government was the product of a particular mode of production, namely, industrial capitalism, but more particularly, the advanced Fordism of the post-World War II period. The present era of capitalism, characterized by global markets and computer applications, demands a different structure of government; the growing global economy is fettered by the enormous size and inertia of anachronistic national bureaucracies.[54]

Insofar as the "downsizing" of government refers to a reduction in the functions of government, it embodies a *political rationale* that is somewhat involved but can be laid out briefly and schematically as follows. The functions include all state interventions in the economy and social life of the nation that have grown with the development of capital. Many of them are reforms won, after years of struggle, suffering, and loss of life, by the working class for its own protection and advancement in the face of capital. Gradually, but especially after World War II, conditions made more reforms necessary and possible. One of the conditions from an earlier era was a political system allowing for a change of government at more or less regular intervals, a system that developed in an age of competitive capital and reflected this competition by providing for alternations in control over the public purse. The rationale of modern politics became the contest over which party, representing a sector or sectors of civil society, would possess state power to enact its policies, to dispense public funds in accordance with its policies. In an age dominated by transnational conglomerates and consortiums, however, a national political system allowing for alternations in power of party and policy is no longer needed and, more to the point, forms a potential problem. What internationalized capital needs is either the removal of the possibility that state power can be won by a party opposed to neo-liberal policies,[55] or the redefinition of the role of the state (its interventions) so that the state cannot be used in the future in the way it was in the past. Here lies the political motive for downsizing the functions of government.

Downsizing in this sense means the abrogation of government responsibilities for the social and economic well-being of society; it means the redefinition of public duties by the state or the reshaping of the boundaries between civil society and the state so that intervention by the state in the affairs of civil society are hereafter constitutionally or legally restricted. Hence the importance of the constitutional enshrinement of the rights of private property.[56] Social and economic reforms are to be reduced to a minimum and the state prevented from re-establishing them. The objective is the minimal state on the one side and the mythical market on the other – the "market" being simply another name for the unrestrained power of corporate private property. The autocracy of private property is the utopia of the neo-liberal.

The Restructuring of Local Government

Some of the reasons for the restructuring of local government that has taken place in the 1980s and 1990s are similar to those for the downsizing of government in general, but others are specific to the issue of regional or municipal government. It is, however, more difficult to generalize about this level of politics because of the enormous variations across nations. Local governments have remarkably different histories, constitutional positions, ranges of powers, financial resources, and, it follows, size and influence.[57]

There have been several attempts, nevertheless, to draw out similarities and trends. First, although the origin of local government may vary from mere statutory creation to medieval free or chartered city-states, they all possess a similar rationale. Levels of government arise or are created in order to administer or direct the use of resources in a defined jurisdiction, and local or urban government is no exception. Until the 1970s and 1980s local governments existed for the purpose of local capital accumulation, of developing local conditions conducive to business investment. To achieve this they have political powers (including regulations over housing, zoning, planning, certain taxes, social services, transportation, education, health care, policing), and they can marshal local resources (including, variously, tax revenues, grants, pension funds, labour power, energy sources, transfer payments, and local state indebtedness). For these reasons, whatever their history, local governments have usually been dominated by local business interests. In the present age of highly mobile capital, however, much of the historic rationale for local government has begun to dissipate.

Related to this point is the second, namely, the political contradiction at the centre of local government: its powers and jurisdiction are subordinate to those of higher levels of government and yet there is a certain potential for independent action resting on local elections and sources of revenue.[58] This limited degree of local autonomy has in turn meant at least the possibility of asserting community needs and values in opposition to the demands of capital or the "marketplace." Such "politicization" has taken place at one time or another in most of the Western nations. In France in the 1970s and England in the 1980s, for instance, several municipal governments attempted to promote local development, not just to answer local needs but more significantly to serve as model alternatives to capitalism.[59] In other cases, local government served as a base for political opposition to central authorities and corporate interests.[60] Even if uninformed by a broader social or community "mission," however, a degree of local control can still mean local barriers to regional or urban development in the mere existence of regulatory and taxation powers, or social service obligations, at that level.

As a counter to the assertion of local control, central governments have introduced a number of direct and indirect changes. The indirect changes take forms such as restricted criteria for the allocation of national funds, a system of "targets and penalties" to direct local government spending, and changing limits on taxation powers. The direct changes come as reductions in national funding, restrictions to or redefinition of powers, or specific legislation forcing local government to carry out certain actions.

These changes amount to a restructuring of local government, the impetus for which comes from the need to override local democracy, such as it is, because it can present barriers, favour local business, and potentially be employed to create alternatives to the "free-market" agenda. The restructuring would appear to be intended to make local government responsive to the neo-liberal agenda. Paradoxically, such changes can take the form of centralization or decentralization.[61] In either case, local control over local resources and powers may be shifted to other administrative levels. It may be moved to administrative agencies and commissions often with quasi-independent status and responsible to the central government or its departments, or be redefined to narrow their impact. In these ways, among others, the central government can dampen or prevent locally based and financed small-scale development, reduce the power of local government over social policy, divert funds and other resources away from local needs and small business to local developments with non-local objectives, and in general increase its own control, while at the same time it can shift financial responsibilities to the local or regional levels.[62]

Since the 1980s many countries have followed this agenda at the local level. It has led to the development of free economic zones, the discouragement of social redistribution policies, the privatization of municipal services, and general pressure for the diversion of public funds from public facilities to the furtherance of accumulation in the private sector.[63]

Dismantling the Welfare State

The dismantling of the welfare state or, to put it euphemistically, "unburdening the state of the social agenda," began in many nations in the late 1970s and early 1980s, but is now taking place in every industrial nation. There is everywhere a shift to privatize as many aspects as possible of the health, educational, and social security systems.[64]

Because the private sector now cannot possibly meet the demand for social services provided by the welfare state, and because of the obvious political difficulties, much of this dismantling has taken the form of a "blurring of boundaries," a process that gradually introduces the private sector into arenas that previously seemed to be the sole preserve of the state. In the eyes of the Friedmans, this partial but expanding privatization is a "second-best alternative" to outright private-sector ownership.[65]

Privatization of the welfare state can take several avenues.[66] One route, for instance, involves government attempts to transfer the production of a service or a good from the public to the private sector while maintaining public financing. Examples of such transfers include the contracting-out of services such as cleaning, maintenance, laundry, or catering; the shift in social care of the elderly, handicapped, or mentally ill to private, voluntary, or non-profit organizations; and the selling of prisons or reformatories to "security" firms. These transfers create the illusion of a developing market, but because the transferred production usually remains dependent on state financing its viability continues to rest on the vicissitudes of government policy and revenue generation. Contrary to the rhetoric, moreover, private provision has often proven to be more expensive than public provision of the same services and benefits; but this, of course, is beside the point.

Another avenue of privatization takes the route of state-regulated services and benefits that are mandatorily provided by the private sector. Privatization here amounts to legislation obliging employees or individuals to have certain kinds of insurance or pensions, available only or partially through the corporate sector. Automobile insurance is the most easily recognized and common example, but the principle can and has been applied to unemployment and industrial accident insurance, sick pay, maternity leave, pensions, and even a range of health services.

The least visible and yet a widely taken route of privatization is the policy of incremental degradation of benefits and services. By increasingly restricting public services through rising eligibility criteria or declining quality, and by allowing income benefits to fall behind the rate of inflation, the policy eventually reaches its objectives: to create pressure for improved quality and benefits to be met by the private sector. The public health-care systems provide good examples of this form of privatization with the growth of user fees, deductibles, and restricted treatments, operations, and facilities, while at the same time a variety of incentives encourage private insurance and medical treatments. The interim goal of many governments would appear to be a two-tiered system: private but publicly supported medical treatment for the well-off, and a degraded state program for those who cannot afford to pay for private care.

Other examples are social assistance programs and insurance for unemployed and injured workers, when there are increasing qualifications and restrictions and the payments do not keep pace with the cost of living. Yet another is the government moving to restrict grants to state schools while increasing funding to encourage the growth of private schools. Similarly, the universities have experienced restrictions on grant increases, causing a rise in student fees, lower standards, and restricted eligibility, along with the need to pursue greater links to private enterprise.

In contrast to these undeclared policies of erosion, governments have taken up open policies of incentives. They use tax deductions as a form of inducement to move people towards the private provision of benefits, and the privatization of pension plans and medical insurance is a common objective of such schemes. Another method is the use of "vouchers," when, for example, the state educational budget is dispersed in the form of vouchers to parents with children, enabling them to choose public or private schools, with the ultimate goal of undermining the public system and providing private schools with state funding, of making a universal social program of benefit to the private sector. These incentives all involve a form of subsidy to those who can afford private provision at the expense of those who are and will remain completely reliant on state provision. The incentives will, moreover, encourage existing two-tiered systems in which those who have the means to set aside money or afford private fees are assisted in doing so.

In general, there is movement away from state provision of social services and programs, especially those that are "universal" or characterized as "social rights." In place of these rightful entitlements there is the reinstitution and reinforcement of the principles of the poor laws, the welfare schemes of preindustrial times.[67] In modern welfare states some of these earlier principles have been eclipsed by that of "universality," an attribute of many modern publicly provided programs, but others were retained and merely modified.[68] The current trends, however, present a revivification of the concept of the "deserving" versus "undeserving" poor, and of the principles of means testing, familial liability and responsibility, qualifying moral conduct, temporary benefits, deterrent eligibility criteria, targeting the "needy," and the workhouse ("workfare").[69]

The more that these principles are put into practice, the more the principles of universality and social right are undermined or consciously rejected; and the more the failures and omissions of the system are presented as the responsibility of the individual rather than of the state or corporation, the more every aspect of the welfare state can be made into an instrument of social control. Deterrents can, for example, force people to work for subsistence or below subsistence wages; the qualifications can counter the readiness to go on strike by making the benefits conditional on reasons for being out of work; and conditions for benefits may oblige relocation, doing menial work, or eventual acceptance of low-paid jobs.

There are many reasons for these changes in policy, most of them similar to the reasons for privatization in general. Again, the policies have several overall goals: to "shrink" the state by reducing state responsibilities and employees; to "open up" state sectors to private accumulation; to divert to the private sector the revenues spent on health, education, and welfare, which represent a large percentage of national budgets; and to discipline the working classes by undermining union achievements and eroding their social security in the face of rising permanent unemployment. One of the immediate causes would appear to be the decline in the available state revenue, but this is more consequence than cause: the decline is due mainly to declining national growth, the shift in tax burden, and greater demands from capital. The broader context of these changes is the need to "harmonize" national social security reforms, which constitute barriers of varying degrees to the needs of the international market, and to open the state sector to private accumulation.

As long as the welfare state remains relatively intact, providing a wide range of services and benefits, there also remains a political aspect, albeit modest, to the determination of the kind and nature of these policies and to the disposal of the necessary public funds. With a privatized system of welfare, this element of political determination is replaced in theory by market principles – impersonal, apolitical forces beyond the control of the state, especially when stripped of its economic management policies. The effect of a privatized welfare system not only removes the future possibility of political control, but also makes the provision of essential aspects of the reproduction of the working class subject to the vagaries of market forces. As the market goes, as it follows its booms and slumps and creates ever higher rates of chronic unemployment or underemployment, so too go the benefits and services so necessary to a healthy working population. Just as stock markets can collapse, businesses go bankrupt, and corporate theft and embezzlement on a grand scale continue, so too will the elements of a privatized welfare system bear the consequences not only of the business cycle, but also of a system of contradictory class interests.[70]

The Promotion of Charities

Thousands of charities exist in the industrial nations, and many more are added each year, including educational facilities, hospitals, and a range of social services previously funded by the state. There are several important trends that form the context for this vast growth in the size and number of charitable institutions and non-profit organizations and for the conscious efforts by government and the corporate sector to promote that growth. One trend has been the multiplying social needs that have accompanied increasing long-term, structural unemployment, among other forms of social disintegration; another the growing limits on further expansion of the social wage;[71] and a third the planned reduction and privatization of the services of the welfare state.

As these trends accelerate, the entire sphere of social reproduction, embracing all aspects of health, education, and social services, will increasingly be moved into the realm of service markets, one part of which takes the form of charities or trusts. The fostering of such institutions and agencies is but another means of privatizing public facilities; and their expansion is an attempt to shift the responsibility for the human costs of an inhuman system from the state to the individual and to transfer the means of redress from the social wage to private "gifts."[72]

Although charitable donations amount to only a small fraction of state social expenditures, they are playing an increasingly larger role as the current trends continue to build. With this expansion, the implications of their role will become more obvious. The very existence of charities and volunteer organizations and indeed their extension tell us, first of all, that capitalist "society" is in effect a mere marketplace, and that if one is not an active employee or employer, membership means very little. Only those considered "productive" in an economic sense have a place and are considered real members, while all others (to wit, "homemakers," the handicapped, the ill or injured, the old or young, the unemployed, the artist) are in one way or another marginalized, deemed external to the social system.

Moreover, it becomes evident that society as marketplace does not provide all of its members with the basic elements of life such as employment, housing, food, and health care. Society has no mechanism, aside from social reforms or charity or volunteer work, which are anomalies to the system, to provide such "amenities" to those who are not working or who are "non-productive," or, for that matter, even to the working poor.[73] With the decline of the welfare state and the growth of charities, all of the marginalized will increasingly become dependent on the purported benevolence or good will of others; and this in a society that looks upon altruism as abnormal.

By "dealing with" its "non-productive" members in this way, society as marketplace relies mainly on individual donations and tax revenues, that is, on deductions from the wages of those working, to shore up the chronic social destruction that takes place under capitalism. But now, increasingly in the form of charity, social redistribution becomes a "voluntary" matter and indeed tax-deductible. This means that the more that goes to charity, the less goes to the state for redistribution. It is a planned paradox: charities are both a substitute for and an instrument in the demise of the welfare state.

To the degree to which charitable institutions and non-profit or volunteer organizations become the prevailing form of social redistribution, moreover, the existing "social rights" or universal entitlements to state-funded social services will be narrowed. In part in the name of charity, the erosion of the elements of "social citizenship," never fully realized anywhere, has everywhere begun.

Circumscription of Civil Liberties/Human Rights

Civil liberties or human rights are popularly understood to be God-given, inalienable, or absolute, as if standing above the real world of conflicting material interests. They are, however, the outcome of a long history of contending forces, which makes them relative to time and place. Their continuing existence in modern capitalist society is likewise relative to and dependent on a certain balance of organized class or sectorial interests. Without this balance, civil liberties can be curtailed in favour of the interests of the stronger of the contending forces. Everywhere in the world where the organized resistance of the subordinate classes has been suppressed or eliminated, there is a corresponding abnegation of human rights. The ruling classes, without organized opposition, are no respecters of civil liberties when the pre-eminent power of capital is threatened.[74]

Civil liberties are considered fundamental rights in advanced industrial societies, and in general they are enshrined as such in constitutions. These liberties vary somewhat across nations but normally comprise a range of rights, including the freedom of speech, religion, security, movement, assembly, protest, and due process of law. Most of these civil liberties have a reality, a practical application, only in conjunction with another "right," and that is the right to private property. In a system of private property, many of these freedoms *depend on* the possession of private property. That is, the financial wherewithal is more or less a requirement for their realization. Without it the freedoms remain, but only as abstractions, as unrealizable principles. With it the freedoms can be realized, but even then only to the limits established by contact with the freedom of others possessed of private property. The freedom of one is contradicted by the exercise of the freedom of another.

In abstract, then, these freedoms are shared by every citizen; in reality, their realization is extremely limited without money – and, increasingly, considerable amounts of money. At present, for instance, for the right of freedom of speech to have a reality, to make an impact on society, it would require at least the ownership of a journal, newspaper, or radio or television station. To use another example, given the costs of hiring a lawyer and of taking a case to court, the right to due legal process is now everywhere severely compromised for those without the means.

Implicitly recognizing this problem and the potential consequence of a loss of legitimacy for the justice system, many industrial nations introduced state-supported legal services and human rights commissions to allow those without the financial means to be represented in court or to find redress for violations of their civil liberties. Both the services and commissions have been tacit acknowledgements of the contradictions within a system of private property, in which the rights of those with property can be exercised while the rights of those without are circumscribed or blocked. In fact, the promulgation, defence, and expansion of civil liberties or human rights can and do restrict the activities of the corporate sector. From the point of view of business, the exercise of civil liberties by subordinate classes is nothing less than a fetter to the unrestrained use of the power entailed in private property by owners over non-owners.

In practice, subsidized legal services and human rights commissions have served, however inadequately, those without financial means, in particular the poor and dispossessed, to resist in a limited way encroachments on their rights by the owners of the means of production, distribution, housing, and so on. They have provided a modicum of protection for those without means from those with means, and in the process they have placed restrictions on the powers of the possessors of substantial property. Given the present decline in the possibilities for capital accumulation, these restrictions become less and less tolerable because they encroach on the powers of ownership and present the possibility of modifications or an end to practices that are immensely profitable – to name one example, unequal pay for women and minorities.

Given the negative current and potential effects for capital of these state-supported instruments of defence of civil liberties for the powerless and disadvantaged in society, the state has begun to reduce their financing, powers, scope, and independence from government. In the United States under Reagan, both legal services and the human rights commission were substantially restricted, as they were in several Canadian provinces during the 1980s and in Britain in the early 1990s.[75] Although the budgets and powers were cut, the form of these services and commissions and even some of the legislation were left in place, thus guarding against criticism that these governments were evading their responsibilities to those without the power of capital. The abstract freedoms remained (although these too are coming under attack), while the practical possibility of the powerless realizing them was further restricted. Legal protection for the poor, for women, for minorities, was undermined, while it became easier for the corporate sector to do as it pleased. Another route for legitimate protest was narrowed.[76]

As these restrictions are legislated, other circumscriptions to civil liberties also take place. The laws passed to increase citizens' access to information about government have been progressively restricted in practice or in law.[77] Although the right to know what one's government is doing is not as a rule enshrined in constitutions, such a right is at least implicit in the notion of democracy. These laws, then, do point to a contradiction, namely, the fact that so-called democracies operate in relative secrecy from their own citizens, and that citizens have at best only limited and narrow access to government information.[78]

Far from becoming more accessible to its citizens, governments are increasingly employing powers to restrict access to information about their activities. Most of those nations referred to as liberal democracies are expanding mechanisms such as official secrets acts, national security laws, public order bills, and highly restrictive definitions of the public interest.

A further circumscription is implicit, and that is the increase in police budgets and powers taking place throughout the industrial world.[79] Police intelligence work and surveillance grow with little regard for accountability, while other aspects of government activity meet with financial restraint.[80]

As a counter to the growing "national security state," the courts cannot be expected to act as a "check or balance." The manner in which judges are chosen in most countries remains profoundly undemocratic, and considerable abuse of judicial power can be traced to the selection process itself.[81] Given this process, and the "politics" of judicial decisions (some of the most draconian restrictions to civil liberties recently have originated in the courts and not in legislatures), as well as the declining access to legal aid, the future of the judiciary will most likely remain one of the pillars of a system of growing inequalities. Citizens will increasingly need a means to protect themselves from the abuse of judicial powers.

To understand the current restrictions in civil liberties or human rights it is necessary to see them as the political reflection of an earlier system of private property, from a time when ownership meant the individual ownership of the means and product of production. In the transition from feudalism to capitalism, civil rights represented the transformation from existing political privilege based on heredity and landed wealth to that of political equality of all citizens before the state. The later rise to pre-eminence of capitalist private property, for the most part a development of the nineteenth century, changed the basis of these civil rights in that this property became "the right, on the part of the capitalist, to appropriate the unpaid labour of others or its product, and the impossibility, on the part of workers, of appropriating their own product."[82] Civil liberties, then, became fully realizable only for the capitalist and more or less abstractions for the working classes. The degree to which civil liberties became and have remained realities for the working classes – those with little or no significant real property – has usually borne a strong relation to the organized power of those classes or to their threat to the "public order" within the nation-state.

The apparent persistence of civil liberties or human rights for the working classes in the industrial nations, long after the property basis for those rights had been transformed, has rested on the historical conditions of a certain stage in the development of capitalism, namely, the national, social, and economic foundations of liberal democracy. As these conditions have declined or disappeared with the coming of the global economy, so too have the respect for civil liberties and these liberties themselves. A world dominated by global transnational corporations without supranational political control provides little basis for civil liberties for the working classes, except as abstractions for ideological reasons or when capital has been forced to acknowledge them.[83]

Circumscription of Trade Union Powers

As representatives of the organized sector of the working classes, trade unions have been all-important to the achievement of social reforms. In general, the size and militancy of the trade union movement have been closely related to the amount of social reform and state intervention in the economy. Within the nation-state the entire range of workers' rights and protective legislation, including employment standards, workplace regulations, social benefits, minimum wages, pensions, and union rights – much that is fundamental to the standard of living and degree of social justice for working people – owes in large part its achievement to the strength of trade union organizations.

Although often perceived as unassailable, many of these accomplishments were premised on the measured accommodation of the trade unions and working classes by national capital within the nation-state in the postwar period of rapid growth. They were, then, always in a sense provisional, maintained by a certain balance of social forces and economic "well-being." When and where they presented a threat to capital accumulation, they suffered contraction or restriction. Since the 1960s, governments throughout the West in periods of crisis have enacted legislation intended to curb the exercise of union powers that had been won progressively since the late nineteenth century. Among the first of the contemporary curbs to be legislated were limits on wage settlements. Often euphemistically called "prices and incomes policies," these systems of wage control stretch back into the 1950s in some countries (Sweden and Holland), but by the 1960s there was hardly an industrial country that did not have some mechanisms for monitoring and regulating wage increases.[84]

Since the 1980s all the social and legal achievements of national trade unions and working classes have come, if not under attack, then at least into question. In most of the advanced industrial countries, albeit with variations, labour legislation covering trade union rights and union security, recognition, and financing has seen the introduction of numerous restrictions.[85] Similarly, the broad category of employment standards, including holidays, length of work week, minimum age, grounds for dismissal, redundancy regulations, and retirement age has suffered increasing restriction or contraction in most of the industrial countries.

To these restrictions can be added legislation banning strikes, excluding certain categories of work or geographic areas from labour code provisions, expanding the definition of "essential" workers, introducing "right to work" laws (as in the United States), and easing decertification or increasing restrictions to certification. Court rulings and fines, moreover, have heavily penalized unions in several countries, and employers have created more union "substitutes" (works' councils, joint labour-management committees) and engaged in a variety of "union suppression" activities. All of these factors make it increasingly difficult for unions to organize, to strike or bargain collectively, or to represent workers' interests for wider social reforms.

In an immediate sense these changes are the product of state suppression of social reform and trade union organizations, but the state has few if any interests of its own to motivate such actions. The underlying reasons rest in structural changes, transnational corporate policy, and the present character of trade unionism.

The coming of the global economy has created a global labour market that has brought pressure for global wage levels and an implicit and abundant world supply of labour power, both of which in turn have reduced the ability of trade unions to exact higher wages and benefits for their members. ("Hourly compensation costs for production workers in manufacturing in the Republic of Korea, Singapore and Taiwan . . . surpassed those of Portugal in 1989; in 1990, per capita income in Singapore was higher than that of Spain; that of the Republic of Korea was close to that of Greece.")[86]

New technology has created smaller and more mobile production units and spawned selective recruiting policies, thereby inhibiting the process of unionization. The continuous incremental growth of structural unemployment in industrial countries has made strike activity as well as union recruitment more difficult. The decline in the powers of the national state in the face of the global economy has lessened the leverage for exacting reforms and diminished the jurisdiction in which reforms could be enacted and enforced. The increasing introduction of free trade zones is often accompanied by restrictions on trade unions and employment standards.

International freedom of movement for capital across national borders, moreover, has no counterpart for the movement of trade unions. The point was well made many years ago: "The true correlative to an international agreement securing to capital the right to move and, therefore, organize across the boundaries of national states would be an agreement securing to collective organizations of workpeople the right to take common action in negotiating, bargaining with and, if need be, striking against the multinational enterprises. . . . It is not free movement of labor but free international trade union action which is the true counterpart to free movement of capital."[87] Insofar as labour can be said to have mobility this applies to workers as individuals or as contractual labour. National labour legislation and employment standards, in short, are the product of national working classes, trade unions, and capital and not reflective of economic activity with global arrangements dominated by transnational corporations and characterized by high technology. Being at odds with a world economy, these laws and standards in fact become increasingly insupportable within nation-states and also divisive factors for trade unions and working classes, separating them as national entities and fuelling the divide between the industrial and lesser developed countries.

From the point of view of TNCs, the rights of trade unions, even the very existence of unions, and high employment standards generally appear as so many barriers restricting the "freedom of the market," as restrictions to capital accumulation. Through "global strategic management" – multiple-sourcing, international subcontracting, blackmail, financial manipulation, physical relocation – TNCs are able to pressure governments to level employment and other standards and to restrict union rights.[88] They are also often able to move their operations to avoid or escape such legislation, or simply to refuse to obey national laws.[89] And their collaboration in or instigation of the conscious suppression or deradicalization of trade unions is an important factor in the growing difficulties faced by unions. In its annual survey of violations of trade union rights, the International Confederation of Free Trade Unions reports: "260 activists were killed and 2,500 arrested in 1992 for carrying out legitimate trade union activity. This compares with 200 deaths and 2,000 arrests in the previous year. . . . The reported killings were the result of repression by government, security services and death squads. Most of these crimes remained unpunished."[90]

In this historical juncture, trade unions are finding their own organizational structures a hindrance to their ability to respond to the changes taking place. Because they are social structures corresponding for the most part to a post-World War II Fordist mode of production, the new technology is making many of them appear as anachronisms. They are facing a transition, as they did in the second half of the nineteenth century in the shift from craft-based manufacturing to large-scale machine-based industry. This time it is from the relative stability of Fordism to the flexibility of computer-integrated production. The enormous administrative-state once required by the Fordist mode of production, moreover, is no longer necessary, and it follows generally that the strength of public-sector unions begins to decline. Unions are organized, furthermore, on a national basis for the most part, whereas the largest formations of capital are now mainly international in their operations. This means that laws defining and delimiting union activities present restrictions to the possibilities of concluding international agreements. It also means that their structure as national organizations is becoming more clearly a limitation to the struggle for the internationalization of trade unions.

On the national level, trade unions are preoccupied with these numerous checks and tethers on their activity and on their declining numbers. On the international level, they have little if any real strength or organization to confront the transnational corporations and their representative associations. And there is no supranational jurisdiction in which they can exercise leverage. When attempts were made in Europe to establish a regulatory system for transnational collective bargaining and union activities, the transnational corporations spent considerable effort to ensure that this would not come to pass.[91] Even the attempt to establish common employment standards and trade union rights in the European Social Charter was fought by the European employers' confederation and has amounted to minimal standards, cast in terms of individual rights, without protection for the right of association or to strike and lacking any enforcement mechanism.[92] Without substantial organizational strength at the international level the unions could expect little else. Capital was not about to subordinate itself willingly to political control.

We are left with a picture of diminishing national trade union membership, increasing restrictions in labour law, and serious opposition to international structures allowing for trade union activity at that level. Mired in bureaucracy and defensive activity, and often bourgeois nationalist in outlook, the unions seem somewhat unaware of the political meaning of the global economy or of the forces arraigned against them.[93] As products of the postwar period of Fordism, Keynesianism, and the nation-state, they are ill prepared not only for the challenge of the new right, which is upon them in the form of deregulation, privatization, and anti-union legislation, but also for the realities of the global economy, advanced technology, and the supranational organizations representative of the interests of capital. Unless the continued decline of trade unions is reversed and the unions resist becoming a mechanism for dividing the working class (by negotiating two-tiered contracts, among other developments), this important bulwark underlying social reform in the nation-state will become increasingly ineffectual as a social force, and the working class will lose its main representative voice.

Preparing for the Consequences:
The Growth of Prison Facilities

As neo-liberal policies have come to be adopted across the industrial nations, as they have started the process of dismantling the welfare state and downsizing the size and role of government, one clear countertendency stands out: the expansion of forms of coercive social control in almost every country. In many jurisdictions police powers have been broadened, and in some cases police budgets have been increased or police allowed sources of finance independent of public authorities. Most strikingly, there has been a large growth in prison facilities and inmate population.[94]

These tendencies, most marked in the United States, are present in many Western nations. According to Andrew Rutherford, prison systems in several industrial countries:

> remain set on a relentless expansionist course despite expenditure cuts on schools, hospitals and social services. Indeed, imprisonment has emerged as a growth industry even in periods of economic stagnation, and some prison systems are geared up to redoubling their size over the coming decades. Far from protecting citizens from crime, the massive growth of incarceration undermines the essential values which distinguish free societies from authoritarian ones.[95]

Despite falling crime rates, the prison population in the United States continues to grow and is expected to reach about two million in 2001, making the country's rate of incarceration among the highest per capita in the world. In keeping with this growth, it has been argued that "corrections will represent the largest single item in many state budgets."[96] In many U.S. states the rate of increase in corrections expenditure now far exceeds that for non-coercive social expenditures. While the United States is in the forefront of the expansion of penal institutions, other countries are pursuing similar policies. Britain, France, West Germany, and even Holland have begun large construction programs to increase the number and capacity of penal institutions. In Britain new prison construction represents "the largest expansion programme undertaken this century. Twenty-six new prisons between 1983 and 1995 will be provided, at an estimated total capital cost of £870 million at 1987 prices."[97]

Assuming that crime and imprisonment are related, one might at first glance also assume that the explanation for the present expansion programs is due to a rise in crime. There is, however, no direct or consistent correlation between the amount of crime and the prison population. A survey of data and literature on the relationship illustrated that rates of incarceration and of crime may, but equally may not, correspond. Rutherford concluded that the size of "prison populations" is "primarily the consequence of policy choices and practice. The use made of custody, prison population size and other aspects of the prison system are the result of decisions made throughout the criminal justice system and the wider political sphere."[98]

This point was made not simply by showing the lack of a consistent correlation between crime rates and rates of imprisonment, but also by looking at how the German Nazis and Italian fascists carried out an expansion of prisons and their populations in the 1930s. In both countries, the governments openly advocated policies of expansion and intended them to be part of their national "development" programs, as part of a solution for dealing with dissenters to the "reconstruction" of those societies.

It can be argued, then, that the growth of penal facilities today similarly reflects a conscious choice, one that rests on a particular philosophy and is by no means directly or solely related to the amount of crime. While government policy largely determines the present expansion, governments also by and large determine judicial processes and sentencing practices both of which are partly responsible for the size of the inmate population.

The very definition of crime is also largely a matter of state policy and practice. Crime is a certain act defined by legislation as prohibited by the state under the law. Because it is formulated by a state authority, the definition is a social and political construct; it is a decision by a government past or present that some acts are to be labelled criminal and others not; and this, in turn, determines how much or little crime of a certain sort will exist. A certain definition of crime, moreover, will determine the activities that occupy police agencies and, in part, judicial processing and sentencing, as well as popular perceptions about crime.

The definition of certain acts as criminal, then, is relative to the social system in which they are found; and typically, they are acts that run counter to the principles of that system. In a capitalist society, for this reason, many corporate activities – even though the financial cost to society and the harm caused to individuals far exceeds that of individual crime – are not perceived or treated as criminal because they are not defined as such.[99]

The questionable and even scandalous activities of many TNCs beginning in the 1960s gave rise to numerous attempts to modify a near vacuum of definition, let alone regulation, of acceptable international business practices. The UN, OECD, ILO, ICFTU, UNCTAD, ETUC, EEC, the Group of 77, the United States, and even the International Chamber of Commerce, among others, all put forward guidelines, codes of conduct, rules, regulations, and charters in an effort to control the extensive unethical and illicit practices of TNCs. Bribery, extortion, non-disclosure, restrictive practices, environmental destruction, money laundering, the disregard of human and trade union rights, and con-sumer health and safety and national laws were among the activities these organizations and governments sought to define and then control. These efforts have resulted in more precise guidelines and definitions, but they have had little effect on actual corporate activities. There is no overall international agreement or jurisdiction, no authoritative inter-national institutional machinery, and no agreed-upon sanctions or means of enforcement.[100] The small and mildly reformist United Na-tions Centre on Transnational Corporations (UNCTC), set up in the mid-1970s, was subjected to attack by right-wing groups and corporate representatives over the years for its attempts to define an "international code of conduct" for multinationals, until it was dismantled in 1993.[101]

The actions of corporations are, in effect, the principles of the sys-tem; therefore if companies harm the environment or human health, take away livelihoods, or blackmail governments, they are carrying out these actions in the name of the system. If they break the law, they are seen as having been overzealous in the pursuit of the accepted "legiti-mate" goals that all corporations pursue. Since the existence and growth of the corporation are fundamental to capitalism, to engage in corporate law-breaking or amorality is to sin *within* the system. For a person with little or no property to break the law – that is, laws established for the most part to protect private property – is to sin *against* the system.

To a large degree it is the various individual acts against private prop-erty that are perpetrated out of need, out of deprivation, that are defined as criminal and dealt with harshly by the judicial system. Very high percentages of defined "criminals" in all capitalist countries are from the poorest strata of society, and for the most part their "crimes" are acts against property, that is, theft of one sort or another, actions by those with little against those with much. The negative impact of corporate crime and unethical corporate behaviour, however, is vastly greater in all ways on society than individual crime, but these corporate acts are committed *within* the spirit of the system of private property. "In Canada there is one homicide roughly every twelve hours, but even conservative estimates indicate that a worker dies from a preventable employment condition every six hours."[102]

Because the prison expansion programs do not necessarily correspond to actual crime rates, they beg for an explanation beyond a mere correlation. Since they are the product of government policy, and since the expansion is widespread amongst the industrial nations, it would appear that there is something of a common policy. Although the rationale has not been openly stated, some speculative reasoning about the purpose is not out of place.

In general, the reliance on coercive forms of social control, instead of non-coercive measures, is a policy taken up by authoritarian or conservative regimes. Coercion in the form of police actions and incarceration can be used against political dissent, as it is in dictatorships and was in the former U.S.S.R. and Eastern European countries; or it can be employed against a working class that has been plunged into poverty and hopelessness, thereby constituting a threat to private property and the social order based on it. In most Western nations the extensive use of police force has not been typical, and extensive incarceration has not been necessary, except against the lowest strata of the working class. This is because since World War II the continual economic expansion of capitalism has made possible a relatively high standard of living for most of the working class, and the welfare state has provided a tolerable existence or economic "cushion" for the "non-productive."

In the industrial nations, however, the standard of living of the working class has been in slow decline for many years (since the late 1970s in North America), and the protection and programs of the welfare state have been in decline for almost as long. With the adoption of neo-liberal policies has come a conscious attempt to do away with the postwar social programs, to deny the state its role as a collective or social conscience, and to minimize the state itself. The mechanisms of the marketplace are to replace all aspects of a society of socially responsible human beings, at least in theory. There has been, moreover, a secular dissolution of traditional institutions of social integration such as the family, church, and small community. In short, most of the non-coercive bases of social control have been eroded as a natural consequence of the development of capital or as the intended consequence of government policy. In their absence there arises the need for more coercive means.[103]

If state policy choices determine the number of prisons and the size of the inmate population, then, policy implies a plan, and a plan implies an analysis of a situation. Because the need for more prisons does not necessarily correlate with present crime rates, it may correlate with expectations of higher rates, revisions in sentencing, or redefinitions of crime.

If, however, crime (and punishment) is largely a matter of state definition and embraces for the most part those acts that contradict the principles of the system, and if increasing numbers of people are left with few choices but to contradict those principles, then it would seem obvious that "crime" cannot be "solved" by adding police, expanding their powers, or increasing the number of prisons and rates in incarceration. It is even more obvious when the social system in question refuses to provide economic and social well-being for its members, when it allows poverty and deprivation of all sorts to grow to encompass sizeable percentages of the population. This is a system that increasingly creates the need for its outcast members to violate its principles to survive.[104]

But more, the principles of a system that promotes self-interest in opposition to social interest and allows its own population to be degraded are hardly worthy of support. In this context, those who sin *against* private property, and are defined as criminal for it, have done so out of necessity and can hardly be condemned for it. Those who have sinned *within* private property or in its name, and have become successful for it, have done so in the interests of the self. One is defined as being criminal because the interests of private property must be protected as the bastion of the system; the other is excused as being overzealous in pursuit of socially defined and accepted objectives, individual wealth and power.

Restrictions to Democracy

The commitment to market principles and practice as embodied in neoliberalism is antipathetic to the principles and practice of democracy.[105] The reason is straightforward: the free market and democracy represent *in principle* two contradictory forms of resource allocation for society. On the one hand, the free market implies a form of social distribution of goods and services via the exchange of private property, which is free of mitigating morality and sometimes captured in the phrase "economic justice." Democracy, or more broadly politics, on the other hand, implies a certain political determination of economic activities, as implied in the notion of "distributive justice."[106]

In practice it is difficult to point to any example under capitalism of the unmitigated operation of either politics or the free market in the social allocation of resources, and this is because the state has always played a role in distribution even if the market has determined the broad parameters for political decision-making. The point is that there is a contradiction between market and politics. The market implies priorities in accord with the demands of capital; politics implies priorities in accord with some form of social, or ethical, determination. In capitalist society, the two have had an uneasy co-existence, each representing in essence the antithesis of the other. Within this contradiction lies the rationale for the neo-liberal interest in a "minimal" state.

There is little doubt, despite this co-existence, as to which principles have prevailed. In the West, even with the coming of universal enfranchisement, for the most part a post-World War I phenomenon, political decisions have never seriously challenged the demands of capital. At best, politics has achieved reforms to the system. We have experienced, after all, "democracy" in the context and form of a capitalist state, not democracy as human beings determining and controlling their own destinies. The system is democratic more in form and rhetoric than in content.[107] Nevertheless, the enfranchisement of the non-owners as well as the owners of capital has made for a political system in which it has been possible to impose certain mitigating effects in the shape of reform on the operation of the market.

Although the welfare state has done little to redistribute wealth from capital to the working class, it does represent a certain degree of protection and security that the working class has achieved for itself via political means.[108] It embodies elements of "distributive justice" that temper the "economic justice" of the market. Distributive justice, however, has always been preceded by extraparliamentary demands made by a sector of civil society (usually the working class), and the degree to which this intervention has played a role has constituted a compromise between a national capitalist class and the citizenry. Since the 1980s, even this limited assertion of political considerations over the economic has become both restricted and superseded.

As capital moves beyond its national character and foundation, it forces as a natural consequence a supplanting of national and local jurisdictions in favour of its own injunctions or international administrative authority. Organizations such as the WTO, the UN, IMF, and World Bank increasingly pre-empt national and local laws and standards in spheres such as health and welfare, workers' rights, environmental protection, food quality, capital flows, and ownership. In fact, these international organizations touch on most aspects of the national jurisdiction. They continually diminish even the right to curtail certain kinds of exploitation of resources or to encourage economic development in certain directions. National and local governments are increasingly powerless in a growing number of spheres; national sovereignty is being reduced, in effect, in almost every arena of national jurisdiction. More and more national policies become subordinate to the demands of the global market and to the regulations, laws, standards, and enforceable deregulatory powers of these international organizations.[109]

At the international level the elements of democracy or the mechanisms of political access to decision-making are far more limited than the already narrow access at the national or local level. The main influence is without question the interests of international capital, promoted by costly lobbies and international agencies and commissions; and the main principles set forth are those of the market.[110]

Although there has been an unmistakable decline in the jurisdiction of the national state due to the pressures and influence of TNCs and the acceptance of the authority of international agencies, the political institutions of the industrial nations remain in place and continue to possess the *possibility* of political control by social forces opposed to the interests of capital. Corporate representatives have been quite aware of this possibility, but their more immediate concern has been the increasing demands within the terms of the various programs and institutions of the welfare state. As early as 1975 the Trilateral Commission had identified "democracy" as the Achilles heel of the industrial countries. The "democratic ethos" was making it "difficult to prevent access and restrict information" and the postwar years had seen "the expansion of the demands on government from individuals and groups." The result was "an 'overload' on government and the expansion of the role of government in the economy and society."[111] The solution was to begin the process of restricting access (in part by "reinvigorating political parties" as the main instrument of "interest aggregation"), of reducing information (in part by encouraging government secrecy), and of lowering social expectations (in part by limiting enrolment in higher education). Most of their solutions, as well as other changes, were gradually introduced during the 1980s to lessen access to decision-making and to reduce the condition of "too much democracy."

On the other side, corporations and their collective associations successfully rebuffed the various attempts to subordinate TNCs to international political control with respect to labour standards, union rights, and illicit and unethical practices. Aside from some voluntary guidelines and a few international agreements (the Montreal Protocol and the Rio Declaration, for instance), which do not constitute political control properly speaking, there is no *political* regulation of TNCs. The coming of the global economy has brought with it the "sovereignty of capital," more or less unimpaired except by remaining national powers and jurisdictions.[112]

In other words, politics in the form of liberal democracy in the national sphere enabled a citizenry to modify – and made it both necessary and advantageous for capital to compromise on – the exercise of the property rights attached to capital. But at the global level there is no comparable political structure or jurisdiction, and there the accumulation of capitalist private property can be pursued without political interference – though not without certain regulation or restrictions emanating from such organizations as the WTO, IMF, WB, and BIS. These constraints, however, are not political, but rather are the formalization of the rules of global competition between capitals. From this level and with the advantages of global self-generation, capital has little need to compromise with national political policy, and indeed it is positioned to demand broad policies reflecting its own needs – hence, neo-liberalism.

The political dilemma for capital is how to maintain the trappings of democracy in the West, as crucial to social control, while economic inequality and long-term unemployment increase, chronic decline of living standards sets in, and the powers of national and local government decline. The consequent growing loss of legitimacy is exacerbated by several other factors, including decreasing political access; widening corporate blackmail over jobs, pollution, and taxes; expanding numbers of single-party or coalition political systems; an increasingly obvious meaninglessness of party alternations in power; and spreading political corruption. Among the industrialized countries, Italy and Japan are

probably the most notorious examples of national governments characterized by political corruption, but they are hardly alone.[113]

The loss of legitimacy in turn will have an increasing number of
effects. Voter apathy will be the least important, while a range of
extraparliamentary activities will grow, encompassing forms of direct
political and economic action, both legal and illegal, and perhaps more
terrorism.[114] The future of social control, given the declining legitimacy
of government and growing unemployment, is almost certainly going to
rest increasingly on forms of state coercion. If market principles are to
prevail, imposed from the international level, it is not plausible to imagine their co-existence with democratic principles, except where these
principles exist in form only.

The quaint idea of self-regulating social control under market principles presumes a wide and relatively equitable distribution of property –
the foundation of the Jeffersonian vision of a democracy of small propri-
etors. This romantic neo-liberal vision of a democracy of private property holders is somewhat out of touch with the real trends in capitalist
private property. If there ever were such a society, there is certainly none
at present. The irony is that the operation of the capitalist market itself
destroys small businesses; they are squeezed and ultimately bankrupted
by the effects of the very policies they have supported. The operation of
the market, even given the "distributive justice" of the welfare state, has
produced a very unequal distribution of wealth. Since the coming of
neo-liberalism there has been a striking increase in this inequality.
"Economic justice" is rapidly eclipsing "distributive justice" everywhere, and without organized resistance the unmitigated tyranny of the
market may come to prevail sooner rather than later.

• • •

The promulgation and progressive realization of the neo-liberal agenda
are not to be grasped as an "ideological victory," as if a set of political
ideas were sufficient to cause such profound changes. Rather, the
changes are best viewed as the consequence of the arrival of the global
economy, and as such they form the political assertion of the demands of
internationalized capital in search of new avenues of accumulation. The
agenda comprises policies for a new age, a genuinely "new reality," a
global economy characterized by enormous conglomerates, oligopolies,
and cartels, intense competition between them, new modes of highly
capital-intensive production, pervasive fluctuating "excess capacity" in

every sphere, vast capital funds in constant search of profitable investment,[115] an attenuated national state, the growth of trading blocs, and increasing numbers of international and multilateral agreements, laws, and agencies.

If the national economy is to remain capitalist, the agenda must be accepted by the world's governments. Yet, at the same time, such acceptance will harmonize the national with the international; it will spell the end of the national economy and of the nation-state as we have known it. In their place will be global economic power, maintained by the "dull compulsion of economic necessity" and arbitrary governing structures of administration and coercion.[116]

The realization of the agenda will also bring a kind of completion to the development of capital because it will mean that the entire sphere of societal reproduction will have become capitalized. Those aspects of the reproduction of labour power now fulfilled by the welfare state, that is, "paid out of deductions from the social revenue," will be transformed into commodity relations, thereby more or less completing the subjugation of social life and societal needs to capital. In addition, those aspects of the reproduction of collective necessities previously underwritten by the state (public works or infrastructure, such as roads, rails, water supply, and sewage) will be transferred to the private sector if there is a profit to be made. The coming minimal state will be defined by the tax revenues necessary to finance only those public necessities in which capital cannot make a return on investment. These necessities will be defined not in human terms but in strict commercial terms: what is essential to the furtherance of the conditions of capital accumulation.[117]

The future will not bring a neo-liberal paradise of free buyers and sellers, however. There will be, rather, a continuous growth of the global system of enormous social and economic inequalities that already exists – a natural consequence of the more or less unrestrained accumulation of capitalist private property.

VI

The Era of the
"Triumph of Capitalism"

The Meaning of the "Triumph"

The "capitalization" of the world

Spurred by advanced Fordism and massive state investment after World War II, national capitalism expanded outwardly and "inwardly" to capture or create markets that had remained unopened or under-exploited. There were several key elements to the outward or geographic expansion. Even before the war had ended, the institutional basis for the coming international regime of capital under the "leadership" of the United States was being laid. By the end of the 1940s, the United Nations and its associated agencies and commissions, such as the IMF, the World Bank, and GATT, were engaged in opening markets, reducing barriers, and standardizing regulations for world trade.

The process of decolonization was strongly promoted by the United States and aided by United Nations' offices and peacekeeping forces as a means of opening the former colonies to U.S. and indeed international investment. Independence, "assisted" by the United Nations and the United States, freed the colonial world from its subordination to particular metropolitan, national capitals, making it accessible to penetration by other national capitals, especially U.S., and helped to circumvent the widespread move to socialism.

Common markets, in particular in Europe, were urged upon groups of nation-states as a means of increasing capital concentration and centralization through mergers, oligopolies, cartels, and specialization. The consequence was to give pre-eminence to the powers of capital by increasing the market size, by reducing the authority of national governments (and so liberal democracies) over the operation of business, and by facilitating the cross-national supply of labour and lessening trade union power and militancy.

A further component of the geographic expansion was the so-called "containment of socialism." Here was the motive for the immense arms buildup over several decades after World War II, for the formation of NATO and other regional military alliances, and for several localized wars and interventions, for instance, in Malaysia, Korea, Vietnam, Indonesia, the Dominican Republic, the Congo, Cuba, Chile, Angola, Nicaragua – the list could go on. The point of these efforts was to prevent the expansion of socialism and to enhance and enlarge the avenues for capital accumulation. They were the historic machinations of the struggle between the forces of capitalist private property and socialized state property.

The "inward" expansion of capital refers to the development of the consumer market. Although modern consumerism began with the coming of Fordism in the early twentieth century, its totalizing or all-embracing thrust dates from the era of advanced Fordism in the post-World War II period. Its foundation was mass production and the consequent development of mass advertising.

Consumerism is the commodification of socio-cultural needs; it is the penetration of capital into all facets of human need – satisfaction previously fulfilled outside the realm of contract. It is, in other words, the commodification of everyday life, of culture in the broadest sense. Such subjection to the demands of capital means that all socio-cultural dimensions of life become dominated by corporate interests; the corporation comes to determine broadly the main cultural boundaries and to define and structure human needs so that they correspond with society as marketplace.

By the early 1970s, given the postwar structure of capital in the form of the national Keynesian welfare state, the expansion of capital geographically and "internally" was more or less complete. For the most part, the non-"socialist" world had been opened and subordinated to the domination of international capital; and the "socialist" countries had been effectively "contained." Capital, moreover, had penetrated and conquered most aspects of socio-cultural life, creating a comprehensive internal or consumer market. Furthermore, postwar military production had produced war goods stockpiled to the point of absurdity.

The nearing of these limits to further expansion was coterminous with the arrival of global capital and the growth of new modes of production based on microelectronics and computer applications. These two developments increased the pressure then building to expand the possibilities for global accumulation. By the end of the 1970s the trends that were to characterize the next decade were already visible. In the industrial world, the ongoing corporate merger movement commenced and attacks on the welfare state in practice and theory were initiated; in the Third World, debt dependency grew and "structural adjustment policies" made their debut in Chilean blood; and the Soviet-aligned "socialist" countries were soon to find their own internal contradictions exacerbated by a U.S.-inspired arms race.

All these trends possessed a common underlying motive: the subordination of the world to the demands of capital. Wherever capital has taken the form of state ownership, as in the so-called socialist countries, in the welfare state, and all forms of "public" property, it has presented limits to the accumulation of capital as corporate private property. Wherever the working class has defended itself against the depredations of capitalist enterprise, by means of trade unions and the organs of liberal democracy, it has created limits to its exploitation by capital. With the coming of global capitalism the pressure to overcome these restrictions has increased as the opportunities for accumulation have approached certain limits; at the same time, the globalization of capital has provided the possibilities for surmounting or overthrowing many of these political and economic restrictions to increased accumulation.

The end of the industrial nation-state

In the early stages of national industrial development, unencumbered by social or economic reforms, horrific excesses were committed in the name of accumulation – particularly in the treatment of workers, especially women and children, and in the despoliation of the environment. As the degradation grew beyond tolerable limits, resistance by working classes to these excesses and to the effects of economic depressions, albeit in different periods in different countries, brought respite little by little in the shape of state-legislated social and economic reforms.

The reforms represented compromises in periods of capital expansion between more or less organized subordinate classes and national, competitive capitalist classes. As capitalism came to embrace the economic totality of the nation-state, the continuing reproduction of labour power, nature, and capital increasingly *required* restraints in the shape of reforms to protect these elements from the consequences, and to ensure the perpetuation, of the system itself. In the years after World War II, these accords reached their most coherent expression in the industrial nations as the Keynesian welfare state.

Despite the continuing currency of the notion of reformed and democratic capitalism, the Keynesian welfare state has remained only a set of compromises, attenuating and obscuring but not resolving underlying contradictions. It was intended as mitigation for the class struggle, which had intensified during the depression of the 1930s, and as a counter to the postwar power and popularity of socialism, the then-apparent answer to economic crises and capitalist wars. Keynesianism and the associated social reforms, premised on the extensive postwar possibilities for accumulation, were an attempt to offset the cycles of boom and bust, to provide a bridge over the cyclical gap between "excess" productive capacity and aggregate demand. By means of government interventions, it was thought, the extremes of economic slumps could be moderated, while high levels of employment and social security could be touted as government policy. The legitimation of capitalism and its political system, based on a rising standard of living and a degree of security from the vagaries of the labour market, was thereby confirmed in the eyes of the working classes, allowing for a quasi-unity of capital and labour to restructure the war-destroyed capitalist economies, to "liberate" and reconquer the colonies, and to counter socialism as a viable alternative. For these "achievements" of the postwar period, the KWS was necessary.

However important these reforms were to postwar prosperity and economic stability, they were themselves a product of that period of expansion. They rested on a number of historically evolved prerequisites and, together with them, provided the basis for these unprecedented postwar developments. Far from immutable, the conditions underlying the existence and reproduction of the welfare state and the relative prosperity of the industrial nations in the postwar period continued to evolve, and since the 1970s they have been undergoing a transformation.

Pre-eminent amongst these conditions has been the existence of the nation-state, the geographic and political construct of a national bourgeoisie. As capital loses its national distinctiveness, becomes more concentrated and international, and establishes its dominion on a supranational level, the consequences for the nation-state become quite visible. Most of the variables determining national policy are now beyond the control of national governments; and common markets, free-trade areas, political unions, and international treaties, agreements, laws, organizations, and agencies all contribute to the declining *raison d'être* of the nation-state.

As the geopolitical context for reform erodes, so too does the political means for reform. The institutions of liberal democracy evolved as the governing compromise reflecting the national contradictions, at first between capital and capital and, later, between labour and capital in the era of industrialism. The compromises were manifest in reform legislation and became embodied in the institutional allowance for alternating political parties. Since the coming of industrialism, the expansion and persistence of liberal democracy have been predicated on an expanding national economy and a class structure characterized by partially organized, structurally complex subordinate classes and a divided, competitive capitalist class. Political choice, it followed, generally gravitated towards two main parties representative of these classes, yet committed to the principles of the system.

In recent years capitalist classes have become increasingly monolithic or supranational, while the trade union and other social movements have generally weakened and remained distinctly national.[1] In such circumstances, a political system with alternating political parties is not only no longer necessary but also a potential hazard to the interests of new configurations of capital. Indeed, the adoption of neo-liberal policies has patently begun to negate the compromises between labour and capital, and the global economy has made national and local access to state power and the public purse less meaningful. Rule by executive fiat grows, with perfunctory regard for due process, and arbitrary government reflects more than ever the transnational economic pressures and corporate lobbies that grew enormously during the 1980s.

Continuous economic growth in the form of national capital accumulation was another condition of the welfare state and postwar prosperity. The rate of growth in many industrial countries, however, has been falling for several years. Although the industrial world still receives the majority of global investment, increasingly investment also goes to the Third World, for it is there that the rate of growth has been increasing. The reasons for this shift in investment patterns include a relatively high wage structure, the high cost of the KWS, and a degree of working-class political access to state policies and the public purse in the industrial nations. Although these "deterrents" to investment are more or less absent in the Third World, they are also waning in the industrial world, producing commensurate positive effects for investment.

In the industrial nations the vast increases in productivity due mainly to microelectronics and computer-integrated systems have increased the number of long-term or permanently unemployed and underemployed. These same changes in productivity have also transformed the class structure: among other movements, there has been an absolute and relative decline in blue-collar workers, a general shift to the service sector from the primary and secondary sectors, a levelling of work hierarchies, and a relative decline in the need for highly skilled and well-educated workers. These changes have also produced the increasing female participation rate in the workforce, resulted in a decline of full-time work with regular hours and high benefits and a growth of subcontracting, and accelerated the growth in wage and wealth disparities. All of these changes dampen consumer demand and reduce tax revenue while increasing the need for social expenditures and more taxation.

The real power of the working classes and the principal counterforce to the negative social effects of capitalism have been the trade union movement. Although union membership is holding its own in a few countries, in most it is falling due to the introduction of new modes of production and to concerted attacks by government and capital on trade union rights, on the ability of unions to organize and negotiate, and on relative income levels. Moreover, the limited attempts by trade unions to develop strong organizations, regulations, and collective bargaining law on the international level, complementing the development of capital, may well further hasten their declining membership and social importance as they find themselves locked into the political and policy arenas of an increasingly circumscribed nation-state. This weakening of the political role of the trade union movement makes it progressively difficult to defend reforms, let alone advance them.[2]

The very existence of the nation-state and the prerequisites that made the KWS possible, then, are in visible decline. Certainly the possibilities for extending domestic markets as national markets and hence for the continued growth of the surplus that makes up the "social wage" – the economic and fiscal foundation of the welfare state – are limited and without a future. The political and economic premises of the postwar era are at an end.

If the nation-state as the political and territorial embodiment of national capital reached its highest development as the KWS in the post-World War II period, this period also saw the beginning of its transformation to supranational political and geographic units. In other words, the completion of the development of national capital was at the same time the beginning of its transfiguration into global capital.

End of socialism as state capitalism

In the late 1970s China began to open itself to foreign capital investment, and by the early 1990s the states that had formerly made up the U.S.S.R. and all the Eastern European countries had abandoned their state capitalist regimes and embarked on the road to "market economies." The most significant aspect of these "revolutions-in-reverse" was the privatization of a vast amount of socialized capital (albeit as state capital) in the context of an emerging system of global capitalism. It signified the end of a form of capital that was politically controlled and, in name at least, accumulated in the interests of the working people. Now it was to become accessible to private accumulation on the global level.

In the former U.S.S.R. the move to a market economy has combined privatization of state property with consequent forced unemployment and the progressive destruction of the welfare state. In China the same attempt to transform a state capitalist system into one of corporate capitalist private property has been more controlled. The same privatization of state enterprises has taken place, albeit more slowly, but the acceptance of foreign investment and the development and expansion of free-trade zones have been much more restrained.

Perhaps the fundamental difference between these two former "socialist" states is the form of government bringing them into the capitalist world. In Russia the attempt at liberal democracy has increased the instability of a disintegrating economic system. In China the persistence of the Communist Party and its autocratic resistance to the principles and practice of liberal democracy have provided the political security required by foreign investment and made for a more successful and staged transition to capitalism. At the national level, autocracy in the political realm is far from undesirable for global investments.

For global capital, the demise of "actually existing socialism" has meant formidable new potential for accumulation. Massive new possibilities for commodity markets have arisen, and hundreds of millions of workers have been or will be added to the world labour market, a market characterized by low wages and poorly or non-regulated working conditions. Global capital has been given enormous new scope for expansion.

End of the Third World

Throughout the history of capitalism, the non-European world was progressively conquered and subordinated to the national interests of metropolitan capital. After World War II the colonies and dependencies gradually won their independence, although they remained, with some exceptions, subordinate to the interests of the industrial nations. By the early 1970s, with the coming of global capitalism and a transformation of transportation and communications technology and highly automated production processes, this relationship began to change.

It was not that the former colonial world was achieving economic independence from the industrial nations; it was that capital was losing its national allegiances and, aided by technological changes, was able to intensify the subordination of Third World economies to its demands at the international level. It was to be the beginning of the end of the division of the world into East and West, North and South, and developed and underdeveloped. The world division between metropolis and hinterland would remain, but the metropoles would increasingly be stripped of national distinctions.

There were several means by which international capital intensified its exploitation of the Third World after "independence." Among the earliest was the promotion (especially by the United Nations) of free-trade zones. Although these experiments did not produce the promised effects, they did establish beach-heads in the Third World for global capital, bringing more Third World workers into the global labour market and making these countries more a market for global commodities.

The use of the state to promote capital accumulation in the Third World was widely adopted, and this element goes far to explain the "success" of the so-called "Four Tigers" in Southeast Asia. Throughout much of the Third World an unaccountable and repressive state has been employed to build infrastructure, promulgate anti-union laws, enforce limits on wages, grant tax concessions to corporations, and use the police or military to suppress trade unions and certain political parties. This type of state has largely ignored industrial pollution and provided little by way of welfare policies or employment standards for working people.[3] Under these conditions it is difficult to imagine how capital could not "succeed."

Another means of increasing the possibilities for accumulation in the Third World has taken the form of conscious policies to proletarianize or urbanize that part of the population outside the capital relation: peasants, small farmers, farm workers, aboriginal agriculturalists, herders, and hunters and gatherers – all those who constitute semi-autonomous local communities or cultures. Where their subsistence and security have rested on land usage as the means of production in the form of small holdings, communal property, or ill-defined aboriginal title, there have been multifaceted efforts to separate these often large percentages of the population from their means of production, making them dependent on wage-labour for their livelihoods and, at the same time, transforming their property into capitalist private property or subordinating it to corporate use.

Some of these efforts take the form of the weight of the state (as laws, police or military action, physical expropriation, and forced transmigration), and some as the intrusions of corporate agents (miners, lumber workers, road builders). Others appear as the creation of pasturage or plantations, and yet others come as fomented civil wars to depopulate the rural areas (Angola, Mozambique, Rwanda). Still others come as the promise of high technology (the "green revolution" and World Bank projects). All have the effect of appropriating and depopulating land held in precapitalist forms of property, of decimating local communities, and of depriving millions of people of their means of production and obliging them to find work as wage-labourers, to become the cheap labour foundation for new investments, for global capital accumulation.

While the creation of this enormous labour pool has contributed to a high rate of return on investment in parts of the Third World, this is not to say that working people have benefited. During the 1980s, income disparities increased, external debt rose, and the rates of poverty, illiteracy, morbidity, and mortality grew throughout most of the non-industrial world. These trends were by and large the consequences of "development," not the result of a lack of it.[4]

But it is to say that this proletarianization represents the impending culmination of the more or less violent process whereby the world's population is separated from the means of production in the land and made dependent on wage-labour. At the same time, it is the imminent global completion of "primitive accumulation," the process by which landed property previously outside the capital relation is made part of it, able now to be employed as capital for turning a profit. In short, it is the penultimate stage in the triumph of global capitalism, in which the population of the world is forced into a global labour market and all means of production becomes capitalist private property.

The global labour market

The structure of the labour market has always been determined by the structure of capital. It cannot be otherwise because the labour market is a corollary of capitalism. Given the structure of capital until the early 1970s, as nationally particular and culturally and linguistically relatively homogeneous, the structure of the labour market in the industrial nations was similarly patterned. With the coming of global capital, that is, with the progressive removal of national, cultural, and linguistic barriers to, and the global homogenization of, production, distribution, and exchange, the labour market no longer bore a structural correspondence to the configuration of capital. While capital moved relatively freely around the world, labour remained national, culturally and linguistically specific, and defined by and preoccupied with national laws and history.

Even so, there are global dimensions to the world's labour markets that belie their appearance. Although formally restricted by national and linguistic particularities, they comprise a multifaceted global labour market forged in the interests of international capital. Probably the most visible of these global dimensions are the free-trade zones, which have now been opened up in the majority of the world's nations. With national variations, the restrictions here to the exploitation of labour (employment and health and safety standards, union representation) and to the degradation of nature (environmental laws) are minimized or eliminated, and the state provides concessions and infrastructure for corporate investment and enforcement of labour subordination. While the workers themselves and their activities come under national, albeit minimal, regulation, the value and the product of their labour are integrated into a global system. Inasmuch as commodities are produced for a global market, they internationalize the embodied labour value.

Another and similar component of the international dimension is the "centres" of cheap labour, where corporations can assemble or manufacture goods destined for global markets. Small, relatively impoverished nations with authoritarian political regimes usually serve as these centres. Haiti and the Dominican Republic are good examples, as are Puerto Rico and Hong Kong.

International migration from less developed countries to the more developed is yet another dimension. This movement, involving many millions of people, produces a sort of "underclass," which typically has little or no protection under the host nation's regulations and remains more or less outside the available benefits of the welfare state, if such exists. These people constitute an enormous mass of working poor, semi-excluded by national barriers and therefore part of an ill-defined but de facto global working class.

The current unprecedented process of proletarianization now under way in the Third World is producing enormous reserve armies of workers available to global corporations. For the most part these workers constitute a potential labour force, without much by way of state or union protection, destitute, and often objects of foreign aid until "productive" use can be made of them. This vast body of potential labour acts in much the same way as does the redundant working population in the industrial nations – that is, in general, to advance the possibilities of accumulation, to depress wages, to undermine social policies, to increase the power of capital, to increase competition amongst workers, and to enfeeble the role of trade unions.

An essential part of the definition of a labour market is the nature of the skills and knowledge required by the mode of production. Fordism and, after World War II, advanced Fordism demanded a highly skilled and well-trained and educated labour force. The world division of labour between industrial and non-industrial nations was founded on the location and reproduction of these skills and knowledge in the industrial world. By the 1970s, however, global capital and the mode of production characterized by microelectronics and computer applications could have the same work done by any labour force around the world that had the requisite levels of education and training. The work could be located anywhere given the communications and transportation technology that arose within that mode of production.

The immediate consequences of this implicit global labour market are very significant for increasing the prospects for the accumulation of capital, but decidedly not positive for labour. In general they give enormous advantages to the corporate sector over the rights and remuneration for labour. The state is employed in the legal suppression of trade union rights and activities, and extralegal attacks escalate around the world. Both the state and the corporate sector actively work to inhibit the promulgation of international legal frameworks for union co-operation. The progressive internationalization of the market creates pressure for "world wages" and a gradual levelling of employment standards and work conditions. Global competition between workers grows with no political mechanism for offsetting even the more extreme effects, such as the superexploitation of women and the growth of child labour and other forms of coerced labour (bonded, slave, prison, and military).

Is capitalism sustainable?[5]

The drive for continuous economic growth has always carried an implicit assumption, namely, the ability of nature to absorb the costs of this growth, to withstand its flagrant misappropriation and irresponsible desecration. The ecological limits of industrial growth are everywhere now evident. Environmental degradation of the planet is proceeding at a pace that is not abating despite recent international accords and promises. And the effects, such as global warming, falling crop yields, desertification, deforestation, soil erosion, declining or exhausted fisheries, ozone depletion, air and water pollution, and species extinction, all have an impact on the possibility for continued economic growth.

It has been argued that "pollution and the irreparable loss of resources . . . provide the most obvious and notorious objection to the doctrine that the free play of market forces in a regime of laissez-faire leads to beneficial results for society as a whole."[6] For example, in Europe the cost of treating water to make it potable is now about 30 to 40 per cent of the cost of water, and this percentage will grow as the pollution of the last thirty years increasingly takes effect.[7] Environmental problems will also take their toll on human health, measured in rates of morbidity and mortality and the return of many diseases once nearly eradicated. It is widely agreed that nature is approaching its limit of tolerance.[8]

This impending limit has given rise to attempts, however qualified, to clean up past pollution.[9] It has also caused a growing, albeit narrow, corporate consciousness about the real costs of economic development, that is, of the destruction that takes place in production and the despoliation in waste disposal, of the unaccounted costs of pollution from industrial processes.[10] Even "green" investment funds and "green" products have appeared. A consumer-consciousness has developed as well, although it has been largely restricted to the arenas of recycling and conscientious purchasing. Environmental protest movements have also been a consequence of these approaching limits; while Greenpeace may be among the best-known organizations operating in this sphere, there are many others, as well as green parties in most countries of the industrial world. Numerous aboriginal communities have also been galvanized into action because of the environmental destruction of their land.[11]

Despite this growing consciousness, protest, and resistance, the trends of planetary pollution worsen, and this continued degeneration brings the question of the sustainability of capitalism to the fore. The underlying issue is easily definable: unreformed capitalism destroys the bases of its own existence, namely, the reproduction of nature and labour power. The system has no inherent means of preventing this destruction, and in the past reforms have had to be imposed to save capitalism from its destruction of nature and labour power.

Global capitalism, however, spells the end of many national restrictions to its activity. The reforms brought by trade unions, other social movements, and by capital itself through state policies to protect the environment and to uphold health, safety, and employment standards are eroded or eliminated as national jurisdictions succumb to the demands of international organizations, commissions, agencies, and capital. A review of the Final Act of the Uruguay Round of GATT concluded, "There has never been a concerted effort to conform [sic] the rules and institutions governing international trade to contemporary understanding of threats to natural resources, human health and environmental quality."[12] Indeed, the Final Act might well necessitate the erosion of many environmental laws in the industrial nations as barriers to trade. And there is little or no recourse to other authorities; the present impasse between the advocates of free trade and environmental interests rests in part on the non-existence of an international organization to define and enforce environmental standards and principles for international commerce.[13]

Escaping national jurisdictions, transnational corporations are able to create a world answering to their needs more than ever before. Under these circumstances, there arises the question of the compatibility of unreformed capitalism on the global level with sustainable development. If the latter is defined as the permanent ability of nature and human beings to be reproduced, there is little evidence to suggest that any credence can be given to a positive response. This leads to the question of the sustainability of self-reformed global capitalism. It is difficult to imagine corporations still competitive within their own spheres and between spheres being able and willing to impose upon themselves restrictions that would have an impact on their rates of profit. If these possibilities are improbable, there remains the alternative of politically reformed global capital; but this presumes an authoritative organization with powers to legislate and enforce. At the moment, it does not exist.

145

All of these questions are framed by another: namely, the question of the reversibility of the present level of destruction.

The Global System

All the conditions, then, that made social and economic reforms possible, that allowed for the reproduction of a relatively prosperous working class and its political expression as social democracy in the industrial nations and permitted postwar global dominance by certain national capitals, are in the process of transformation. Internationalized capital can now circumvent the "grand compromise," and indeed it has begun systematically to undermine and transform the "regulated capitalism" and liberal democracy that characterized the KWS. If, however, the KWS was central to the perpetuation of capitalism after World War II, its dismantling and transference to the private sector cast a certain fateful irony on the "triumph of capitalism." For in this victory over all the past achievements of the working classes, won through rebellion, reform, and revolution, capitalism also accelerates the coming limits to its own development.

The introduction of neo-liberal policies around the world is the consequence of this triumph. The policies are intended to surmount the impingements to economic growth presented by national social and economic reforms and political access to the state. They are designed to minimize the effects of an organized working class, a "democratic" national state, and a large public sector, and to allow capital to prevail across national boundaries with minimal restraint. Without these or other reforms and restrictions, the production, exchange, and distribution of goods and services will take place in the form of unmitigated marketplace relations.

Given that all products appear as private property in capitalist society and follow the movement of "competitive" markets, they are necessarily unequally distributed and accumulated by some at the expense of others. Labour power, the products of labour, and nature itself become solely objects of commerce whose purpose in such a system is to provide the means for unequal accumulation of wealth in private hands. In short, the inherent dynamic of *economic* development[14] leads to increasing relative poverty between classes and "nations" and the destruction of nature, on the one side, and ever greater concentration of wealth in the hands of a few on the other.[15]

Unmoderated market principles are incompatible with democratic political institutions and income redistribution motivated by political demands or social ethics, and this incompatibility holds a contradiction in that one side can prevail only at the expense of the other. In the attempt to restructure the relation between economic demands and social welfare and environmental sustainability, capital undermines the conditions of reproduction of the working population and the propagation of nature, which are the two most significant conditions for its own reproduction. International capital has no choice in the introduction of neoliberal policies because they represent its drive to fulfil the logic of its own nature faced with the need to expand and with declining opportunities for accumulation, but their adoption accelerates the consequences of an unfettered reign.

On the one hand, then, capital expands by usurping the role of the state in production and distribution, by undermining and eliminating standards and regulations, and by intensifying competition leading to widespread mergers and takeovers. On the other hand, the working classes experience greater structural and long-term unemployment, lower standards of living, increasing rates of poverty, restricted social security, and weakened trade unions; and the ecosystem becomes pervasively degraded. To some extent increased productivity and cheapened goods and services ameliorate the impoverishment and declining levels of consumption, but ultimately the deterioration of nature and the growing difficulties of working-class reproduction hasten the coming limits to the continued expansion of capital.[16]

If further economic activity ignores these accumulating "costs" to nature and the working classes, and if corporate self-regulation replaces political regulation, there will be continued destruction beyond which nature may not be able to recover, and many strata of the working classes around the world will be progressively reduced to a state of abject poverty.[17] If industrial development were to take these "costs" into account, it is doubtful that there could continue to be growth in the present sense, that is, as accumulation in the hands of a few and relative deprivation for the many. There would have to be a reorganization of production so that it would no longer be economic or market-driven development but rather human development that would be sustainable and therefore qualitatively different.

147

Political Dilemmas

For social-democratic parties, the dilemma in these closing limits is fundamental. If a certain greater interest in social legislation is what has distinguished them from conservative parties, it would appear that the basis of this distinction is disappearing. With few exceptions, since the mid-1970s wherever social-democratic parties have been elected considerable disillusionment and cynicism over broken promises, changed priorities, and an apparent inability to act have quickly set in amongst their members and supporters. The causes of this growing disaffection, as we have seen, lie outside the immediate concerns of party policies and government ministers.

Previously, in times of expansion reforms to capitalism could be financed out of new value in the form of wages sufficiently high to allow for their partial redistribution. In times of recession, reforms were funded out of public debt and higher taxes, or there was retrenchment, or both. Governments also made efforts to stimulate economic growth to provide anew the economic basis of the welfare state. None of these means for perpetuating or expanding the welfare state have, any longer, a long-term future.

Keynesian economic stimulation, for instance, no longer works because the economy has become global, which means that national or local demand can be met by international supply and that the political tools of the national state are being usurped. More economic growth, moreover, can only increase environmental destruction and intensify inequalities in wealth.[18] More state debt is no longer a plausible route, because it is by no means certain that states can increase future tax revenues to service larger debts, and creditors cannot be unaware of this. Transnational corporations, the international markets, and supranational structures are increasingly taking over state planning and administration of the economy. The entire economic and political foundation on which social-democratic parties were able to promote capitalism as reformed is eroding, forcing them to accept what global capital requires, the neo-liberal agenda. As long as capitalism is accepted as the mode of production, there are few possibilities of going against the tide. In fact, there is no significant resistance on the part of any social-democratic party or government in any industrial nation to this agenda.[19]

The social-democratic left has become, in effect, part of the problem. It remained wedded to a notion of reformed capitalism until the 1980s and since then has produced little analysis of or alternatives to neo-

liberalism. Where it has come to power, it has sooner or later introduced new right policies in the face of an electorate desirous of protecting the social security of the welfare state. Yet it has remained the main
political alternative for the working class in most industrial countries.

By accepting this agenda in theory and practice, social democracy has
lost much of its credibility as a party representing the working population, and hypocrisy has become its hallmark. Since social democracy can
no longer promote or expand social reforms but must introduce neo-
liberal reforms, by whatever name, working people in effect lose what
limited representation they had in liberal democracies. The role and significance of social democracy, then, become increasingly only ideological, that is, to maintain, first, the appearance of alternate political
choice, and second, the sense that politics at the nation-state level is
meaningful, that the national state can determine policy in an age of
internationalized capital.

Social democracy as we have known it has no future, because the conditions that gave rise to it are being transformed and because its policies
and programs – the reforms of the nation-state era – were nothing more
than what these conditions allowed or even demanded.

The more radical left parties, long undermined by the viability of social-democratic parties, by sectarianism, and often by the lack of a class
base, were profoundly weakened and discredited by the introduction of
capitalist reforms in the People's Republic of China and then by the collapse of the U.S.S.R. and the so-called socialist states of Eastern Europe.
As for the theorists and intelligentsia on the left, some have become lost
in the morass of postmodernist relativism, some have found hope in the
prospect of a revitalized liberal-democratic politics, some see a future in
linking socialism to markets, and yet others, while acknowledging the
reality of the global economy, still see the path of change in the form of
progressive national Keynesian economic reforms.[20] Very few, moreover, have grasped the singular importance to the future of the planet,
and to the future struggle against capital, of the environmental question
as a global demand for common rights, for the common heritage of
humankind, in opposition to the continuing extension of capitalist private property.[21] Throughout the world an enormous theoretical and institutional vacuum has appeared on the left of the political spectrum.

The green parties and movements, furthermore, have not had the
success that they should have had, given the state of the environment.
There are several general reasons for this failure. One is the difficulty of

seeing the interconnectedness of all things in a society in which disconnectedness is the norm. Another is the problem of jobs versus environmental protection when employment rests on industries predicated on not taking into account the costs to nature and society. In addition there are the problems of poor organizational structures, conflicting agendas, and an unrealistic appreciation of capitalism. The green consciousness embedded in these organizations, moreover, has often not moved beyond the level of reformism.[22] Since the structure of capitalist society presents no social forces whose immediate interests rest in sustainable and non-polluting production, the greens have been unable to extract fundamental reform or change from the powers that be.

The conundrums of the left are not shared by the right. The loss of genuine political alternatives, decline of political legitimacy, weakening of trade union movements, the dismantling of the welfare state, and rapid increase in long-term unemployment have all contributed to the recent growth of right-wing movements.[23] This right-wing will most likely retain and even strengthen the political initiative it now appears to have as long as the conditions for its growth are there and the forces providing resistance and alternatives lack an analysis of the present situation and a general program to guide and unify activity.

Given these trends, the neo-liberal agenda is the only agenda on the political table anywhere. No other set of policies or programs appears as plausible. Socialism and communism as ideas for the future are now associated with corrupted state-capitalist regimes whose record on social welfare, workers' rights, political accessibility, civil liberties, and pollution compares badly to the liberal-democratic, capitalist regimes of the West. We have arrived at the end of the period of independent national politics, and the neo-liberal agenda is so far the only agenda taking us into the era of the global economy.

Many aspects of the current political dilemma can be found in the movements against free trade that developed in response to the North America Free Trade Agreement (NAFTA) in Canada, Mexico, and the United States. While the agreement was a product of North American/ international capital requiring a larger production base and home market, the resistance was founded on the negative implications for labour, namely, the loss of jobs and the decline of wages, social security, and employment, health, and environmental standards. Unless the resistance were advocating a socialist alternative, which it was not and which in any event does not appear plausible at the moment, it was an implicit argument for the status quo ante – the KWS of the postwar era. But this was a status quo from a past era in which a national capitalist class required a nation-state and a national compromise with "its" working classes. The structure of capital is today quite different, and a struggle against free trade with no perspective or alternative other than the maintenance of the status quo could hardly hope for success. To fight against free trade on a national basis is not to understand the era we have now entered.

(Opposition to NAFTA should have accepted the reality of transnational capital and fought to have certain guarantees for labour and mechanisms for representation added to the agreement. With these in place, organized labour would have had a basis from which to confront capital now mobile across North America. As it stands, there is no North American-wide provisions for trade union organizing, labour mobility, collective bargaining, health and safety standards, workers' rights, or environmental protection. There is, moreover, virtually no access to decision-making powers at the treaty level. All of this compares unfavourably with the European Community, even though the EC does not facilitate the activities or advance the rights of organized labour.)

Many of the traditional social and political means of resistance to the depredations of capital are failing because the conditions for their existence are disappearing. The fundamental dilemma now concerns the nature of political action in the nation-state, which is losing its sovereignty, and in the global arena, which does not yet have a political authority. The problem is how to construct new means to confront international capital in a new age.

The Possibilities

The forces of international capitalism are not the only forces now at work. Experiments in both alternative ways of doing things and new forms of resistance to capitalist expansion have begun to develop around the world. In the industrial countries the resistance appears in a number of forms, some as yet often poorly organized and with consciousness limited to particular issues, but the counter-efforts are unmistakably there. The most prominent are actions of the trade unions, the environmental organizations, the women's movement, and Aboriginal alliances. To these can be added consumer protection groups, old age advocacy coalitions, unions of the unemployed, cultural forms of protest, civil liberty associations, and anti-nuclear groups.[24] Many of these also exist in Latin America and elsewhere in the Third World, where other organi-

151

zations inspired by liberation theology and the need for self-defence have existed for some time, and where there has also been an increase in politically informed, organized armed resistance to repressive regimes.[25]

Some of these forms of resistance, particularly the environmental, aboriginal, women's, and liberation theology movements, gained sufficient strength to merit counter-resistance by capital, government and church.[26] Organized insurrection, moreover, such as in the state of Chiapas in Mexico, has encountered intense military repression. To these examples must be added the organized reaction to other forms of resistance, including the financing of counterorganizations, contrary advertising, right-wing parties or movements, attacks on free expression and the liberal arts in the universities, and coercive state repression, among other direct or covert actions. With the exception of the insurrectionary movements, these relatively new movements have yet to suffer the same persecution that has been increasingly experienced by trade unions and their leaders. If the degree of persecution is a measure of the significance of the resistance, trade unionism remains by far the most important of all the present social movements. This is probably because it represents the most significant contradiction to the principle of capitalist private property.

The alternative developments are expanding largely but not exclusively to occupy the gaps left by the declining ability of capitalism to provide employment, maintain the welfare state, or provide answers to environmental degradation. Self-help groups, community economic development programs, co-operatives or worker-owned companies, and recycling projects are examples. Insofar as these alternatives have a co-operative element and a degree of social and political counter-consciousness, they form another aspect of resistance.[27]

Both the resistance and the alternatives face enormous odds as long as, first, the current system continues to provide a tolerable material existence for the majority and, second, control over the ideological and political systems remains a monopoly of the powers that be. These movements also face other barriers, such as the persisting legitimacy of the system and national identity, the ideological power of the mass media, the bureaucratism of the trade unions, the paucity of financial resources, the corporate and state counterattacks, the sense of disillusionment and cynicism, the spread of pornography, the fear of unemployment and fear for personal safety, and the absence of a coherent analysis of the current transformation. Without a countercritical analysis or means of promoting it, the ideology of the status quo possesses a firm hold over the working population, leaving the forms of resistance uncoordinated and the alternatives often as so many ways to weather a slump or to provide a means of getting by.

Despite these odds, the will to resist expands, though often hidden or latent. In countries throughout the world, the introduction of neo-liberal policies has precipitated demonstrations, strikes, and even general strikes. The consequent increases in the disparities of wealth, in unemployment, homelessness, and poverty, have engendered a new political awakening and at the same time a decline in moral and political authority. In general, it has been more the poverty of opposition leadership than the will of the people that has prevented this resistance from developing.

Resistance and alternatives will, nevertheless, continue to spread as the ability of capitalism to provide for the material, let alone human, needs of the populace declines, as destruction of the environment becomes more obvious, as political legitimacy fades, and as the potential for economic crisis increases.

The Coming Tyranny

Neo-liberal policies mark the transition between two eras, from a world of national capitals and nation-states to a world of internationalized capital and supranational organizations, commissions, and agencies. They represent the coming transformation of long-established social and political institutions in the industrial nation-states. They embody a shift *from* the expansion of social reforms, rising national wealth, and limited political alternatives *to* the dismantling of reforms, the supersession of national economies, and political reaction. While they consolidate the triumph of capitalism over the world and increase the possibilities for expanded accumulation, they also accelerate its consequences.[28] Capitalism must increasingly confront the world it has made, the results of its own expansion: seriously degraded nature, an increasingly impoverished working class, growing political autocracy and declining legitimacy, and new forms of resistance.

As trading blocs develop without responsible political mechanisms, as capital accumulation takes place in the international arena more or less free of national constraints, as access to national political and legal systems declines and undemocratic decision-making processes at the international level come to dominate and the possibility of levering reforms from national governments weakens, we will be increasingly confronted by the tyranny of corporate decisions minimally qualified by political considerations. We will also have little or no recourse to the elements of political or distributive justice. The relatively unrestrained paramountcy of decisions made in the corporate boardroom will have pervasive and formidable effects. These consequences, albeit in another context, were noted by Friedrich Hayek many years ago:

> Economic control is not merely control of a sector of human life that can be separated from the rest; it is the control of the means for all our ends. And whoever has sole control of the means must also determine which ends are to be served, which values are to be rated higher and which lower, in short, what [we] should believe and strive for.

> Any international economic authority, not subject to a superior political power, even if strictly confined to a particular field, could easily exercise the most tyrannical and irresponsible power imaginable.[29]

In these striking terms, Hayek excoriated the practice of central planning over the economy at the national and international levels. With the globalization of capital, the demise of state capitalism, and the growing realization of neo-liberal policies, the object of his dread has more or less passed into history. But the irony is that his argument is now fully suited to another "authority directing all economic activity," that is, to an ever decreasing number of cartels, oligopolies, and transnational conglomerates in a global economy.

This is not a market, Hayek's counter to the "planned" economy, in any genuine sense, for one can speak of a market only when there are numerous competing corporations for any given product, and no corporation with a dominant share of the economic activity. Only under these circumstances does the theoretical market operate independently of the competing firms and, it is claimed, in the interests of all. There is no longer any economic sector that fits this description; there is only more or less monopoly power, constrained by varying degrees of conglomerate, sectorial, or vestigial national competition.

Here, largely unfettered by political considerations, is a tyranny unfolding – an economic regime of unaccountable rulers, a totalitarianism not of the political sphere but of the economic.

VII

Globalization as the Second Bourgeois Revolution

If the foundation of the modern nation-state was the territorial assertion of the will of capital at a certain stage, then, it follows that as capital changes in nature, so too, sooner or later, must the character of the nation-state, its property relations, and the state policies that reflect these relations. And just as the character of the nation-state has changed historically within the same shell, when its foundation in the circuits of capital moves to the global level, the very rationale of the nation-state becomes attenuated. When the accumulation process is no longer predominantly national, the historical role of the national framework for capital becomes not only largely redundant but also an impediment to the growing global framework.

After World War II, as we have argued, all the elements for a global regime of accumulation were gradually established, and particularly since the early 1970s the means of production and their corporate ownership have outgrown the institutions of the nation-state. The economic rationale of the nation – capital at a certain stage in its development – has been transformed by radical technological changes. A national framework no longer corresponds to the present stage of development of the broad forces of production, and for that reason the nation-state has experienced an ongoing restructuring.

If the "first" bourgeois revolutions represented the creation of the nation-state, the political consolidation of capitalism, this "second" bourgeois revolution represents the transformation or globalization of national regimes of accumulation.[1] It entails a shift from a mitigated framework for capital (liberal democracy, the KWS) into a more or less unmitigated framework (supranational agencies for capital alone).

The Restructuring of Economic Units

Just as capital had to create the nation-state to further its development, to come into its own, to assert its pre-eminence over other modes of production, now it must construct and oversee larger economic units for the same reasons. Ironically, it is the national political structure that is employed to do this, while the creation of new supranational administrative frameworks gradually usurps much of the role of the national state.

The creation of a coherent domestic market within a certain territory was the substance of so-called nation-building. The task amounted to the abolition of "internal" tariffs, tolls, custom duties, and the destruction of precapitalist property relations, among other barriers to a "regional" free-trade system. It also required the establishment of a single legal jurisdiction, a corresponding political system, and a common national identity. In the early stages, nation-building could follow two paths, the political and the economic. One of the first tasks of the French Revolution, for instance, was to forge an internal national market out of the numerous regional and jurisdictional divisions that characterized France and thwarted its economic development. The German Zollverein of 1834, by contrast, was a customs union initially uniting some eighteen states, principalities, cities, and other jurisdictions, and it preceded political union. Similar customs unions antedate the rise of the modern nation-state throughout much of Europe.[2] In each case the new economic unit provided the foundation for the further development of capitalist relations and the suppression of precapitalist forms of property.

The current restructuring of economic units is a product of World War II. Postwar reconstruction and continuing capital growth could not be contained by its national form; the two world wars were testimony to the contradiction between this growth and its national administrative framework. In 1945 the economic ruin or exhaustion of Europe alongside U.S. economic pre-eminence made self-evident the need to create new economic units appropriate to the power of the Fordist mode of production. These frameworks were constructed on two related levels, the regional and the international. Despite the creation of new nation-states and the persistence of existing ones after the war, almost all countries entered into some sort of regional common market or multilateral trading bloc. At the same time, a global framework for free trade was being constructed under the auspices of the United States. The objective was an integrated world system free of trade barriers, a system for capital in its corporate form, not an inter-national system. While periodically at loggerheads in the struggle for certain advantages, these two levels, global and regional, were in principle compatible; both were advances towards larger coherent and uniform markets.

The "State" and "Civil Society" at the Global Level

The birth of the modern nation-state is at the same time the debut of the first completely political system. The political is defined as the resolution of a social formation into two distinct realms: civil society and the state. On the one side, civil society becomes the realm of "private" affairs, the world of personal, familial, religious, and work-related and corporate interests. On the other side, the state becomes the sphere of "general" affairs, the arena of government in which the prevailing property relations are defined, made into law, and enforced. In principle, at least, the political system that marks the capitalist nation-state allows for leverage over state policy through the exercise of political right by a citizenry. The postwar KWS may be seen in part as a product of this political right.

With globalization, this divide between civil society and the state is re-created at the global level, but the "content" of each side is transformed. The "state" becomes a relatively coherent multiplicity of supranational agencies and organizations, dominated by the U.S. state, that oversee the broad reaches of the global economy in the interests of corporate private property, of the TNCs. Global civil society includes not only TNCs and INGOs (such as Greenpeace or Amnesty International), but also, and importantly, national states.

This shift in the global makeup of civil society has several implications. First, representation and access to the superstructure and policy-making at the global level are mainly by means of the national state or TNC; together, they have become in a sense the "citizenry" of the globe. In other words, the national or regional representatives of capital now comprise one of the two main constituents of the global divide between state and civil society. Second, representation by the national state in the most important global agencies is not by equal right but accorded by economic importance. In other words, representation is weighted: the privileges of wealth have returned to have a direct voice in policy-making. Third, as part of global civil society, national states can be disciplined in a variety of ways by the supranational organizations if they counter or step outside the boundaries of global corporate relations. Fourth, the actual link between global civil society and the supranational structures is mainly via a process of appointment, political or bureaucratic, and is composed of national government representatives, corporate nominees, or global bureaucrats. Fifth, the real citizens of the world and their representative organizations are left voiceless in the global superstructures. Their political right, such as it may be, remains defined as national and does not extend to the global. And so while capital becomes self-supporting at the global level and creates a system of global governance, the world's working and other subordinate classes and peoples have no access to this "government" and no legitimate basis for leverage. Finally, in this global divide lies one of the reasons for the rapidly growing disparities in wealth: capital accumulation takes place at the global level within global policies, while the working classes remain defined as national with political rights and influences that extend no further. The ability to force wage increases, to demand social redistribution of wage income, or to increase taxes on profits, once possible at the national level, is now complicated by the global operations of the TNC and a growing transnational regulatory regime.

The Decline of Liberal Democracy

The origin of modern democracy lies in the demand by representatives of different amounts and kinds of capital for voice and vote in the general affairs, in "public" policies, for the fullest extension of legislative powers, for constitutional guarantees of citizen's rights, and for an independent judiciary. Its development represents stages of accommodation of contradictory interests in civil society pressing for representation as the "general." With the rise to pre-eminence of capitalism and the concomitant growth of the modern state, political right (the right to vote and be elected) was extended to possessors of moveable capital and, later, to those whose only capital lay embodied in labour-power. Those outside these mainstream property relations (usually women, children, aboriginal peoples, racial or ethnic minorities, marginal peoples) were generally not granted political rights – at least not until much later.

Liberal democracy reaches its apogee in the post-World War II period with the nearly complete resolution of the national economy into two classes representing labour and capital. The lessons of the war were embodied in part in the UN Universal Declaration of Human Rights; the 1930s failure of capitalism and fear of socialism were addressed in the "social citizenship" of the Keynesian welfare state; and political right was ultimately extended to all adults regardless of status in property relations. Historically, this period represents the first universal enunciation of the sanctity of the individual ensconced in a set of principles regardless of ethnicity, colour, religion, gender, or origin, among other factors. Given the need to legitimize capitalism in its national form and provide the conditions for its reconstruction after the war – in particular to reconcile an organized working class – the principles of social citizenship and individual rights were partially realized, albeit reluctantly, by means of state intervention in the economy.

In the transition to a global economy, however, the TNCs need not accommodate the pressures and leverage springing from nationally delimited labour markets and organized subordinate classes. The supranational agencies created to oversee globalization are not fashioned to be accessible by countervailing interests, rather, only to reflect the interests of capital. The rise of a policy framework that gives global economic considerations pre-eminence over national politics has led to a corresponding decline of the political powers of the national state.

As national political systems become increasingly circumscribed in their possible interventions, it follows that the liberal-democratic system of alternating parties representing more or less mitigating influences on capital becomes decreasingly significant. In the non-industrial world the promotion of "democracy" becomes more than ever an instrumental use of politics to legitimize globalization, to give an illusion of political choice while the economic dictates, and to employ the element of social control implicit in the formalities of liberal democracy.[3] When the possibility arises that such democracy may benefit the people or advance national interests, it is quickly and unmistakably undermined or overthrown. Military or police interventions into politics characterize the entire non-industrial world wherever legitimate political decisions have promised to make a significant difference for the non-owners of the means of production, challenged the rights of corporate ownership, or promoted national solutions to economic problems.

By limiting the influence of politics over the economic, the process of globalization now presses national governments everywhere in the direction of the minimal state, a government structured mainly to frame economic relations and defend the rule of law. In this shift, the very meaning of citizenship begins to be redefined. Although the definition of citizenship has always been an arena contested between classes,[4] it is formalized by the state as enforceable rights and obligations of the citizen and state. The rights of the citizen – namely, individual property rights, political rights, and social security – are at the same time the obligations of the state vis-à-vis the citizen. And the obligations of the citizen – mainly to pay taxes or perform military duties – are the rights of the state vis-à-vis the citizen. Globalization undermines the obligation to serve in the military for national goals; it progressively dismantles or shifts to a supranational level the system of social security; and it enforces corporate property rights over the rights of the citizen or state. With all of these issues, the European Union provides a good example in blurring the meaning of citizenship by making the union's own institutions the final guarantor of citizens' rights, by creating a European parliament, and by giving military priority to NATO.

At the founding of the nation-state, citizenship was conditional on property qualifications, and only later did it evolve in the direction of universal political right and social citizenship, principles eschewing property considerations. As globalization challenges this notion of citizenship, property models of citizenship are gradually being re-established; the link to society can be defined not by political right but by "stake," that is, according to amount and kind of capital possessed.[5] Citizenship as "stakeholder" implies a reintroduction of economic elements into the political arena. In practice it means that those who have a material interest or investment in some activity or object also have privilege in determining policy pertinent to it. The principles of equality and universality that characterize political right and social citizenship are subordinated to the principle of citizenship as a property right, to models implying that some can have a greater or lesser "stake" or say in "general affairs" according to the nature of their capital.[6]

In effect, globalization brings into the open the contradiction between the principles and practice of the so-called market and of liberal democracy. Despite their co-existence in practice, these two modes of resource allocation in society – the economic and the political – are in principle contradictory. The economic pre-eminence that comes with globalization overshadows the political allocation of social "goods" and neutralizes the political expression of a citizenry.

Securing the Economic Unit

In the making of the nation-state, once an integral market over a certain territory had been defined by a customs union or political revolution, it became an economic necessity, a "national" interest for capital, to se-

cure these borders, and indeed to expand them to include other territory, especially if it was still defined by precapitalist relations. The first
bourgeois revolutions required the creation of standing armies based on
universal national service or conscription. Their ideological rationale,
military "duty," lay in some form of nationalism, resting on the ideals of
private property in the American and French revolutions or the asserted
"national" superiority or corporatism of British and German capital.
Such military mobilization put an end to precapitalist troop levies based
on the corvée, the press gang, or mercenaries. The consolidation of the
nation-state as a market society in the eighteenth and nineteenth centuries also gave rise to the modern police.

In the current "second" transformation, the issue has become one of
establishing and securing the global market. An integrated supranational market implies uniform and universally held economic principles, a harmonization of the rule of national and international law or
national subordination to global trade and financial agencies, *and* the
absence of socialism, nationalism, and certain forms of favouritism. One
way of achieving and maintaining these conditions for a global market is
paradoxically the affirmation or imposition of some form of liberal democracy at the national level. This governing mechanism not only lets
citizens "do it to themselves" but also incorporates structural limits to
politically motivated restrictions on the market.[7] But the instrumental
use of liberal democracy is hardly sufficient to secure the global market
when forms of nationalism and socialism resist such harmonization or
are even adopted by means of liberal democracy.

The move from national to international police and military forces
began early in the postwar era. Dominated by the United States, the
operations of NATO, UN peacekeeping, and multilateral forces have all
been employed for the defence and expansion of capitalist markets. The
United States, moreover, has not been adverse to acting unilaterally, as
it has done particularly in Central and Latin America; its actions, however, should be understood not simply as securing markets and resources
for U.S.-based TNCs but also as safeguarding the interests of capital in
general. With the coming of a transnational system, these activities have
been described as "police actions," often justified on the basis of alleged
transgressions of international law, and so obviating the need for declarations of war.

The more that armed forces are required to secure the general interests of capital globally, the greater the shift from conscripted armed

forces to professional or volunteer forces.[8] Conscripts may be employed in the defence of the nation or to advance national interests, but professionals or volunteers are needed for tasks without a distinct national interest, that is, for "jobs to be done" with no higher motive than to obtain the conditions for capital accumulation for specific corporations or global capital in general. Indeed, modern mercenary forces have been proposed to do jobs that national armies are no longer suited for.[9] Whereas national armed forces once acted in the interests of national capital, multinational "professional" forces (and mercenary companies) provide the soldiers for capital *sans* nationality.

Securing the nation-state also meant laying down the foundation for economic activity. As the first customs unions and nation-states came into existence, the delimited territory had to be made open and accessible as a market. For this reason, improvements in transport and communications systems became an issue of signal importance. The construction of roads and canals and later railways and the telegraph became synonymous with "nation-building"; it was but the building of the infrastructure for a territorially defined regime of accumulation. In a similar manner, the infrastructure for a veritable global system came with the technological revolution of the early 1970s. Shipping, trucking, railroads, and airplanes, along with harbours, roads, and airports, all saw substantial improvements in speed and volumes of freight handled in that decade. Communications were utterly transformed with the new linkages between satellites, computers, and telephones. If the earlier improvements consolidated the nation-state, the changes after 1970, although often promoted by national states, made the global economy possible, indeed necessary, while making the nation-state redundant as a delimited market.

Much of this initial construction of infrastructure, or nation-building, was financed through state mechanisms.[10] The state's taxation powers underlay the borrowing of vast sums in the form of the "public" debt, constituting a massive initial and continuing accumulation of capital for use by the corporations whose *raison d'être* the state was. The ongoing national debt was employed in the pursuit of national policies and markets that created obvious advantages for national corporations. As long as the productive power of the corporation could be realized within the nation-state and its external reach, this modus vivendi of the national state was the necessary complement to a certain stage in the development of capitalism. But once the corporation became transnational the national debt began to detract from competitive advantages on the global level. It created an "uneven playing field," to use the spurious language of the free marketeers, in that it allowed for national policies in contradistinction to global ones. Here lies one reason for recent pressure on government to reduce or eliminate the national debt, or at least the current account deficit, if for no other reason than it embodies the nation and demands a percentage of tax revenue to service.

In the formation of the nation-state the state had to determine and proclaim a common standard for weights and measures, as well as a single currency. Perhaps the classic example was France, where the metric system and decimalized franc were introduced to displace several different existing weights and measures and currencies at the time of the Revolution. With respect to the global economy there was the dramatic rise up to the early 1970s in the standardization of all facets of production and distribution. Although created before World War II, the International Organization for Standardization (ISO) has overseen during the last fifty years the growth of global standards on goods and services that have been extended to the entire range of production. Other global agencies more or less completed this global harmonization in the spheres of telecommunications, transport, and energy, among others. As for a global currency, the coming of the Euro points to the fate of national currencies – a fate that the U.S. dollar already foreshadowed after World War II in becoming *de facto* an almost universal currency.[11] Even now the use of the U.S. dollar continues to spread in countries outside Western Europe, and it constitutes more than one-half of the world's reserve currencies.

Transformation of Property Relations

In the first bourgeois revolutions, it was the precapitalist property relations that had to be transformed in order to make way for the assertion of capitalist relations. The present restructuring of the geography of accumulation calls into question the property relations that obtain within the nation-state. These are the relations that define the specific character of the nation and its people; and they are the product of the nature of national capital and the particular national history of class struggles. From the point of view of the process of globalization, however, these relations suffer from two defects: they are national, and they are not all in the form of corporate private property.

To address these "shortcomings," global policies began progressively from the 1970s to be adopted by national states through legislation and even constitutional change to reflect the demands of transnational corporate property rights. In general, these changes amounted to increasing the pre-eminence of corporate rights, circumscribing property privileges for national capital, and privatizing "public" and other forms of collective or social property. The principle of these policies was the reduction of all property relations to relations of unmitigated corporate private property and non-restrictive access to national capital from the global level.

Together these policies have come to be known, among other names, as neo-liberalism in the industrial nations and structural adjustment policies in the non-industrial nations. In concert with the promotion of corporate property rights, they include policies to deregulate, privatize, popularize capitalism, transform the tax structures, reduce the national debt, dismantle the welfare state, circumscribe trade union and workers' rights, and restrict the powers of national constitutions. Even science, technology, and culture are pursued within the form of corporate intellectual property rights. In short, all forms of property not already in the private corporate form are moved in this direction.

The ideological rationale of the policies is the rhetoric of the "free market," but this is more fictional construct than reality. While the policies do introduce the conditions for global competition between corporations, they also entail highly circumscribed competitive conditions, favouring the largest companies and allowing for vast systems of bribery, corruption, influence-pedalling, and cartelization, and their effects do not amount to a market in any genuine sense. The rhetoric, moreover, obscures the fundamental difference between private property in consumables and private property in the means of production – a veiled difference that conceals the basis of class contradictions and the limits of liberal democracy.

The Decline of National Cultural Identity

At the founding of every nation-state, as capital asserted itself over a given territory, there was a greater or lesser need to create a coherent national identity, and to subordinate sub-regional or diverse ethnic identities, in order to complement ideologically the economic union. Much attention was paid to the homogenization or hybridization of language as the most significant means of creating a common culture.

But the symbolic trappings of a unified whole also had to be set in place. National anthems, flags, pledges, "heads" of state, and commemorative holidays were all more or less invented or given new meanings to embody the "nation."

The processes of globalization call into question and begin to dissolve all existing social relations and structures belonging to the nation-state and previously existing modes of production. Time and space in a computer-based mode of production are compressed as if to make the world a singularity; and history, which is the history of nations, becomes for the first time irrelevant to the future – a global future and commodified life have little to do with a national past or persisting precapitalist relations. In place of the relative stability of social institutions comes only a sense of permanent change, a new world without rest or respite. In short, globalization brings in its wake the loss of our social "referents," the underlying source or cause of every hitherto accepted aspect of identity or social definition. "Things fall apart," as never before.

More specifically, what is lost, obscured, erased, transformed, or destroyed comprises the foundations of our notions of god, nation, citizenship, race, ethnicity, language, gender, class, career/work, family, culture, and history. Expectations surrounding the countervailing property rights associated with the Keynesian welfare state increasingly dissolve; the employment patterns of Fordism disappear daily; and corporations, schools, and governments become "de-institutionalized" with the coming of their "virtual" existence. Nothing with respect to the traditional means by which we define ourselves remains undisturbed by globalization, and there are no prospects for the continuation of past certainties and stabilities into the future.

Although the dissolution of these historical, real-life, "referents" leaves us in a world with no apparent foundation to social and cultural patterns, it is also a world that is being made over, reconstructed, in the image of global capitalism. This is done largely through the production and promotion of so-called cultural commodities – in food, clothing, furnishings, entertainment, ideas, and information – all of them increasingly produced only as commodities. Tourism completes the picture, as those with surplus means commodify the life experiences of those outside their own national domains.

Global commodification of the cultural, the ideational domain, leads to a more or less rapid homogenization or hybridization of world cultures. This consequence is not in itself negative, given that no existing culture can pretend not to be the result of previous hybridizations. The problem lies in the process of commodification because this substitute form detaches everything as commodity from its historical or human meaning. It destroys the elements of humanity in cultural artifacts and practices, makes profit the principle motive for cultural creation, and defines the cash nexus as the only means to a social existence. With the demise of nationally distinctive and real "referents," the production of a commodified global culture makes rapid levelling inroads everywhere and brings an attitude of detachment from reality.

With a rationale of profit and legitimation of the system, the commodified culture is also a synthetic culture: it is culture invented or created for ulterior motives, without empirical referent other than the values of global capitalism; it is not the ideational expression of an aspect of genuinely human sentiment; it is qualitatively distinct from culture as an emanation of human communities. The products of the Disney corporation epitomize commodified culture as synthetic culture, and this commodification increasingly embraces all aspects of life from birth to death.

The process of globalization also brings a single dominant language – English, the language of business – and because the economic prevails, English becomes the language of science and technology and of international politics and media, and even literature. While its almost universal adoption in these spheres does not necessarily exclude the use of other languages, it does subordinate them, and, in many cases, it reduces them to kitchen languages, putting an end to their growth and renewal as evolving languages.

In contradistinction to the ideas and ideals that embody the nation-state as something more than the mere sum of the parts, globalization brings with it a simple notion that corresponds with the process. With minor variations the idea of society as marketplace and its members as atomized actors whose social life consists of exchange relations is widely promoted. Its strength lies in its consistency with the commodification of life and the globalization of commodities. In some countries its promotion has become a celebration of greed, selfishness, and individualism. Indeed, this celebration is an integral part of the "civil religion" of America. It has also not infrequently been used as a counter to the ideas surrounding Keynesianism, social citizenship, and state and corporate responsibility.

The more that this neo-classical vision or exchange theory gains acceptance, the more it appears that the end of ideology has arrived. It is, we can agree, the end of ideologies, of the nationalisms, that were developed to reflect the nation-state and were promulgated to help secure its integrity.[12] It is not the end of ideology, however, because the many nationalisms are simply supplanted by the single ideological notion of the marketplace that corresponds to the global commodification of life. Still, there may be a positive note in this, and that is that one consequence of this substitution is the end in principle of the ideological expression and use of national differences.

Another consequence is the end of national history. There is an end to this in two senses: national history actually does come to a close as globalization dissolves the integrity of the nation-state as a delimited market (the end of national geography is the end of its history); and the knowledge of history as part of self-definition and understanding becomes irrelevant to the individual defined as economic maximizer and to social relations conceived as rational choices. Increasingly commodified global culture becomes the dominant source of our identity as national/ethnic differences dissolve.

VIII

A Critique of
the Sceptics

In little more than a decade an enormous literature on the subject of globalization has appeared. Yet, despite the wide exploration of this concept, there is little consensus as to its meaning. Indeed, there is no small amount of scepticism as to its empirical referent and there is much criticism surrounding its use – especially on the left of the political spectrum.

A great deal rests on demonstrating that there is a reality to globalization and on grasping the nature of that reality. Since the early 1970s, much of the intellectual and organizational disarray in the movements of subordinate classes and other groups has been a product of the radical changes brought about by globalizing capital, transformations that have seemingly overturned all former certainties. Class structures and legal and political systems of the recent past are undergoing more or less rapid modification; and the critical theories and objectives of the left have all come into question. As a consequence, resistance and alternatives to current economic and political developments are necessarily being rethought, but their success can only come with an understanding of just what it is that is happening.

Without a clear analysis of globalization there can be no effective resistance. It is crucial, then, to clarify the concept and the reality underlying it; and part of this task can be done by addressing some of the criticisms made of it.

Globalization as Mere Rhetoric

Some critics of the concept of globalization dismiss it as not reflective of real or significant change in the world economy; we must therefore begin our discussion here, at the very least to make some important distinctions. If we cannot go beyond the claim that it is empty of content, the discussion stops and we are left with a vision of a world of nation-states and their attendant concepts.

A common criticism of globalization makes it out to be a merely ideological concept, a sort of instrument of the powers that be to demand concessions from subordinate classes. As one sceptic observed, "The 'globalization thesis' here became a powerful tool to beat upon socialists, welfare statists, nationalists and so on."[1] A non-sceptic refers to the same point: "In much of the Left's anti-globalization writing, globalisation is seen as an ideology that is sapping the working class of its power ('paralysed by the bogeyman of globalisation'); it serves to quash the 'socialist project,' and play into the hands of a resurgent capitalist class."[2] Another critic goes further, asserting that the "idea itself is suspect"; it is simply an attempt to find "an alternative to the existing Marxist vocabulary."[3] There is little question that corporate and political leaders have used the idea that "there is no alternative" to the current trends in these ways, but we must make a distinction between the political use of the term "globalization" and its conceptualization of a reality. This is perhaps a small point, but apparently necessary to make: a critique and rejection of the ideological use of a concept should not lead to the dismissal of its possible reference to a reality.

The notion that globalization is but an ideology connected with large corporations and compliant politicians and academics has led some writers to the conclusion that as mere ideology it can be countered by similar means. In other words, if the phenomenon is simply ideological it will be enough to change the ideological perspective of those in power or at least to resist only on the ideological plane. But even if globalization were merely an ideological weapon without real content, it is no longer clear that any ready counter-ideational weapon is at hand. All the previous givens about the welfare state, about socialism in the nation-state, about the contradiction between national capitalist and working classes, and about the nature of the national state and national markets are being transfigured; they are no longer the same as they were even a short generation ago. Similarly, in the Third World the previous contradictions between centre and periphery no longer hold. The meaning of imperialism, furthermore – when applied to a country or organization in the age of transnational corporations, globalized production, distribution and consumption, and supranational agencies and regulations – is no longer clear.

The sceptics not infrequently point to the rhetorical promotion of globalization as a "recipe for prosperity,"[4] and rightly show that except for a minority this claim is patently false. Numerous studies, national and global, show that globalization has brought more or less rapidly increasing disparities in wealth everywhere. One of them concludes, "Global integration is among the main causes of rising inequality and poverty in any nation-state."[5] Little counterevidence has been offered. Just because the process itself does not bring benefits for all as claimed, however, is again no reason to dismiss the concept, along with its purported "promise" and theologue-like advocates.

As a variation on this theme, there are those who have argued that something is indeed happening, but whatever it is, it is not globalization. In this vein, the book-length treatment of the issue by Paul Hirst and Grahame Thompson contends with qualifications that globalization "is largely a myth," despite providing evidence for a certain reality behind the "myth."[6] Another study argues that far from being a new world in the making, globalization is about the old world order coming apart – as if the two could be separated.[7] The works by Hirst and Thompson and David Gordon comprise serious efforts to explore the empirical evidence for the phenomenon; but there are now too many authors and too much evidence pointing to pervasive qualitative global shifts to suggest that globalization is merely a myth. The debate can only be about how to understand and characterize it and what to do about it; it can no longer be about whether or not it is happening.

Nothing New – Plus Ça Change . . .

Given that the rhetorical use of the concept does not deny the underlying reality of new global conditions, the question that follows for the sceptics concerns the nature of that reality. A notable stream of criticism of the concept globalization makes the case that it does not reflect any significantly new development and is in fact simply the continuing "logic of capitalism." One notable analyst, David Harvey, writes: "Certainly from 1492 onwards, and even before, the globalization process of capitalism was well under way." Paul Sweezy concurs: "Globalization is not a condition or a phenomenon: it is a process that has been going on for a long time, in fact ever since capitalism came into the world as a viable form of society four or five centuries ago." He adds that globalization has been "the always expansive and often explosive capital accumulation process."[8]

Ellen Meiksins Wood agrees: "What they are calling a new epoch may be just the basic logic of capitalism asserting itself again after the exceptional, anomalous moment of the postwar boom. They may call it globalization or postmodernity, but it is really capitalism." Earlier she wrote, "The only concept we need to deal with this new reality is capitalism." W.K. Tabb reiterates: "The most significant features of what is called globalization have always been part of capitalist development, even if the forms are different in different periods (including our own)."[9]

Such positions are widely accepted on the left and amount to saying that the present changes are but the continuation of the expansion of capitalism down through the ages, or that capitalism is capitalism is capitalism. At a high level of abstraction this is true enough, but truisms do not make us much wiser; they do not help to explain either the stages in capitalist world development or the present shift in this expansion to the global level. Few if any writers on globalization, moreover, have said that it is not capitalism; most would agree that it is a stage in the development of capitalism. The problem is to identify the defining characteristics of the particular stage as opposed to other stages.

These positions may well rest on a certain reading of Marx, who writes: "The world market itself forms the basis for this [capitalist] mode of production."[10] But this says nothing about the stages of development of capitalism or its world market; it merely points to a necessary relationship. In the same vein, we can say that a social system is the precondition for the individual human, but this does not bring us any closer to an explanation of the stages of human social development.

If not derived from Marx, these positions seem implicitly to assume Immanuel Wallerstein's notion of a "world-economic system."[11] Yet in this concept he has reified an international capitalist trading system, given it an autonomous reality separate from the historically developing national capitals that have constituted its parts. The assertion of an independent reality for the world economy is to hypostatize the market, to give it a life outside of its actors. It is, in other words, to grasp only one side of a relationship, to miss the very dependency of this market on the competing national capitalist/managerial classes, corporations, and states that are/were its embodiment. The effect of positing the "world-economy" as an independent variable stretching forward from the sixteenth century is to impede an understanding of distinct stages in its growth, of its relation to its member nations, and of the transition from nationally based capital to capital increasingly free from or indifferent to national interests.

The point is that there is no such thing as capitalism pure and simple. Only in the most general, abstract sense is capitalism the same phenomenon down through the ages. If its fundamental characteristics are com-modity production, production for profit, corporate private property, social labour, a world market, and the law of value, none of this says any-thing about the developmental stages of these characteristics or about how any of these elements manifest themselves in a given age or coun-try. Similarly, there is no such thing as an independent world market, except as an abstraction. Just as there is no society without its constitu-ent members, so too there is no market without its member capitals, and no international market without nation-states.[12] And just as the history of capital evolves through many qualitatively distinct stages, so too does the corresponding world market.

Prior to the 1970s, capital was largely national in character and the world market was still more or less international, a trading system by and large framed by inter-national relations. Only with the current process of globalization is there the actual establishment of "self-gener-ating"[13] capital at the global level, in the form of the TNC, where the national character is of little consequence. Only now has capitalism become independent of its previous political and economic restrictions and developed a reality as self-generating capitals, as a system *sans* na-tionality. In all previous stages, capitalism had national characteristics, a national bourgeoisie, and its own specific history. Contra Wallerstein, national capitals always produced a fractious, warring, international sys-tem rather than an integrated, coherent one. After the early 1970s, how-ever, globalization became the growing realization of Wallerstein's "capitalist world-economy," that is, as a world market in transition – on the way to becoming a unified, unfettered global trading system.

Global capital has no national bourgeoisie and no national alle-giances; it has declining national characteristics and increasingly the characteristics of capital per se, as framed by the current global condi-tions. Its history begins after World War II with the creation of a supranational framework for the global market. Just as the national mar-ket was created by eliminating trade barriers over a certain territory in the bourgeois revolutions of the eighteenth and nineteenth centuries, so too the global market is being created by the systematic reduction of national trade barriers worldwide. In this way the global market is quali-tatively different from the national capitalisms and the international sys-tems of the previous eras. Historically, the world market evolved through stages marked by the growth in the relations of its constituents, namely, national states and national corporations; now there is movement towards a global market, and its members are TNCs.

In every stage in the development of capitalism, its fundamental characteristics appear in different ways, in strikingly different class structures and relations, labour processes, social, political, and legal relations, and organizations representing labour and capital. The differences between the stages such as "manufacturing," "large-scale industry," and Fordism, for example, represent nothing less than transformations of the whole of "society" – with profound differences in the manifestations of the contradictions of capitalism. To call it all capitalism is to add nothing. In fact, that view hinders the analysis of transformed conditions of accumulation and the new social, political, and legal landscape that accompanies them. It is one thing to argue that globalization is *not* a new stage of development and that there is *no* new regime of accumulation; but to say that it is all just capitalism is merely an empty truism intended only to dismiss.

To make the case that what the world is experiencing now is nothing new, some sceptics point to the period between 1870 and 1913 as a time of similar or greater international economic integration than the present. Over those decades labour migration from Europe to North and South America, it is argued, was unprecedented; citizenship was granted easily to immigrants; capital mobility and profit "repatriation" were more or less unrestricted; exports grew faster than domestic production; the gold standard governed foreign exchange; a free-trade philosophy dominated international relations. Yet, even if we accept these points (though most are open to debate), we can see that the critics miss out the significance of the event that brought the period to a close. If the international integration of that era amounted to globalization, then, the meaning of World War I is not at all clear.

Undoubtedly, that period was a time of extensive international economic integration, but the integration took the form of the expansion of national capitals. It was the age of "nation-building," or the consolidation of the domestic market, and of the extraterritorial extension of the national market characterized by colonization and imperialism. Both the First and Second world wars represented the limits of an *international* expansion that took the shape of the near destruction of much of the world due to the contradiction between the form and content of capital at a certain stage in its development. Globalization has nothing to do with the expansion of territorially exclusive markets; it is about making the world into one market.

The sceptics who deny that the present era is any different are missing a key characteristic of the phenomenon. Globalization can be described as the unfolding resolution of the contradiction between ever-expanding capital and its national political and social formations. Until the 1970s the history of capitalism had been the history of the nation-state; and the expansion of capital came always in the form of national capital – capital with particular territorial and historical roots. This development was characterized by colonial conquest and conflicts between nations, culminating in the two world wars. By the 1970s, however, capital was expanding in the form of, simply, the corporation; ownership corresponded less and less with national geographies. Just as at one stage capital had to create a national state and a defined territory in order to come into its own, now in the form of the TNC it has to remove or transform this "shell" to create institutions to ensure and facilitate accumulation at the global level. The national history of capital has come to a close, and the history of the expansion of capital *sans* nationality has begun.

Technological Revolution

Aside from the matter of the postwar construction of a global market framework, a significant part of the case for globalization as a "new reality" has rested on the perceived technological revolution based on the coming of microelectronics, computers, and biotechnology, and their applications from the early 1970s. One of the main critics of the so-called globalization thesis, Ellen Wood, takes issue with the argument:

"So what is new about this so-called new economy is not that the new technologies represent a unique kind of epochal shift. On the contrary, they simply allow the logic of the old mass production economy to be diversified and extended. Now, the old logic can reach into whole new sectors, and it can affect types of workers more or less untouched before."[14]

Wood argues here that, first, there has not been a significant or qualitative change in technology sufficient to talk about an "epochal shift" or "historic rupture"; and, second, given that there are new technologies, they only advance "the old logic" of cheapening production and increasing managerial control. The second point is a non-point: given that technological change under capitalism in general has been brought about for these reasons, what we have here is a non sequitur – that technological change contains capitalist logic has no specific bearing on whether or not it brings into being a new stage in capitalist development.

The first point, however, calls for more examination. Published criticisms of the argument for globalization do not often address the question of the technological aspect of the shift, in theory or in practice, but it is here that the crux of the differences lies. Because most of the critics are on the left, it is not unfair to borrow from Marx to map out conceptually why there is a transition from one stage of development to another. On the level of the mode of production, referring to broadly coherent systems – that is, communal, Asiatic, slave, feudal, or capitalist – Marx saw the *differentia specifica* as resting in the nature of the labour process, that composite of purposeful work, "raw" materials, and the instruments of production. To differentiate modes of production at this level of abstraction, however, does not address the need to differentiate historical changes within them.

The stages of development in the history of capitalism are characterized by significant changes in class structure, government systems, ideologies, and so on. These stages, as Marx argues in several places, are similarly delineated by transformations in the labour process, principally in the instruments of production. Hence, the shift in capitalism between "manufacturing" and "large-scale industry" – the only two stages that Marx discussed and could have known about – is laid at the feet of the coming of the machine.[15] And it is the introduction of machinery that Marx argues as transforming the relations of production and exchange within a given social formation and causing the shift in regimes of accumulation. The class structure, its mediating mechanisms, the state, ideologies, the works – are all more or less revolutionized in the process.

When the scientific and technological changes of the late nineteenth century brought new sources of energy, new branches of industry, and new means of communication, the stage was set for a transformation in the labour process of the day. The coming of Fordism in the first decades of the twentieth century rested on these developments and can be demarcated by major shifts in the labour process. "Scientific management" transformed the organization of labour at the point of production, the assembly line revolutionized the instruments of production, and science transformed the material of labour. There followed a consequent transformation in the structure of the capitalist and working classes, along with the rest of the social formation. Mass production ushered in "mass" society with the rapid growth in proletarianization and the ability to satisfy and expand needs as never before via commodity production.

The 1940s and 1950s ushered in another stage – advanced Fordism – in which the wartime advances in science and technology and their subordination to capital grew in an unprecedented way. For the first time in history, scientific and technological innovation became central to the labour process; and capital accumulation became more than ever dependent on research and development. As in previous shifts, major social changes took place: the class structures and social and political relations were more or less transformed;[16] increased productivity allowed for the laying of the economic basis for the Keynesian welfare state, and also made necessary the first genuinely supranational experiment in governance. It was not for no reason that in the aftermath of World War II there was talk of a "new world order."

The same argument underlies the so-called globalization thesis. With the coming of computer technology and its many applications in the early 1970s, a veritable revolution in the labour process began to take place.[17] In this case, however, each of its three components was transformed in a very short time. Unlike any previous instruments of production, the computer and its applications made the robotization or automation of every conceivable aspect of work a real possibility: they possessed the potential for minimizing and even eliminating human beings at the point of production, distribution, or communication. The raw material of the process, moreover, became less the existing forms of nature than the elemental building blocks. Increasingly, unlike any earlier period, the product of the process became wholly or partially synthetic. More than just transforming the labour process, the computer allows scientific and technological change to develop into what can only be deemed a permanent technological revolution. With the vast increase in productivity and "flexibility" stemming from this transformation, the entire structure of production, distribution, and consumption moves to the global plane, increasingly indifferent to national considerations except to overcome them as impediments to commerce. And more, there is in the computer the potential for the elimination of all the divisions of labour that previously determined the history of our social relations.[18]

The transformation of the national relations of production and the political shell, a result of this revolution in the labour process, is now evident everywhere. National class structures and agencies, the labour and capital markets, systems of government, culture, family, precapitalist social formations, and the nation-state and its political geography all come into question. All face the process of disintegration and reconstitution in new forms.[19]

From this perspective, it can be seen that the concept of globalization actually refers to the consequences of the transformation of the labour process. It refers to the growing denationalization of capital and to the expanding supranational regime of accumulation, and is therefore not an appropriate label for characterizing the material basis of the distinctive era that we have entered. Similarly, the concepts of lean production, "just-in-time," flexible manufacturing, and even bio-technology all point to consequences of the new labour process and not to its foundation in computers. We have entered *the age of the computer* with unprecedented and comprehensively revolutionary consequences.[20] Yet it is still an age based on a capitalist mode of production with all of its contradictions, albeit in new forms and at new levels. It is unquestionably a new world, but one that the sceptics do not acknowledge.

The Transnational Corporation and the Global Market

The TNC is the chief carrier and user of the new technology in all spheres of the economy; and as the corporate embodiment of this technology, it is the TNC and its demands that become the central motive for the systematic changes to the nation-state as we have known it. The new technology makes national relations of production, and corresponding political, legal, and ideological structures, all reflecting the national character of capital, seem increasingly redundant, antiquated, and even antagonistic in relation to its powers to reduce the dimensions of time and space. But the sceptics challenge the very concept of the TNC.

Before their objections are addressed, we should attempt a definition. The TNC is a corporation whose productive and distributive capabilities span the jurisdiction of many nations, minimizing its national character, and for which national labour, consumer, and capital markets have more or less lost meaning, except to take advantage of their differences or impose harmonization. Its location and decisions are based on global market considerations and not national ones. While its management and ownership need not be transnational, they are indeed transnational in outlook, objectives, and interest. In principle if not in practice, the TNC stands as a contradiction to national sovereignty, that is, its interests are served better by a supranational, and not national, regulatory framework. This is not to say that it does not remain a national legal entity or no longer operates within national regulatory regimes; there is at present no alternative to certain national delimitations. Essential to this definition, however, is an established and growing coherent and comprehensive transnational regulatory regime and rapid national harmonization with it.[21]

Drawing on these characteristics, globalization can be defined as the arrival of "self-generating capital" at the global level: that is, capital as capital, capital in the form of the transnational corporation, increasingly free of national loyalties, controls, and interests. This is not to be understood as the mere internationalization of capital, which assumes a world of national capitals and nation-states, but as the supersession by capital of the nation-state as its historically necessary but now redundant social and political framework. It is a process in which the main actors become the TNCs and all the circuits of capital become global in nature, with a distinct global framework; and the national economy – and its associated borders, policies, and programs – becomes a fetter.

No corporation, national or transnational, stands on its own; there are always many, and they always develop in relation to a market. Although the firm or corporation is not often grasped in this way, the market is always a necessary component of its definition. Prior to the pre-eminence of the TNC, the market had both national and international dimensions. The national market was by and large a politically unified, economic union without significant barriers; and the international market was a system characterized by multilateral and bilateral agreements and treaties, foreign exchange rates and mechanisms, imports and exports between national jurisdictions, trade barriers and wars, international loans and debts, and diplomacy and warfare between nations. The last significant war between capitalist nations was World War II,[22] and in its immediate aftermath there began the process to transform the international market into a transnational or global one. This is the historical significance of the formation of the United Nations, the Bretton Woods agreement, and GATT. They comprised the first systematic attempt to end the hitherto international market and provide the institutional beginning, the "core enabling framework," for globalization: the staged and negotiated process of creating a single, unified, global market without significant national barriers. In the early stages of development the framework provided the precondition for the rise of the multinational corporation; at a later stage in the reduction of national barriers, in the early 1970s, it became the precondition for the TNC and its growing employment of computer-based technology.

Given this transformation of the market, globalization may be seen as the shifting of the main venue or site of capital accumulation from the national to the supranational or global level. This shift, captured in the phrase "the end of (political) geography," implies the realization of a global market as such, which requires the establishment of administrative bodies at the global level and a transformation or harmonization of national relations of production that have become barriers to the global accumulation of capital.

The global market and the TNC, then, are qualitatively different from the prewar and postwar international market and MNCs. The global market has been constructed through the systematic dismantling of national barriers to trade and investment and by the creation of supranational regulatory agencies to advance and maintain the emerging global system. National and regional markets become merely the component parts of the global market, and their specificity declines in relation to the realization of the global. In tandem with these developments, the TNC expands its global assets, sales, employment, perspective, ownership, and management. Both market framework and TNC develop in a reciprocal relationship; with the staged systematic diminution of national barriers comes an increase in transborder operations, a growing preponderance of foreign direct investment over commodity trade, and large numbers of transnational corporate mergers and takeovers, joint ventures, share agreements, cartels, and oligopolies. The degree to which all this is realized challenges the sovereign economic powers of the national state.

The sceptics are reluctant to use the concept of TNC and prefer the label MNC. The most thorough critiques to date, by Hirst and Thompson and Linda Weiss, use MNC throughout their book-length works, and they even convert the label TNC to MNC without argued justification when citing statistics designated "TNC" from the UN Centre on TNCs and other sources.[23] What is at issue is the reality of the TNC, and this cannot be addressed by evading the concept in order to retain a vision of a world of nation-states and nationally based MNCs.

Several of the sceptics also seek to minimize not only the reality but also the size and number of TNCs,[24] but without providing the appropriate evidence. As long ago as 1974 the UN Centre on TNCs began to report extensively on the size, growth, and operations of TNCs. In the early 1990s the Centre estimated that there were about 37,000 TNCs and that they controlled about one-third (and rising) of all the private-sector assets in the world.[25] Other studies by the World Bank, the IMF, and the OECD all reiterate the existence, size, and economic significance of TNCs. One writer points out, "The number of these [TNCs] based in 14 major developed home countries more than tripled . . . from 7,000 in 1970 to nearly 24,000 in 1990. The total number of foreign affiliates stands at 200,000, a dramatic acceleration over the 3,500 manufacturing affiliates established between 1946-61."[26] The *World Investment Report* for 1998 states: "In 1997, the value of international production, attributed to some 53,000 TNCs and their roughly 450,000 foreign affiliates, was $3.5 trillion as measured by the accumulated stock of FDI, and $9.5 trillion as measured by the estimated global sales of foreign affiliates."[27]

The assets and revenues of the largest TNCs are greater than the GDP and tax revenues of the majority of nation-states; and the enormous size, pervasiveness, and power of TNCs are sufficient to raise the question of the very meaning of the "national economy." Although for the most part economic measures and statistics collected remain largely national, this condition reflects a certain "institutional lag" and belies a changing reality. If a national economy implies a national capitalist class and interests, those elements can hardly be said to exist today with any significant degree of effect and integrity, with the possible but declining exceptions of the United States, Japan, and Germany. TNCs dominate in most spheres of most national economies; and given the extensive "import penetration," increasing affiliations, intracorporate trade, intercorporate collaboration, and foreign direct investment, TNCs make the possibilities for persisting national economies increasingly dubious.

The sceptics also appear to have a preference for the concept of the international market rather than the global, again suggesting a reluctance to admit to the changing nature of the world market. The emergence of the global market is now far advanced and is qualitatively different from what is meant by the international market. The evidence of an emerging transnational economy is overwhelming. Hardly a single country is not at present a member of one or another trade zone or customs union. The progressive economic integration that accompanies such unions, along with membership in GATT (now WTO), makes the idea of persisting national economies in an international market appear to be an exercise in nostalgia. In Europe, moreover, the replacement of national currencies with the Euro signals the consolidation of the European economy and the end of the national economy in any significant sense in Europe. Much of the rest of the world has already embraced the reality of "dollarization" or currencies "pegged" to the dollar. And the dollar increasingly dominates as a foreign reserve currency, bringing the world closer to a single currency in trade and investment. Indeed, the degree of global interfirm collaboration and intrafirm trade is sufficient in some economic sectors even to foresee an eclipse of the market and its replacement by corporate planning – a form of "central planning," but for profit.

As a counter to the concept of the TNC and rationale for using MNC, several critics raise the question of a "home base" for the "footloose" MNC.[28] They suggest that most corporations have a "home base," which in itself is an indication of less "transnationality." They do not consider, though, the meaning of the home base. If the case can be made that it refers to national interests, then, indeed, they have added to the argument against the idea of globalization. Having a home base in itself, however, is neither here nor there; it indicates nothing about national as opposed to global interests. Indeed, it would be odd for a corporation not to have a home base. Similarly, the nationality of ownership and management is no indicator of corporate national interests. Moreover, as more corporations develop a "virtual" existence, as many financial institutions have already done, the existence of a home base and nationality of management become meaningless. The rapidly growing "electronic economy," moreover, attaches no significance to nationality or the notion of a home base.[29]

One of the hallmarks of the global economy is the vast and growing movement of equity capital or foreign direct investment (FDI); its significance lies in its connection with ownership and control and the decline of the integrity of national economies. The 1998 *World Investment Report* makes the point rather directly:

The ratio of inward and outward FDI stocks to global GDP is now 21 per cent; foreign affiliate exports are one-third of world exports; and GDP attributed to foreign affiliates accounts for 7 per cent of global GDP. Sales of foreign affiliates have grown faster than world exports of goods and services, and the ratio of the volume of world inward plus outward FDI stocks to world GDP has grown twice as fast as the ratio of world imports and exports to world GDP, *suggesting that the expansion of international production has deepened the interdependence of the world economy beyond that achieved by international trade alone.*[30]

To counter the idea of globalization the sceptics must find a way of diminishing the obvious significance of foreign direct investment. To do this they make several distinctions within FDI; they argue, for instance, that aggregate data on FDI do not tell the whole story.[31] Some of them suggest that non-manufacturing investments have a higher rate of growth than do manufacturing investments. Even if this is the case, it is a non-issue; such a shift might be expected when manufactured goods and key services are already largely controlled by transnational oligopolies and cartels. The issue is the degree of non-national control and/or ownership over a corporation. Another distinction the sceptics make is between FDI and portfolio capital, which would be a significant point to make if capital were still national in character. But the Eurodollar market has been in existence for a long time now and represents the more or less complete integration of the world's capital markets, outside the control of individual national governments or central banks. The distinction the sceptics make is not significant in the context of the global capital market.

Another point that sceptics make concerns the high degree of FDI that goes into mergers and acquisitions (M&A), suggesting that investment in "existing ventures" rather than new ones is somehow less globalizing. Such a trend would be precisely what would be expected with globalization; it marks the concentration and centralization of capital through competition at the global level. If anything, the rapid progress of M&A is a strong indicator of growing TNC control. The 1998 *World Investment Report* states, for instance:

World-wide cross-border M&As, mostly in banking, insurance, chemicals, pharmaceuticals and telecommunications, were aimed at the global restructuring or strategic positioning of firms in these industries. . . . Valued at $236 billion, majority-owned M&As represented nearly three-fifths of global FDI inflows in 1997, increasing from almost half in 1996. . . . One outcome is a greater industrial concentration in the hands of a few firms in each industry, usually TNCs.[32]

The problem for the sceptics is that FDI has continuously been greater than the growth of GDP and trade, bringing more and more economic activity under the control of TNCs, and that, furthermore, FDI statistics do not reveal the actual degree of global corporate inter-penetration. TNC collaboration in research, marketing, and production continues to expand,[33] and intracorporate trade is increasing as a pro-portion of all trade. Investments in the world stock and financial mar-kets are close to being fully integrated; food production and distribution of major staples are highly monopolized by a handful of TNCs;[34] indus-trial manufacturing of appliances, vehicles, airplanes, computers, tel-ecommunications, clothing, and arms is dominated by the TNCs; and mergers and acquisitions continue to grow.[35] By most accounts, the TNC and the global market have arrived; and the adoption of neo-lib-eral policies and the expansion of TNCs develop in tandem. The global market is so integrated in so many spheres that it is no longer possible to identify or measure nationality in some industries in a meaningful way.[36]

Global Governance

The institutions of the postwar rapprochement – the United Nations, the IMF and the World Bank, and GATT – constituted the 'core ena-bling framework' that would underlie the coming of a genuinely global market as such, distinct from an international one. The TNCs that grew in response then required further continuous transformation of the pre-vious international system of nation-states. The whole postwar period down to the present day has seen the continued expansion of this frame-work for the global market with the progressive removal of national bar-riers to trade and investment, the creation and consolidation of global oversight and enforcement agencies, the freeing of currencies from na-tional control, and a system of global security.

Despite the growth of this framework, historically novel because it operates at the global level, the sceptics are reluctant to admit to their significance. One of them writes: "The world shows almost no signs of moving from a high level of economic globalization towards the forma-tion of a serious global state."[37] It is not clear what a "serious global state" is, but it is not possible to have global economic integration with-out a governing framework, and there can be no doubt that a comprehensive, albeit multilayered, institutional framework has been set in place to govern the global activity of corporations. It is of course for capital only; it is a system for governing economic relations without any means of "access" by subordinate classes and groups.

While it is not possible to determine precisely the relative significance of the given parts of the system, it is clear that they are united in their underlying principles and operate within a certain division of labour in global governance. They are not without their internal and cross-institutional disputes, reflecting vestigial national or regional interests and intrasector and intracorporate conflicts. But such contradictions within the global framework do not belie its role as the emerging system of governance at the global level; and they did not prevent its rapid expansion, particularly after 1970.[38]

The rise of global governance can be understood by analogy to the rise of the nation-state in that many national economies were unified and made coherent in the same way. Numerous and disparate sub-national territorial units were often first brought together as customs unions of various sorts, frequently with mainly bureaucratic supervision; and then, only later, were broader political mechanisms added to give voice to and mitigate growing and changing class interests. Governance of the nation-state, nevertheless, was and remains first and foremost the administration of economics. In this sense, the growth after World War II of a supranational enabling framework for capital at the global level has been no different.

While there may be disagreement about the hierarchy of authority, or the division of labour, amongst these levels and agencies, there is certainly considerable agreement about the main components of supranational governance. Certain broad policy matters are determined by the heads of the major national governments in the G-3/7/8 forums.[39] Several pivotal agencies (such as the UN, WTO, IMF, World Bank, OECD, and BIS) staffed in part by government appointees play a significant role in supranational regulation, policy formation, standardization, and credit facilitation. State membership in common markets or trading blocs (such as the EU, NAFTA, and MERCOSUR [El Mercado Común del Sur]) goes a long way to create supranational control over the economic. Multilateral agreements (such as OPEC, and UNCTAD commodity agreements for key staples) also diminish national powers over the production and distribution of major commodity exports. The growth of international law after World War II, moreover, provides another level of supranational governance. Not least, since 1945 the growth of an international regime of individual and "human" rights has increasingly allowed national sovereignty to be challenged by "rights" defined at the supranational level.[40] If these are the main layers of global governance, the mechanisms of enforcement and advancement of the rule of capital should be added; UN peacekeeping operations, NATO, and several bilateral and multilateral military pacts, as well as mercenary operations, complete the global system.

One can talk of such governance only after World War II.[41] It is still an evolving system whose parts are coherent in principle though somewhat disparate in origin and function. It can be understood as levels of administrative agencies and institutions controlling, directing, regulating, and facilitating the activities of TNCs and the shape of the growing global market. Although not without differences and conflicts, it is comprehensive and united in principle and through subordination to the U.S. government. It has been labelled "governance without government,"[42] which is meant to imply an authoritative administrative apparatus without the political and legal legitimacy of an elected government purportedly responsible to its citizenry.

That the U.S. government has tended to play a dominant role in all these agencies at all levels is not strictly an example of national control. To be sure, there has been an active element of national interest, but more importantly this role is a consequence of the U.S. position as the world's dominant capitalist power and so the initiator and "overseer" of the global enabling framework. This position in turn is a consequence of a series of historical junctures, in particular the outcome of World War II and the end of colonialism that allowed for the initiation of this framework. China's shift to the "capitalist road" and the demise of the U.S.S.R., furthermore, opened the way for the entire globe in effect to be subordinated to the U.S.-dominated capitalist market and framework, ended any significant resistance or alternatives to the market by states representing socialized property relations, and left the United States unchallenged militarily.

The development of a global framework for transnational capital required it to be secured, defended, and advanced, while socialism had to be contained. Where peaceful maintenance of, or transition to, capitalism could be obtained, diplomatic or other non-violent means could be employed. Where there has been resistance to capitalist property relations, military or police actions have been used. In these cases, the

United States (and other powers) employed unilateral interventions, bilateral and multilateral military pacts, the UN peacekeeping operations, economic blockades, and the arms race, as well as a variety of covert means. Underlying the establishment of the global enabling framework during the whole of the postwar period to the present was the principle of *Machtpolitik*, and its chief proponent has been the U.S. government and the military-industrial complex, whose interests are served both as capital in general and a particular sort of capital.[43]

Role of the National State:
"Convergence" versus "State Capacity"

Despite the emergence of a distinctly global framework for capital and the dominance of TNCs in every major economic sphere, the national state has by no means disappeared. Given this, there are many who would make an argument for a world of viable nation-states, of states, that is, with "varieties of state capacities" or persisting "national priorities" and significant remaining powers in the face of global capital and its supranational representatives.[44] Others, more circumspect, would admit conflict between the three hegemons, the United States, Japan, and a German-led Europe,[45] with the rest of the world subordinated in one way or another to those powers. Contrasted to these positions is the argument that globalization brings with it an inexorably progressive transnational "convergence."[46] We would argue that the issue is not one or the other, but that in this current interregnum between two eras we are confronting the transition from national interests to global convergence. What lies at the heart of these different views, however, is the implicitly conflicting views on the nature of the state.

Underlying the view of convergence is the notion that with the rise to power of the modern capitalist class, the modern national state was born. It comprises the machinery of government that embodies the property relations of this class and mediates class relations and conflict with other classes and strata embodying different forms of property. The character of the state, it follows, changes with the changing class structures, which in turn reflect the level of capital accumulation and development of technology. Besides representing this formation of capital and its consequent class relations, the state has no specific content of its own. The very existence of the state is relative to the demands of capital accumulation and to the character of class conflict; it exists only in relation to its civil society and is defined in terms of this relation.

When at different stages of development the capitalist class pursues its interests outside the nation-state, the state similarly extends its policies and security as "national" policies, hence colonialism and imperialism. But when the assets, production, sales, and employees of corporations have become increasingly transnational, and so too their interests, then national policies must be circumscribed, subordinated, eliminated, or asserted as transnational, as "universal." The degree of persistence of national policies and the degree of their subordination to universal policies are largely determined by the amount, ownership, and control of nationally accumulated and productive capital. From this point of view, the role of the national state principally follows the development of the capital whose interests it represents (mitigated by national class conflict). And when this capital expands as transnational capital, the state must also adopt transnational policies, which are determined in global forums and reflect the contradictions of capital at that level. This perspective conflicts with those who want to make states into the "authors" of globalization or globalization into a product of state strategy.[47]

Underlying the view of persisting "state capacities" is a state-centric notion of the relative autonomy of the state, with a stress on the side of autonomy. It is largely a vision of the state as an independent variable, hence the description of a state as "strong," "weak," "catalytic," or "competitive,"[48] as if the state itself is the source of these characteristics rather than the capitalist class or class relations it represents. The focus on the state as actor suggests that it has interests of its own, other than the merely bureaucratic. Its ability to act appears to be without reference to the characteristics of the capitalist class and the contradictions that define its civil society. The view ignores or evades the question of the origin of the interests of the state.

From this perspective there appear to be political means to counter the effects of globalization. Examples of Asian economic development are often offered.[49] The "state-led path to development" taken by the "Four Tigers" of Southeast Asia and Japan are pointed to as instances of state-induced national economic success, as if the role of the state were independent of its own civil society and the larger world market. The problem is that, in general, it is in the nature of capitalism that the state is employed by national capital to further its own ends. It is a question of how it is done, the degree and character of the involvement; but it is never a question of the state having its own agenda – except when political decisions become pre-eminent, as under fascism or socialism, albeit propounded in different ways and for different reasons.

Representative of this same perspective is the position that sees globalization (or aspects of it) as "reversible." One writer on finance argues that the reasons for "financial liberalization" were specific in time and place and are now changing, opening the possibilities for a reassertion of national control; and that the crises in the financial markets in the 1980s fostered an interest in a return to national control for the sake of stability. He concludes that this reasoning is a "challenge [to] the argument that the globalization of financial markets is irreversible."[50] Unfortunately, no aspect of the speculated "reversal" has come about; if anything, financial liberalization expanded enormously in the 1990s. Deregulation of these markets has now been carried out more or less across the world, global bond and equity markets are firmly established and joined electronically, the majority of industrial nations now accepts the Euro as a single currency, the largest reserve currency remains the U.S. dollar, and the "dollarization" of the rest of the world continues apace. Very few financial analysts would not agree that the world's financial markets are irretrievably integrated.[51] Not only is the possibility of a reversal in the structure of the global financial markets implausible, but also the power of these markets over national governments is greater than ever.

These are quintessentially political views; they arbitrarily assign a certain primacy and independence to political actions by the state without an attempt to account for these actions by identifying the source of state interests. They lend themselves to the view that globalization is really "internationalization";[52] and they obscure the possibilities of a supranational existence beyond the nation-state. They also want to make globalization into "a politically rather than a technologically induced phenomenon."[53] In other words, the acceptance of the demands of the global market, "willingly or unwillingly," is still a determination by the state. They try, moreover, to outline several possible strategies or policy options the state can choose to follow, without seeing that the idea of choice obscures what are merely certain optional arrangements for the most advantageous integration into the global economy.[54] Such possibilities are to be expected in the transition from an international to a global system, but they do not point to a national strategy for confronting global demands.

Such perspectives do not admit that an enormous proportion of world capital, especially finance capital, no longer has national or domestic interests and has for several decades worked to create a system of supranational administrative structures, including the political independence of central banks. The growth of these agencies for capital at the global level cannot but gradually usurp and subordinate the role and powers of the national state; and this because such structures represent the largest and most powerful capitals that have penetrated, with minor exceptions, all the world's national economies. As a consequence, the national state is subsumed in larger political and/or economic units (EU, NAFTA, MERCOSUR, among others); and, moreover, it adopts under pressure or for ideological reasons the neo-liberalism of the global market.

State counterpositions and policies can only be sustained under the circumstances of a relatively independent capitalist class, or defiant or well-organized subordinate classes. Even so, such positions can generally be maintained only as secondary to the primacy of the most powerful sector of capital, be it national or transnational. The present role of the state can only be to follow the interests of its capitalist class – mitigated in its policies by the necessity to take into some account counterforces within its jurisdiction. For the most part, the direction of the contemporary state follows the lead of globalizing capital, and its relative autonomy is prescribed by new contradictions at the global and national levels. To put this point another way: state sovereignty rests on the relative coherence of a national bourgeoisie, but with its transfiguration into TNCs a relative shift in sovereignty occurs from the national state and bourgeoisie to the supranational framework and the TNC.

These developments should not be seen as merely the "restructuring" of the national state but as the redefinition of the state because its original definition was the political expression of a national bourgeoisie and its subordinate classes. This is not to say that the national state apparatus will disappear in the near future – only that it will be subordinate to the demands of an increasingly integrated global system. There continue to be important roles for it to play. (In this sense the state is not powerless, but it is if one is suggesting a persisting capacity for independent counter-hegemonic activity.) One of the state's key tasks will be to facilitate the harmonization of national with global policies; another will be to build more of the infrastructure for global processes; a third will be to promote the accumulation of global capital; and domestic

190

social control will also be an obligation. But while the state was once the monopoly of the "whole" in the face of civil society at the national level, it is now a "part" of the global civil society, with only weighted voting rights in its relation to supranational governing structures. Once the embodiment of national corporate property rights, the state must increasingly harmonize those rights with global corporate rights, and in the process transform itself.

The North-South Divide, or the Core and Periphery

On the question of globalization and the Third World, sceptics frequently point to world trade statistics showing that the largest share of trade and investment continues to be within the industrialized world. The persistence of these patterns is said to be "inconsistent with a globalization tendency."[55] Because FDI remains "highly concentrated" in the industrial nations and limited in the Third World is another reason, argue some, that globalization is "largely a myth."[56]

A focus on aggregate data for trade and investment flows, however, never reveals the entire picture. The value of imports and exports might remain relatively stable, while the volumes might see large increases due to radical currency devaluations in Third World countries. The composition of the capital invested and its purpose and destination, moreover, changed considerably in the 1980s and 1990s. Even the meaning of national statistics is open to question given the substantial and growing amount of intracorporate trade. Above all, the use of trade and investment statistics does not address the changing nature of the relation between North and the South.

The continued use of the concepts of internationalization and MNCs in the context of the North-South divide implies the persistence of one or another "development model" for the Third World. The view remains that, although exploited by industrial nations, the "developing" nation-states still retain domestic markets and the potential for independent economic growth. This argument ignores the effects throughout the "undeveloped" world of years of growing indebtedness,[57] of decades of aid programs intended to modernize, and of the widespread enforcement of structural adjustment policies (SAPs) beginning in the 1970s. By the 1980s, in the words of one observer, "a *substantial change* in the dependency relationship between the South and the North" could be seen.[58]

As neo-liberal policies for the Third World, the SAPs are the policy side of globalization imposed progressively with every new loan or foreign exchange crisis. The consequences have changed the character of dependency for the Third World. They have effectively ended state-led national development strategies.[59] The "import-substitution model" for industrialization, for instance, that once held a certain promise for independent development, has all but been eclipsed. The SAPs have eliminated protectionist measures and the domestic market "as a factor in development"[60] and have gone far to transform the "unit of development" from the nation-state to free-trade zones, local areas or cross-national regional markets. Continued trade policy discrimination by the industrial nations against the Third World at the global level has consolidated these developments.

There are many examples of this transformation of the Third World.[61] Chile might well have been the first significant case in which the policies of state intervention for national development were brutally replaced in a coup d'état with policies promulgated by military intervention for the benefit of the TNCs. Here, the role of the U.S. government as guarantor of the global enabling framework was to become plainly visible, but there are numerous instances of U.S. unilateral intervention to end national strategies around the world, particularly throughout Latin America. Moreover, the so-called "Asian crisis" that peaked in 1997-98 presented the opportunity, taken through the IMF and World Bank, to undermine certain Asian national development strategies, particularly in Korea and Thailand.[62] Even the suggested Japanese solution to the crisis to establish a regional development strategy was nipped in the bud, and Japan too was forced by the circumstances to revamp many of its protectionist policies.

Besides ending in general the possibilities for national development, the imposition of SAPs opened the possibilities for TNCs to increase Third World dependency by integrating food production, distribution, and consumption into a global system. This deepening of dependency is being accomplished in part through the increased capitalization, subsidization, and vertical integration of food production and distribution in the industrial countries, making ever cheaper food staples available for export.[63] A more significant means, however, is the transformation and use of property rights over the genetic makeup of plants and animals and humans. The patenting of life forms means that the reproduction of plants and animals that constitute the world's food supply is placed into the hands of a few large TNCs, a shift that amounts to the "corporate enclosure of the genetic commons." This enclosure is affirmed in certain agreements in the WTO and the Convention on Biological Diversity that legalize and codify the right to patent the plant and animal resources of the world and furthermore "restrict the ability of governments to control and regulate the process."[64] It is the most complete and profound mechanism ever devised for economic dominance, allowing corporate private property to be the direct means of control over the world's population. The use of food as a weapon has a long history, but never on the global scale, or so completely, or in such an apparently legitimate or legal way, as is now occurring.

For the Third World the implications of these means of creating increasing global dependency on global sources is the destruction of independent food supply and distribution, of entire ways of life, and of the livelihood for many millions, as well as a massive increase in migration and urbanization. For the world as a whole, they contribute to the growth of the global capitalist labour market and so-called "industrial reserve army," increased pressure to level wages, further ecological destruction, and the standardization and adulteration of food supply, among other consequences.

In effect, this changing relationship between North and South marks the "end of the Third World" in the sense that we are witnessing the end of national development strategies for Southern countries and their direct subordination to the TNCs through the transformation and globalization of property rights, enforced by a supranational regulatory regime. SAPs signal the end of the possibility for independent economic development and the demise of Third World nations as national characters on the world stage – before they got to play anything but a minor role. Still, the industrial nations face much the same fate. Many of them have already subordinated their national independence to the demands of a transnational (or at least regional) economy in the European Union and NAFTA. The process of globalization subordinates all economies to an increasingly unified single economic process.

IX

The Question of
Resistance and Alternatives

There are many who still agree with the position argued 150 years ago[1] that the struggle against capital is at first national. The idea remains current in many circles, and some theorists argue that the national state is a possible instrument for confronting the processes of globalization.[2] Such positions usually rest on the persistence of Keynesian beliefs about the interventionist state, without an understanding of the economic rationale of the state or without perceiving that such a model has lost its foundation with the demise of Fordism.[3] We have entered the era of global capitalism, and attempts to employ the chief instrument of what was national capital against now-global capital are not likely to succeed.

The struggle to change oppressive conditions can no longer be framed in strictly national terms because the nation-state is more or less rapidly losing its integrity as a system. With globalization, national forms of struggle are increasingly less effective against global corporate demands. In the present early stages of the global era, the decline of national sovereignty, powers, and laws all go hand-in-hand with the demise of a national bourgeoisie. The state as a meaningful national political institution begins to slip into history, just as precapitalist political forms did with the coming of the bourgeois revolutions.

Most of the movements, political parties, and organizations that represent property forms other than corporate capital were and remain defined in national or local terms, and their perspectives persist within a national framework.[4] Here lies one of the greatest weaknesses of the opposition and a key reason for much of the disarray and division amongst many of the counterforces to global capitalism. The continuing national definition of subordinate classes and groups creates barriers to their thinking about the "new reality"; and the limited development of united or organized global counterforces allows capital to expand without much restraint or significant opposition at the global level.

Continuous developments in global governance and new instruments of production have made a singular, unified global market not only possible but also a growing reality, implying the ultimate subordination of all national economies. On the one hand, national labour markets progressively succumb to global changes. The structure of working classes is transformed; union rights and employment standards are undermined;[5] more or less rapid proletarianization of the Third World takes place;[6] child labour grows enormously;[7] and there are new extensions of the economic oppression of women.[8] On the other hand, orchestrating these changes are transnational classes and strata that own, manage, and administer global corporate interests and that oversee the supranational "enabling framework."

Given these developments, globalization can be seen as the triumph of capitalism, that is, as the ascendancy of economics over politics, of corporate demands over public policy, of the private over the public interest, of the transnational corporation and its global framework over the national state. It represents the approaching completion of the capitalization of the world. The triumph is embodied in and affirmed by global agencies whose sole function is the facilitation of global conditions for capital accumulation, without formal political access and only limited representation by certain interests. It is not the occlusion of national politics but the subordination of national interests and sovereignty to those of the transnational corporation and its supranational framework.[9]

This rise of the transnational economy, misunderstood by those preferring to argue for an international version, points to a significant change in the relation between civil society and the state: the rise of the polarity of civil society and state at the global level. This development makes for two such separations, the first at the national level and the other now unfolding and clarifying at the global level. To understand the new possibilities and problems of resistance to the many aspects of globalization, we need to grasp what is taking place from the perspective of the concept of civil society and the state.[10]

What many attempts to define the concept of civil society miss is that it does not stand alone. The concept, like its empirical referent, the sphere of private interests, appears only as one side in a relation to the state, the sphere of "the general." The two comprise the "resolved" components of society: the private and the public, the particular and the general, the parts and the whole. They represent the chief distinguishing characteristic of society become political as in the modern liberal-democratic nation-state.

In national political systems, the state possesses a monopoly over the general affairs, albeit in the form of law, administrative apparatus, the military, state corporations, and so on. Its polar opposite is civil society, the sphere of particular interests. Here individuals, groups, trade unions, churches, and, importantly, private corporations, among others, pursue their specific interests and advantages, while the formal relation of civil society to the state is limited to the political rights accorded to individuals. This divide between general and particular affairs allows prevailing property relations to be maintained while certain organized parts of civil society (such as trade unions) can exact concessions from the state in the form of countervailing property relations (such as trade union rights, employment standards, and social rights). Political reforms or concessions are all that can be hoped for within this system.

Globalization opens a new transnational divide between general and particular affairs; but at this level the state and civil society have a different content. On the one side, supranational quasi-governmental organizations (and the U.S. state) codify, oversee, and enforce the corporate property relations that define the global economy. On the other side, global civil society is composed mainly of TNCs and national states and, to a lesser extent, international NGOs, including certain religious and environmental organizations; but it does not include the world's subordinate classes, which are restricted to national civil societies. We are faced, then, with the development of a two-tiered contradiction between the state and civil society.

At the national level, the subordinate classes have some, albeit limited, access to and influence over the state by means of the vote, political parties, trade unions, consumer groups, and in general, the mechanisms of liberal democracy. At the global level, however, there are no such representative mechanisms; there the subordinate classes have little institutional presence. Only national states, representing declining national interests (that is, corporate interests), and TNCs have any significant relation to power in this growing global matrix of governing structures. In effect, the world's peoples are disenfranchised in the global arena; there is no formal, institutional, legitimate mechanism for their representation.

Levels of State and Civil Society

National

State
- national states

Mediation
- political parties
- mass media
- citizenship

Civil Society
- corporations
- TUs, religious and
  other groups
- citizens

Global

State
- supranational agencies/IGOs/UN
- U.S. state

Mediation
- size and significance of
  accumulated capital
- national states
- military

Civil Society
- national states & IGOs
- TNCs, NGOs, etc.

The current two-tiered divide between civil society and state has created a series of new contradictions. Among these are the contradictions between the world's subordinate classes, progressive groups and individuals, *and* the global governance framework for capital, *and* their now-compromised national states, *and* the TNCs. Others have arisen between national states *and* the agencies of the global regulatory framework, *and* the TNCs. And yet others now exist between the world's peoples and TNC environmental destruction; between the subordinate classes of the rich and poor nations; and between the organized working classes of the industrial nations and the largely unorganized in the Third World. There is, moreover, the contradiction between political rights at the national level and economic rights at the global. The world is far from what it was prior to the early 1970s.

All this has to be taken into account in the consideration of contemporary resistance and the question of alternatives. When the main object of resistance is no longer only a national state and bourgeoisie, but increasingly the TNC and the global "state," strictly national strategies contain an implicit defect: they are the application of, or search for, old solutions to qualitatively new problems. To fight for the restoration of the sovereignty of a nation-state makes little sense given that the nation-state was the political shell and economic market for national capital. To try to reassert or rebuild the Keynesian welfare state at the national level, furthermore, has to address the problem of a growing global labour market, declining incomes and increasing economic disparities, a dissolving national framework, and TNC pressure to privatize and deregulate. To fight for socialism in this context, moreover, means to fight for it in one country; and the theoretical and practical arguments against this are well known and more pertinent than ever today. As long as the proposed alternatives are steeped in the conceptual frameworks and solutions belonging to previous eras, there can be no successful counterforce, organizational or ideational, to the present conditions.

None of this is in any way an argument against resistance or the development of alternatives. The fact of the "new reality" does not imply that there must be compliance or subordination to its demands. Numerous labour strikes, demonstrations, armed resistance, environmental protests, and many other actions around the world (even the Internet-based resistance to the Multilateral Agreement on Investment)[11] aimed at TNCs and their policies in national guise are all cases in point. The coming of globalization points to the need to reassess the nature of countervailing demands and the means to achieve them in a world that bears little resemblance to what existed even before 1970. New corporate forms, profound changes in class structure accompanying the new technology, and the new global enabling framework means that resistance of all sorts needs to be rethought and reorganized.

It can no longer be assumed that the national, regional, or local state can act independently of global capital, that the state can stand on its own in the face of TNCs or continue to represent national or local capital. The state can be a "site of resistance," but its intrinsic relation to capital cannot be overlooked. Where national resistance, alternatives, or threats have arisen they have met certain similar fates: for example, in Chile, Nicaragua, Libya, Iraq, Yugoslavia, and East Timor. The differences between these cases are not the issue; the point is that each in its own way constituted a national threat to the operations of global capital.[12]

The challenge for subordinate interests and progressive organizations and individuals is, first, to understand the nature of contemporary exploitation and the new contradictions entailed. Second, they must build global mechanisms for representation and expression to overcome their national definition and restriction. It follows that they must also clarify the global demands they are making and will make, and demand a voice in global governance while critically analysing its limits and those of national government.[13]

All the struggles that face the subordinate classes and peoples of the world increasingly find their origins in a system of production and distribution that is global, more and more dependent on science and technology, and situated within the complexity of new emerging contra-dictions.[14] Effective resistance can only be mounted on the basis of an understanding of these current global changes. There can be no answers to problems that are not properly posed or comprehended.

Notes

Introduction

1. S. Edwards and A.C. Edwards, *Monetarism and Liberalization: The Chilean Experiment* (Chicago: University of Chicago Press, 1991); and J.S. Valenzuela and A. Valenzuela, eds., *Military Rule in Chile* (Baltimore: Johns Hopkins University Press, 1986).

   See also P.E. Sigmund, "Chile: Privatization, Reprivatization, Hyperprivatization," in *The Political Economy of Public Sector Reform and Privatization*, ed. E.N. Suleiman and J. Waterbury (Boulder, Col.: Westview Press, 1990). For an analysis of why the coup, see J. Petras and M. Morley, *The United States and Chile: Imperialism and the Overthrow of the Allende Government* (New York: Monthly Review Press, 1975); and J. Petras, "The New Class Basis of Chilean Politics," *New Left Review*, 172 (November/December 1988). For an excellent examination of Unidad Popular, see B. Stallings, *Class Conflict and Economic Development in Chile, 1958-1973* (Stanford, Cal.: Stanford University Press, 1978).

2. There are many articles reviewing these about-faces; see, for example, G. Ross and T. Daley, "The Wilting of the Rose: The French Socialist Experiment," *Socialist Review*, 87/88, 16,3&4 (1986); and several of the articles in *The Socialist Register 1985/86: Social Democracy and After*, ed. R. Miliband et al. (London: Merlin Press, 1986); and H. Overbeek, ed., *Restructuring Hegemony in the Global Political Economy* (London: Routledge, 1993).

3. "There is much greater awareness today of the way that the political and military fortunes of states, empires, and coalitions have, through the centuries, undulated up and down according to their relative economic positions." N. Colchester and D. Buchan, *Europower* (New York: The Economist Books, 1992), p.12.

I Social Reform and Capitalism

1. R. Mishra, *The Welfare State in Crisis* (Brighton, Eng.: Wheatsheaf Books, 1984); K. Banting, "The Welfare State and Inequality in the 1980's," *Canadian Review of Sociology and Anthropology*, 24,3 (1987); and Suleiman and Waterbury, *Political Economy*. For a review of the policies in Britain, see C. Veljanovski, *Selling the State* (London: Weidenfeld and Nicolson, 1988).

2. V. Navarro, "The 1980 and 1984 U.S. Elections and the New Deal: An Alternative Interpretation," in *Socialist Register 1985/86*, ed. Miliband et al. See also I. Gough, L. Doyal, et al., "Socialism, Democracy and Human Needs," in *The Social Economy and the Democratic State*, ed. P. Alcock et al. (London: Lawrence and Wishart, 1989), p.247; R. Mishra, *The Welfare State in Capitalist Society* (Toronto: University of Toronto Press, 1990), chap. 2; and G. Therborn and J. Roebroek, "The Irreversible Welfare State," *International Journal of Health Services*, 16,3 (1986). The periodical *Marxism Today* (1977-92) was a good example of the promulgation by the "left" of ideas critical of the welfare state. Navarro, "1980 and 1984 U.S. Elections," contains other references to the left critique.

   In light of this popular support for the welfare state, the notion that the new right will not "destroy the fabric of welfare institutions" or make only "marginal encroachments and impairments" has been put forward. It is difficult to agree with these somewhat "optimistic" views. In the first place, the new right is not merely the assertion of political ideas but the reflection of major economic and political changes beyond the control of national governments. Second, the strategies of privatization and gradual degradation of services have managed to circumvent popular support. Third, the possibility of mobilizing the public in defence of social reform is increasingly becoming circumscribed. For such optimism, see G. Therborn, "The Prospects of Labour and the Transformation of Advanced Capitalism," *New Left Review*, 145 (1984), p.25; and P. Ruggles and M. O'Higgins, "Retrenchment and the New Right: A Comparative Analysis of the Impacts of the Thatcher and Reagan Administrations," in *Stagnation and Renewal in Social Policy*, ed. M. Rein et al. (New York: M.E. Sharpe, 1987), p.188.

Claus Offe offers a "pessimistic" view, suggesting that a citizenry will begin to accept the rationale for retrenchment; as he puts it: "The neoconservative denunciations of the welfare state are likely to fall on fertile ground." In "Democracy Against the Welfare State," *Political Theory*, 15,4 (1987), p.535. On the contrary, the dismantling of the welfare state has had to proceed very slowly and surreptitiously because of protests emanating from several different classes and strata. To the degree that there is public acceptance, it is likely due to the absence of critical analysis and political alternatives, or perhaps located in select strata.

3. See, for example, K. de Schweinitz, *England's Road to Social Security* (New York: A.S. Barnes and Co., 1961); P. Berton, *The Great Depression, 1929-1939* (Toronto: McClelland and Stewart, 1990); J. Kuczynski, *A Short History of Labour Conditions under Industrial Capitalism in the United States of America, 1789-1946* (London: Muller [1946], 1973); J. Kuczynski, *A Short History of Labour Conditions under Industrial Capitalism in Great Britain and the Empire, 1750-1944* (London: Muller, 1946).

4. See N. Costello, J. Michie, and S. Milne, *Beyond the Casino Economy* (London: Verso, 1989), p.2; and G. Therborn, *Why Some People Are More Unemployed Than Others* (London: Verso, 1986).

5. See W. Bello and S. Rosenfeld, "High-Speed Industrialization and Environmental Destruction in Taiwan," *The Ecologist*, 20,4 (July/August, 1990); M. Beresford and L. Fraser, "Political Economy of the Environment in Vietnam," *Journal of Contemporary Asia*, 22,1 (1992).

6. The strata referred to here are broader than what is usually contained in the concept of "labour aristocracy." See E.J. Hobsbawm, "The Labour Aristocracy in Nineteenth-century Britain," in his *Labouring Men* (London: Weidenfeld and Nicolson, 1964); R. Harrison, *Before the Socialists* (London: Routledge and Kegan Paul, 1965), chap. 1.

   The degree and kind of fragmentation of union structure (that is, craft/industrial, socialist/communist, white/blue collar, and gender and racial divisions) have had notable dampening effects on the extent of social reform achieved.

7. For a brief review of the explanations offered for working-class reformism, see N. Kirk, *The Growth of Working Class Reformism in Mid-Victorian England* (London: Croom Helm, 1985).

8. The decades-long suppression of the labour movement in the United States is undoubtedly a significant factor in accounting for the very limited social reforms that characterize U.S. society. For a review of the extent of this suppression, see P.C. Sexton, *The War on Labor and the Left* (Boulder, Col.: Westview Press, 1991). By the same token, the suppression of working-class organizations in the now-disintegrated U.S.S.R. helps to explain the poverty of its workplace and environmental standards.

9. It is reported that "after the Paris Commune, [Bismarck] wrote to the Kaiser urging that steps should be taken to prevent conditions deteriorating to such an extent that revolution and unrest might endanger the nation." J. Tampke, "Bismarck's Social Legislation: A Genuine Breakthrough?" in *The Emergence of the Welfare State in Britain and Germany, 1850-1950*, ed. W.J. Mommsen (London: Croom Helm, 1981), p.74.

   Bismarck had a clear awareness of the threat posed by the working class to the capitalist state – a threat that arose, he said, from "the insecurity of their very existence." D. Zollner, "Germany," in *The Evolution of Social Insurance, 1881-1981*, ed. P.A. Kohler and H.F. Zacker (London: Pinter, 1982), p.15.

   Also: "Elite fear of social conflict, and ultimately revolution, was the catalyst in explaining social policy making in interwar Britain." P. Whitely, "Public Opinion and the Demand for Social Welfare in Britain," *Journal of Social Policy*, 10,4 (1981), p.455. See also J.R. Hay, "The British Business Community, Social Insurance and the German Example," in *Emergence of the Welfare State*, ed. Mommsen, p.127.

10. The "threat" of these "socialist" countries was also to become the peacetime rationale for the military-industrial complex, as well as police repression of trade unions and various social and political movements. See the essays in *The Socialist Register 1984*, ed. R. Miliband et al. (London: Merlin Press, 1984); and A. Wolfe, *The Rise and Fall of the "Soviet Threat"* (Washington: The Institute for Policy Studies, 1979).

11. Unorganized, "spontaneous" uprisings with widespread consequences can precipitate reforms, but organized protest is the more threatening to the status quo. The "Great Society Reforms" in the United States, for instance, were introduced after ghetto riots or urban rebellions and widespread property destruction in that country. Extraparliamentary protest in the United States tends to be "spontaneous" because of the relative weakness of trade unions, other social movements, and left-of-centre political parties.

12. Such a case is made for turn-of-the-century America in J. Weinstein's *The Corporate Ideal in the Liberal State: 1900-1918* (Boston: Beacon Press, 1968).

13. Tampke, "Bismarck's Social Legislation," pp.76-81; R. Lubove, *The Struggle for Social Security, 1900-1935* (Pittsburgh: University of Pittsburgh Press, 1986), p.57. The context of industry-inspired reform, however, was always the threat or reality of class conflict.

14. "Social wage" refers to state-sponsored partial socialization of income from wages and salaries by means of premiums, taxes, and deferred income; the funds so created are used for redistribution from one strata to another through transfers such as pensions, income supplements, or social insurance schemes. The essence of the social wage was captured in the earlier phrase "averaging mechanisms." See P. Flora and A.J. Heidenheimer, "The Historical Core and Changing Boundaries of the Welfare State," in *The Development of the Welfare State in Europe and America*, ed. P. Flora and A.J. Heidenheimer (New Brunswick, N.J.: Transaction Books, 1984), pp.18-19. See also Bob Russell, "The Politics of Labour Force Reproduction: Funding Canada's Social Wage," *Studies in Political Economy*, 14 (1984).

15. For a rigorously argued and empirically supported analysis of how many of these elements produced aspects of the U.S. welfare state, and for an excellent countercritique of his critics, see G.W. Domhoff, *The Power Elite and the State* (New York: Aldine De Gruyter, 1990).

16. A useful but more narrow definition can be found in A. Briggs, "The Welfare State in Historical Perspective," in *European Journal of Sociology*, 2 (1961), p.228. Other discussions of the definition can be found in: G. Esping-Anderson, "The Three Political Economies of the Welfare State," *Canadian Review of Sociology and Anthropology*, 26, 1 (1989); J. Quadagno, "Theories of the Welfare State," *American Review of Sociology*, 13 (1987); J. Carrier and I. Kendall, "Categories, Categorizations and the Political Economy of Welfare," *Journal of Social Policy*, 15,3 (1986); I. Gough, *The Political Economy of the Welfare State* (London: Macmillan, 1979); and R.M. Titmuss, *Essays on "The Welfare State"* (London: Allen and Unwin, 1958).

17. A.O. Hirschman, "How Keynes Was Spread from America," *Challenge*, November/ December 1988.

18. Keynes's letter is quoted in D. Winch, *Economics and Policy* (London: Hodder and Stoughton, 1969), p.221; for the Winch quote see p.349. A similar argument is made by K. Schott, "The Rise of Keynesian Economics: Britain 1940-64," *Economy and Society*, 11,3 (1982).

19. See F. Harbison, "Collective Bargaining and American Capitalism," in *Industrial Conflict*, ed. A. Kornhauser, R. Dubin, and A. Ross (New York: McGraw Hill, 1954).

20. For a short discussion, see Esping-Anderson, "Three Political Economies of the Welfare State."

21. See G. Esping-Andersen, *Politics against Markets: The Social Democratic Road to Power* (Princeton, N.J.: University of Princeton Press, 1985). This positive case for the expansion of social democracy has not stood up in the face of the actual road taken by Scandinavian social-democratic parties in the late 1980s and early 1990s.

22. W. Muller and C. Neususs, "The Illusion of State Socialism and the Contradiction between Wage Labor and Capital," *Telos*, 25 (Fall 1975), p.80.

23. V. Navarro, "The Limits of Legitimation and Fordism and the Possibility for Socialist Reforms," in *Rethinking Marxism*, 4,2 (Summer 1991), pp.36-37; Rosa Luxemburg was opposed not to reforms but to *reformism* because it made social reforms not the means of class struggle but "the final aim." See her *Reform or Revolution* (New York: Pathfinder Press, 1970).

24. K. Chorley, *Armies and the Art of Revolution* (Boston: Beacon Press, 1973).

25. Weinstein, *Corporate Ideal in the Liberal State*; H.-P. Ullman, "German Industry and Bismarck's Social Security System," in *Emergence of the Welfare State*, ed. Mommsen.

II The Socialism of Social Democracy

1. This is not to suggest "functional prerequisites," but rather such constraints and social pressures as a restricted labour market, a partially organized working class, national political and economic boundaries, nationally based capital, as well as the fiscal foundation in the "social wage."

2. Such was the sentiment of the social-democratic Fabians as asserted by Sidney Webb in 1890. Cited in L. Panitch, "The Impasse of Social Democratic Politics," in *Socialist Register 1985/86*, ed. Miliband et al., p.50.

    Half a century later Friedrich Hayek reasserted the point before launching into his critique of socialism: "If it is no longer fashionable to emphasize that 'We are all socialists now,' this is so merely because the fact is too obvious." F.A. Hayek, *The Road to Serfdom* (London: George Routledge and Sons, 1945), p.3. After 1945 the same sentiment in a new guise became "We are all Keynesians now." By the 1970s the phrase had become "We are all post-Keynesians now," signifying the end of state intervention as acceptable economic theory or practice. A Japanese comment on the 1994 electoral victory of the Socialist Party of Japan to power went: "There are no socialists; we are all capitalists now."

3. Hirschman, "How Keynes Was Spread from America."

4. Social democracy and the KWS are more the product of truncated class conflict in the era of expanding national capital than the expression of some abstract "socialist project." This view and the following arguments are considerably different from those of A. Przeworski, *Capitalism and Social Democracy* (Cambridge: Cambridge University Press, 1985); Esping-Anderson, *Politics against Markets*; and W. Korpi, *The Working Class in Welfare Capitalism* (London: Routledge, 1978). These authors share the assumption that social democracy is in essence socialist with the goal of socialized property and workers' control, rather than a form of liberalism with a social conscience. The first sees reform and compromise as judicious political choices under adverse conditions rather than inherent political limits to a fractured, heterogeneous working class; while the second sees reform in the form of social citizenship as the crucial step to a genuine economic transformation. They all see the parliamentary road, reform, and class compromise as merely strategic choices in light of the persistent of capitalism, rather than as the sole means and the final goal of social democracy.

5. Even the most advanced welfare state has been compatible with, indeed necessary to, the development of national capital. See J. Israel, "Swedish Socialism and Big Business," *Acta Sociologica*, 21,4 (1978).

6. U.S. "liberalism" is akin to social democracy in the rest of the world and raises the same vision of the welfare state. The Democratic Party is clearly associated with "social security" in the United States, but its lameness as a party of reform is closely linked to the decades-long war on the labour movement in that country. See M. Davis, "The Barren Marriage of American Labour and the Democratic Party," *New Left Review*, 124 (1980); and Sexton, *War on Labor and the Left*.

7. In most industrial nations this definition would include at least four-fifths of the population; it also indicates their relation to the means of production as non-owners; but it implies nothing about consciousness, a phenomenon often more stratified than the class itself.

8. In the sphere of circulation we would include the commercial, financial, and trade sectors of the economy, the "white-collar" and managerial strata in the sphere of production, and the

government sector. For a good discussion of Marx's position on these developments, see J.F. Becker, *Marxian Political Economy* (Cambridge: Cambridge University Press, 1977), chap. 9.

9. Marx gives the name "industrial reserve army" to this "surplus population," and the term refers in part to the growing surfeit of workers made redundant by the increasing productivity of industrial processes. See K. Marx, *Capital*, vol. 1 (New York: Vintage, 1977), chap. 25.

10. With varying importance, the bases of some of the differences are: status, income, ethnicity, religion, region, seniority, gender, race, age, workplace hierarchies, public vs. private employment, productive vs. unproductive sectors, union vs. non-union, manual vs. non-manual.

11. Many texts review these developments. See, for example, G. Carchedi, *The Economic Definition of Social Classes* (London: Routledge and Kegan Paul, 1977); E.O. Wright, *Class, Crisis and the State* (London: Verso, 1978); and A. Collinicos and C. Harmon, *The Changing Working Class* (London: Bookmarks, 1987).

12. The term "contradictory locations" was first used by Wright in *Class, Crisis and the State*, pp.61-62, and in *Class Structure and Income Determination* (New York: Academic Press, 1979). Here, it signifies the existence of positions within the highly stratified working class, which have attached to them interests resting on the hierarchies and differences arising from the division of labour. These interests have an "immediacy" that the essential class interests do not, as long as the economy continues to expand and the hierarchies and differences promise to remain. Many of these "locations" lose their "interest immediacy" once the continued expansion comes into question and the hierarchies begin to be telescoped. Nevertheless, these "contradictory locations" go some way to explaining the lack of revolutionary sentiment in a working class and wide support for social democracy.

For the debate on this issue and others concerning Wright's analysis of class, see E.O. Wright et al., *The Debate on Classes* (London: Verso, 1989).

13. Several studies, countering accepted wisdom, have made this point about the most advanced social-democratic state, Sweden. See, for example, S. Steinmo, "Social Democracy vs Socialism: Goal Adaptation in Social Democratic Sweden," *Politics and Society*, 16,4 (1988); P. Swenson, "Bringing Capital Back In, Or Social Democracy Reconsidered," *World Politics*, 43 (July 1991).

14. While there are many who would agree with this statement, most of the explanations see the "passing" of social democracy as the product of "intellectual problems" or "changing values" within social democracy, "excessive demands" from citizens or the trade unions, "inertia claims of public spending," or the recession of the 1970s, and so on. I have not seen another argument making the decline a product of a changing reality that rendered the "social-democratic paradigm" an anachronism. For a short review of some of these explanations, see "Introduction," *The Future of Social Democracy*, ed. W.E. Paterson and A.H. Thomas (Oxford: Clarendon Press, 1986).

15. P. Gay, *The Dilemma of Democratic Socialism* (New York: Collier Books, 1962), p.205; E. Bernstein, *Evolutionary Socialism* (New York: Schocken Books, 1961).

16. The Marxist or communist parties in general represented manual or production workers; the social-democratic parties represented the unproductive strata, such as scientific and technocratic workers, quasi-professionals, and public employees.

17. The work of John Stuart Mill was an important inspiration for Anglo-American social democrats or "liberals," but he was strongly influenced by early French socialists (Saint-Simonians among others), as was Ferdinand Lassalle, a major influence in German social democracy. Although the pluralist vision misrepresents essential class interests, the party policies were the political reflection of real, albeit immediate, interests and consciousness.

The confusion of immediate interests for essential interests allowed R. Dahrendorf and D. Bell, in the first assessments of the post-World War II era, to make classes into "conflict groups," to write off the revolutionary potential of the working class, and to find the contradictions of capitalism resolved in reforms. See R. Dahrendorf, *Class and Class Conflict in Industrial Society* (Stanford, Cal.: Stanford University Press, 1959); D. Bell, *The End of Ideology* (New York: Collier, 1962).

18. For a good review of the role of social democracy as an "agency of social control *over* the working class," (p.116) and as a contributor "to the decline in class politics and working class identity," see L. Panitch, *Working Class Politics in Crisis* (London: Verso, 1986).

19. See B. Sims, *Workers of the World Undermined: American Labor's Role in U.S. Foreign Policy* (Boston: South End Press, 1992); R. Radosh, *American Labor and United States Foreign Policy* (New York: Random House, 1969); G. Morris, *CIA and American Labor* (New York: International Publishers, 1967); P. Agee and L. Wolf, eds., *Dirty Work: The CIA in Western Europe* (London: Zed Press, 1981); and J. Scott, *Yankee Unions, Go Home!* (Vancouver: New Star, 1978).

20. Bernstein, *Evolutionary Socialism*, pp.141-45.

21. There are at least three points here: 1) there is in this notion no critical appreciation of the meaning of representation in the present system; 2) the examples of incongruity between new legislation and the general will are too numerous to permit acceptance of the idea that electoral success empowers government and enables the fulfilment of a popular mandate; and 3) the idea that the electoral mandate is sufficient to introduce radical reforms without regard to the "realities" of the economy and class structure has been referred to as the "reformist fallacy," or less politely as "parliamentary cretinism."

22. The extraparliamentary exercise of power by capital is inherent in the nature of the system; that is, the rights of private property are invested with enormous powers in their domains of employment, disposition of the products, location, and investment. Given this, "extraparliamentary" activity is almost always construed as working-class or social-movement activity, not the everyday activity of capital.

23. There are many examples worldwide of social democracy helping to put an end to workers' struggles, especially when parliamentary supremacy was threatened. A particularly good example was the "Solidarity" movement in British Columbia in 1983. See B. Palmer, *The Rise and Fall of an Opposition in British Columbia* (Vancouver: New Star, 1987).

24. For these reasons, among others, social-democratic parties have been anti-Marxist and anti-communist since the late nineteenth century.

25. There is little if any sense of the relative dependency of the political sphere on the economic, the nature of the parliamentary executive as unaccountable, or the meaning of elections or representation.

26. N. Chomsky, *Deterring Democracy* (New York: Hill and Wang [1991], 1992).

27. E.S. Herman and F. Brodhead, *Demonstration Elections: U.S.-Staged Elections in the Dominican Republic, Vietnam, and El Salvador* (Boston: South End Press, 1984).

28. C. Payer, *The World Bank* (New York: Monthly Review Press, 1982); C. Payer, *The Debt Trap* (Harmondsworth, Eng.: Penguin, 1974); N. Ba-Nikongo, ed., *Debt and Development in the Third World: Trends and Strategies* (Washington: Institute for Afro-American Scholarship, 1991).

In 1976 Britain accepted a set of monetarist policies as the condition of an IMF loan. As one commentator described it: "International capitalist discipline had been reimposed upon the British Labour government, which would henceforth recognize the "realities" of capitalism." H. Overbeek, *Global Capitalism and National Decline: The Thatcher Decade in Perspective* (London: Unwin Hyman, 1990), p.172.

Even when countries are not asking for financial aid, the IMF apparently gives unsolicited advice: "The International Monetary Fund secretly urged the Canadian government this year to freeze public servants' wages, slash unemployment insurance in poor regions and stop protecting inefficient farmers, confidential documents . . . reveal. In [the] report . . . the UN agency also urged Ottawa to axe a staggering $6 billion from next year's projected $30.5 billion deficit." *The Vancouver Sun*, November 1991.

29. An international committee drawn from business, government, academia, the media, and labour, founded in 1973 by David Rockefeller among others, to bring together these representatives from Western Europe, Japan, and North America in order to explore and find ways to defend the common interests of the industrial nations, as well as "to mold public opinion and construct a framework for international stability in the coming decades."

H. Sklar, "Trilateralism: Managing Dependence and Democracy," in *Trilateralism*, ed. H. Sklar (Montreal: Black Rose, 1980), p.2.

30. Bernstein, *Evolutionary Socialism*, pp.148-55.

31. J.K. Galbraith, *The New Industrial State* (New York: Signet, 1970). For a critical review at the time of publication, see R. Miliband, "Professor Galbraith and American Capitalism," in *The Socialist Register 1968*, ed. R. Miliband and J. Saville (New York, 1968).

32. Keynesian economics keeps the extremes of the business cycles at bay; sociology provides the conceptual "grasp" of alienated society as alienated society; and social welfare follows with palliatives for the individual casualties of the system.

33. A. Shonfield, *Modern Capitalism: The Changing Balance of Public and Private Power* (London [1965], 1977). However excellent the book is on the level of the empirical, it is very limited in its grasp of the nature of the links between the development of capital and the rise of the public sector and the welfare state.

34. For a review of theories on the expansion of the public sector, see D.R. Cameron, "The Expansion of the Public Economy: A Comparative Analysis," in *The American Political Science Review*, 72 (1978); D. Tarschys, "The Growth of Public Expenditure: Nine Modes of Explanation," *Scandinavian Political Studies*, 10 (1975); and R.M. Bird, "Wagner's 'Law' of Expanding State Activity," *Public Finance*, 26,1 (1971).

35. For a short review of some examples of capitalist planning in the West, see P. Devine, *Democracy and Economic Planning* (Oxford: Polity Press, 1988), chap. 2.

36. The wide acceptance of Keynesian policies after World War II strengthened the *political view* of the capitalist state, which held that the state was in command, that it determined the direction of the economic activity, and that it could influence in significant ways the business cycles of capitalism.

37. Galbraith, *New Industrial State*, p.37. There is a wealth of material on "corporate strategic planning" – all of which contradicts in significant ways the neo-classical model of the firm as "a meeting place for market forces." For an early review of corporate planning, see J.T. Dunlop and N.P. Fedorenko, eds., *Planning and Markets: Modern Trends in Various Economic Systems* (New York: McGraw-Hill, 1969).

38. J.R. Munkirs, *The Transformation of American Capitalism: From Competitive Market Structures to Centralized Private Sector Planning* (New York: M.E. Sharpe, 1985), presents a thorough empirical case for the existence of "centralized private sector planning." This is not to be confused, of course, with democratic planning with a social purpose.

39. For an analysis of the "the premier example of modern capitalist planning," see S. Cohen, *Modern Capitalist Planning: The French Model* (Berkeley: University of California Press, 1977); and P.G. Cerny and M.A. Schain, eds., *French Politics and Public Policy* (London: Methuen, 1980).

40. To interpret Marx on the law of value: the exchange of commodities is regulated by the amount of value embedded in them; this value is determined by the socially necessary labour time required to produce the commodity; this socially necessary labour time is regulated by supply and demand in the market, by the struggle between working and capitalist classes, and by the level of development of productive forces. In short, the social distribution of productive resources (labour and capital) in a capitalist society is determined by forces outside the choices and decisions of individual capitalists or governments.

III The Impact of Social Democracy and the Welfare State on Social Inequality

1. F. Kraus, "The Historical Development of Income Inequality in Western Europe and the United States," in *Development of Welfare States*, ed. Flora and Heidenheimer; R. Robinson and D. Quinlan, "The World Economy and the Distribution of Income within States: A Cross-National Study," *American Sociological Review*, 41 (1976); M. Sawyer, "Income Distribution in OECD Countries," *OECD Economic Outlook*, Occasional Studies, July 1976.

2. J.D. Smith, "Recent Trends in the Distribution of Wealth: Data, Research, Problems and Prospects," in *International Comparisons of the Distribution of Household Wealth*, ed. E.N

Wolff (New York: Oxford University Press, 1987); M.L. Oliver and T.M. Shapiro, "Wealth of a Nation: At Least One Third of Households Are Asset-Poor," *The American Journal of Economics and Sociology*, 49 (April 1990).

3. A.L. Maney, *Still Hungry after All These Years: Food Assistance Policy from Kennedy to Reagan* (New York: Greenwood Press, 1989). See also L. Mishel and D. Frankel, *The State of Working America, 1990-91* (Armonk, N.Y.: M.E. Sharpe, 1991).

4. J. Kozol, *Illiterate America* (New York: Doubleday, 1985).

5. V. Navarro, *Medicine under Capitalism* (New York: 1976), p.86. There is, for example, the resurgence of malaria, cholera, TB, leprosy, among others; and the continuous growth of cancer and aids. "The World Health Organization recently declared the disease tuberculosis a global emergency. . . . It warned that TB will claim more than 30 million lives in the next decade unless immediate action is taken to curb its spread." *The Guardian* (London), May 4, 1993.

6. J.M. Maravall, "The Limits of Reformism: Parliamentary Socialism and the Marxist Theory of the State," *British Journal of Sociology*, 30,3 (1979), pp.274, 277.

7. R.W. Jackman, "Political Democracy and Social Equality: A Comparative Analysis," *American Sociological Review*, 39 (1974). Surveying the relation between political democracy and social equality, Jackman concluded that the former "exerted no significant effect" on the latter.

   C. Hewitt, "The Effect of Political Democracy and Social Democracy on Equality in Industrial Societies: A Cross-National Comparison," *American Sociological Review*, 42 (1977). While the author suggests that social democracy "appear[s] to have reduced inequality in industrial societies," he concludes that such findings must remain "very tentative."

   M. O'Higgins, "Inequality, Redistribution and Recession: The British Experience, 1976-1982," *Journal of Social Policy*, 14,3 (1985). The "redistributive impact of social welfare spending . . . has not brought about greater overall equality during the period studied, but it has combated and significantly modified the effects of pressures towards greater increased inequality" (p.303).

   The evidence more clearly suggests a positive link between greater economic development, as the independent variable, and the existence of social-democratic parties, the rise of the welfare state, and the decline of economic inequality, as dependent variables. See S. Kuznets, "Economic Growth and Economic Inequality," *American Economic Review*, 45 (1955); I. Adelman and C.T. Morris, *Economic Growth and Social Equity in Developing Countries* (Stanford, Cal.: Stanford University Press, 1973); H. Wilensky, *The Welfare State and Equality*, 1975.

8. N. Ginsburg, *Class, Capital and Social Policy* (London: Macmillan, 1979), chap. 4.

9. B. Hobson, "No Exit, No Voice: Women's Economic Dependency and the Welfare State," *Acta Sociologica*, 33 (1990), p.246. See also D. Pearce, "Welfare Is Not *for* Women: Why the War on Poverty Cannot Conquer the Feminization of Poverty," in *Women, the State, and Welfare*, ed. L. Gordon (Madison: University of Wisconsin Press, 1990).

10. These characteristics amount to forms of inhumanity and create the context for much abuse. The same point can be made about the old and the disabled.

11. There are, however, policies in which income is redistributed from capital to labour (to wit, rent controls), but this is a limited example and far from the intent or the operative consequences of the welfare state.

12. Taxes on profits, too, are "redistributed," through differential tax rates on different sectors of the economy, and by negative means, that is, by allowances and concessions to some sectors, industries, or particular corporations. Here again the redistribution is usually upward, from the smallest to the largest.

13. Therborn, "Prospects of Labour," p.184.

14. B. Russell, "The Politics of Labour-Force Reproduction: Funding Canada's Social Wage, 1917-1946," *Studies in Political Economy*, 14 (1984); and E.A. Tonak, "The US Welfare State and the Working Class, 1952-1980," in *Review of Radical Political Economics*, 19,1 (1987).

15. S. Bowles and H. Gintis, "The Crisis of Liberal Democratic Capitalism: The Case of United States," *Politics and Society*, 11,1 (1982).

16. A. Shaikh and E. Tonak, "The Welfare State and the Myth of the Social Wage," in *The Imperiled Economy*, ed. R. Cherry et al. (New York: URPE, 1987), pp.185-87.

17. On "social citizenship," see T.H. Marshall, "Citizenship and Social Class," in his *Sociology at the Crossroads* (London: Heinemann, 1963).

18. See G. Esping-Andersen and W. Korpi, "Social Policy as Class Politics in Post-War Capitalism: Scandinavia, Austria and Germany," in *Order and Conflict in Contemporary Capitalism*, ed. J.H. Goldthorpe (New York: Oxford University Press, 1984); and N. Fraser and L. Gordon, "Contract versus Charity: Why Is There No Social Citizenship in the United States?" *Socialist Review*, 22 (1992).

19. D. Bell, "The Public Household – 'On Fiscal Sociology and the Liberal Society,' " *The Public Interest*, Fall 1974, p.39. Bell was not the only academic to voice apprehensiveness; see H. Wilensky, *The "New" Corporatism: Centralization and the Welfare State* (London: Sage Publications, 1976), where he writes: "The revolution of expectations must be channelled and contained because mass demands for benefits and services are out-running the capacity of government to meet them" (p.9).

20. M. Crozier, S.P. Huntington, and J. Watanuki, *The Crisis of Democracy: Report on the Governability of Democracies to the Trilateral Commission* (New York: New York University Press, 1975). This study attempted to cover Japan, the United States, and Europe; a similar argument pertaining to Britain can be found in S. Brittan, *Economic Consequences of Democracy* (1977).

21. K.S. Templeton, ed., *The Politicization of Society* (Liberty Press, 1979).

22. For discussions of this point, see M. Rein, "The Social Structure of Institutions: Neither Public nor Private," and R. Rose, "Welfare: The Public/Private Mix," in *Privatization and the Welfare State*, ed. S.B. Kamerman and A.J. Kahn (Princeton, N.J.: Princeton University Press. 1989).

23. J. O'Connor, *The Fiscal Crisis of the State* (New York: St. Martin's Press, 1973), remains the best theoretical statement on the fiscal crisis. A series of more specific empirical studies can be found in R.E. Alcaly and D. Mermelstein, eds., *The Fiscal Crisis of American Cities* (New York: Vintage, 1977). See also R.A. Musgrave, "Theories of Fiscal Crises: An Essay in Fiscal Sociology," in *The Economics of Taxation*, ed. H.J. Aaron and M.J. Boskin (Washington, D.C.: Brookings Institute, 1980).

24. The short reign of the New Democratic Party in British Columbia in the early 1970s and that of the Parti Québécois in Quebec in the late 1970s and early 1980s provide good examples of this dilemma faced by social-democratic parties. They are elected purporting to represent a spectrum of working-class interests, but given the nature of the system, fiscal crises, among other problems, are "resolved" on the backs of the working classes. The necessary "economies" are made at the expense of the very electoral base that brought them to power. Such dilemmas open social democracy to the charge of hypocrisy (quite correct in these cases) – a charge that conservative parties rarely have to confront – but more importantly usually end with a defeat at the polls. It is a defeat caused by the impossibility of representing working-class interests within the confines of the system in the face of economic difficulties or against the interests of capital.

25. C. Leman, *The Collapse of Welfare Reform: Political Institutions, Policy, and the Poor in Canada and the United States* (Cambridge, Mass.: The MIT Press, 1980). See also European Economic Community, *Report on Social Development* (Brussels, 1986), which states (pp.viii-1): "The trend in social security no longer involves the extension of coverage to new categories of beneficiaries or higher benefits. Austerity policies barely allow existing levels of protection to be maintained where they do not impose drastic cuts to social security budgets."

IV The Global Economy and the Decline of Social Reform

1. For a good comparative review of the retrenchment carried out in the late 1970s and early 1980s, much of it by social-democratic parties, see M.K. Brown, "Has the Welfare State Unraveled?" in *Remaking the Welfare State: Retrenchment and Social Policy in America and Europe*, ed. M.K. Brown (Philadelphia: Temple University Press, 1988), pp.6-12.

2. K. van der Pijl, "The International Level," in *The Capitalist Class: An International Study*, ed. T.B. Bottomore and R.J. Brym (Hemel Hempstead: Harvester Wheatsheaf, 1989), pp.246-52.
3. There are numerous studies of the Bretton Woods agreements. See R. Gilpin, *The Political Economy of International Relations* (Princeton, N.J.: Princeton University Press, 1987), pp.131ff.
4. W.R. Louis, *Imperialism at Bay: The Role of the U.S. in the Decolonization of the British Empire* (London: Oxford University Press, 1977).
5. Given U.S. economic ascendancy and concomitant sway over the UN, it followed that UN intervention in international disputes would be consistent with U.S. goals. The consistency should not be understated because there have been no UN peacekeeping operations that have not resulted in strategic advantages to the United States. Recognizing this point the U.S. United Nations Association stated baldly: "Each UN peacekeeping operation to date has ... been clearly in the United States' interest." *Controlling Conflicts in the 1970's* (New York, 1969), p.48. Other studies have concluded: "The main reason why the Americans have been the chief supporters of the peace-keeping functions is because each and every one of these fourteen UN operations has been a direct extension of the American national interest." J. Stoessinger, "The Payments Dispute," in *The Future of UN Peacekeeping*, ed. W. Woodside (Toronto, 1965), p.29. And another: "The US commitment to UN peacekeeping has been extensive not for altruistic reasons, but because these operations have served the national interest." A.M. Cox, *Prospects for Peacekeeping* (Washington, 1967), pp.9-10.
6. Following the Treaty of Rome, the OEEC was transformed into a broader organization, which was ultimately to embrace all the developed economies and others in its membership. From its inception in 1960, the Organization of Economic Co-operation and Development (OECD) was principally intended to facilitate and co-ordinate international economic growth and the liberalization of world trade.
7. R.S. Belous and R.S. Hartley, *The Growth of Regional Trading Blocs in the Global Economy*, NPA Report no. 243 (Washington, 1990). The present "two-tiered" systems of multilateral and regional trade policies would appear to be a stage in the transition from national economies to a world economy. For a comprehensive list and brief discussion of these attempts at regional economic integration, see H.R. Jacobson, *Networks of Interdependence: International Organization and the Global Political System* (New York: Alfred A. Knopf, 1979), pp.273-78.
8. Distinct from this dilemma for capital, the relative autonomy of political systems presents a similar contradiction in the political sphere. As economic integration leads to political integration, national political resistance has arisen, yet for the most part it has not formed a serious challenge to economic unions.
9. In addition the postwar period saw significant U.S. interference in European elections, political parties, government policies, and trade union movements. R. Radosh, *American Labor and United States Foreign Policy* (New York: Vintage, 1969).
10. To name some of the more obvious: radar, rocketry, jet propulsion, atomic energy, and numerous chemical and biological discoveries.
11. J.M. Cypher, "The Transnational Challenge to the Corporate State," *Journal of Economic Issues*, 13,2 (June 1979), p.514.
12. Ibid., p.515. Although most of this investment in production went to other industrial nations, a growing share found its way to the developing countries, whose rates of growth in the 1960s began to compare favourably with the advanced industrial nations. It led to what Samir Amin called "peripheral capitalism": the investment of industrial capital in lesser developed countries to create "world-market factories" producing for export. See S. Amin, *Accumulation on a World Scale* (New York: Monthly Review Press, 1974).
13. D. Gowland, *International Economics* (London: Croom Helm, 1983), pp.176, 181.
14. J. Hawley, "The Internationalization of Capital: Banks, Eurocurrency and the Instability of the World Monetary System," *Review of Radical Political Economics*, 11,4 (Winter 1979), pp.82-83; G.J. Cough (and V. Chick), *Transnational Banking and the World Economy* (Sydney, Australia: Transnational Corporations Research Project, 1979), p.31.
15. The 1987 agreement under the auspices of the Bank for International Settlements (BIS) to harmonize national standards was aimed at facilitating the global banking system. See T.M. Chuppe, H.R. Haworth, and R. Ramakrishnan, "Current Developments in Global

Banking and Securities Markets," in *Multinational Culture*, ed. C.R. Lehman and R.M. Moore (Westport, Conn.: Greenwood Press, 1992). For an earlier discussion of the nature of the regulation of multinational banking, see N. Coulbeck, *The Multinational Banking Industry* (London: Croom Helm, 1984), pp.79ff.

16. W.J. Feld and R.S. Jordon, eds., *International Organizations* (New York: Praeger, 1988), pp.269-70. The list of "concerns" over the activities of TNCs that were spelled out by the Group of 77 at the United Nations in the early 1970s is striking testimony to just how much sovereignty these corporations assumed in the face of national sovereignty.

17. There is a considerable amount of literature on the effects of internationalized capital on national economic policies. For some of the issues raised here, see M. Fukao and M. Hanazaki, "Tax Systems and the Allocation of Capital," *OECD Economic Studies*, 8 (Spring 1987).

18. It is curious that there remains considerable debate about the weakening of national power in the face of the growth of IGOs and INGOs, not to mention the fact that there is a certain consensus that the nation-state remains central and the IGOs subordinate. In this regard three points should be considered: 1) Although they are the political products of nation-states, the IGOs and INGOs – and their rapid growth and increasing political and economic prominence – represent the necessity for the harmonization or integration of all standards and regulations as the foundation of further trade liberalization. The degree to which such organizations co-ordinate and oversee such harmonization and integration is roughly the degree of abandonment of sovereignty. 2) Any individual state that wished to maintain independent national standards as its mark of sovereignty in opposition to global harmonization and interdependence would quickly discover the "price" of such sovereignty. 3) To the degree that the global economy becomes self-supporting and self-expanding, the sovereignty of all states, including the most powerful, becomes subordinate.

   For alternative views, see S. Strange, "Supranationals and the State," in *States in History*, ed. J.A. Hall (Oxford: Basil Blackwell, 1986).

19. Van der Pijl, "International Level." See also K. van der Pijl, *The Making of an Atlantic Ruling Class* (London: Verso, 1984); and S. Gill, *American Hegemony and the Trilateral Commission* (Cambridge: Cambridge University Press, 1990).

20. By 1973-74, iniquitous world trade relations had spawned a collective voice amongst former dependencies, colonies, and other Third World countries. Revealing a perhaps naive belief in the primacy of politics, these countries began to demand at the United Nations a "search for a New International Economic Order." It was to come, but not as they imagined. See L.A. Hoskins, *The New International Economic Order* (Washington: University Press of America, 1982), p.18. For a review of the debates and the role of the United Nations Conference on Trade and Development (UNCTAD), see R.L. Rothstein, *Global Bargaining* (Princeton, N.J.: Princeton University Press, 1979).

21. For an early reference to this point, see S. Rose, "Multinational Corporations in a Tough New World," *Fortune*, August 1973.

22. A. Mateland, *Multinational Corporations and the Control of Culture* (Brighton, Eng.: Harvester Press, 1979).

23. Crozier, Huntington, and Watanuki, *Crisis of Democracy*.

24. R.L. Rothstein, *Global Bargaining: UNCTAD and the Quest for a New International Economic Order* (Princeton, N.J.: Princeton University Press, 1979). The fate of the decolonized nations was sealed before they were to taste any national independence. The IMF and/or the World Bank were present at the outset, as was the UN with its promotion of free-trade zones and liberal democracy.

25. By 1970 the entire breadth of societal implications of computer applications was perceivable. See J. Martin and A.R.D. Norman, *The Computerized Society* (Harmondsworth, Eng.: Penguin Books [1970], 1973). In the 1970s the French government commissioned a study of these implications; see S. Nora and A. Minc, *The Computerization of Society* (Cambridge, Mass.: MIT Press [1978], 1980).

26. See B. Bluestone and B. Harrison, *The Great U-Turn* (New York: Basic Books, 1990).

27. Under Fordism the labour content of assembly operations ranged as high as 25 per cent, whereas with computer-aided processes it is now between 10 and 5 per cent and declining.

See K. Ohmae, *Triad Power: The Coming Shape of Global Competition* (New York: The Free Press, 1985), p.3.

28. G. van Liemt, "Economic Globalization: Labour Options and Business Strategies in High Labour Cost Countries," *International Labour Review*, 131,4-5 (1992).

29. Knowledge is first embodied in the worker, then in management (Taylorism) and scientists, and then in machines (computerization). These would correspond to the eras of petty commodity production, large-scale capitalist (especially Fordist) production, and now knowledge-based production. In this last stage lies in principle the technological supersession of the capitalist corporation and market.

30. J.P. Womack, D.T. Jones, and D. Roos, *The Machine That Changed the World* (New York: Macmillan, 1990); R. Kaplinsky, "Restructuring the Capitalist Labour Process: Implications for Administrative Reform," *IDS Bulletin*, 19,4 (October 1988); J. Henderson, *Globalization of High Technology Production* (London: Routledge, 1989); K. Hoffman and R. Kaplinsky, *Driving Force: The Global Restructuring of Technology, Labor and Investment in the Automobile and Components Sectors* (Boulder, Col.: Westview Press, 1987).

31. J. Rifkin, *The End of Work* (New York: Putnam, 1995); and S. Aronowitz and Wm. DiFazio, *The Jobless Future* (Minneapolis: University of Minnesota Press, 1994).

32. International Labour Organization (ILO), *The World Employment Situation: Trends and Prospects* (Geneva, 1994); ILO, *World Employment Report 1998-99* (Geneva, 1998). See also World Bank, *World Development Report 1995: Workers in an Integrating World* (Washington, D.C., 1995).

33. Wm. Davidow and M. Malone, *The Virtual Corporation: Structuring and Revitalizing the Corporation for the 21st Century* (New York: Harper, 1992).

34. K. Marx, *Grundrisse* (Harmondsworth, Eng.: Penguin, 1973), pp.705-6. The end of commodity production is *not* the end of the production of goods and services; it is the end of their commodity forms, their form as private property.

35. D. Harvey, *The Condition of Postmodernity* (Oxford: Basil Blackwell, 1989), pp.165-66.

36. Y. Hayuth, "Globalization of the World Economy: The Transportation Viewpoint," in *The World Economy and the Spatial Organization of Power*, ed. A. Shachar and S. Oberg (Aldershot, Eng.: Avebury, 1990).

37. G. van Liemt, ed., *Industry on the Move: Causes and Consequences of International Relocation in the Manufacturing Industry* (Geneva: International Labour Organization, 1992).

38. Gowland, *International Economics*, pp.180-81. For a concise review of developments in financial markets in the 1980s, see J.E. Spero, "Guiding Global Finance," in *International Economics and International Economic Policy*, ed. P. King (New York: McGraw-Hill, 1990).

39. R. Miles, *Capitalism and Unfree Labour: Anomaly or Necessity?* (London: Tavistock Publications, 1987), pp.145-55. See also S. Sassen, *The Mobility of Labor and Capital: A Study in International Investment and Labor Flow* (Cambridge: Cambridge University Press, 1988).

40. For a good review of the literature on the globalization of the labour market, see R. Cohen, *The New Helots: Migrants in the International Division of Labor* (Fainborough, Eng.: Avebury, 1987). For an earlier, less empirical, more theoretical description of the international labour market, see F. Frobel, "The Current Development of the World-Economy," *Review*, 4 (Spring 1982).

41. "The Emerging Response to Child Labour," *Conditions of Work Digest*, 7,1 (1988); "Child Labour: Law and Practice," *Conditions of Work Digest*, 10,1 (1991).

42. As capital becomes international its mobility creates a tendency for a world rate of return, and in this lies the pressure for world wages. Resistance to this pressure is very difficult given that capital becomes global in organized units, as cartels, conglomerates, and oligopolies, while labour becomes international as so many individuals or in the form of labour-value embedded in commodities. International trade unionism remains very weak.

For a good review of these employment and wage trends in the United States and their effect on the welfare state, see L. Mishel and J. Bernstein, *The State of Working America, 1992-93* (Armonk, N.Y.: M.E. Sharpe, 1993).

43. C. Palloix, "The Self-Expansion of Capital on a World-Scale," *Review of Radical Political Economics*, 9,1 (Summer 1977), pp.11-14.

44. With the decline of "central planning" regimes in China and the U.S.S.R., the global labour market in the 1980s and 1990s increased manyfold. For an analysis of the "internationalization of the industrial reserve army," see M. Godfrey, *Global Unemployment* (Brighton, Eng.: Wheatsheaf, 1986).

45. Palloix, "Self-Expansion of Capital," pp.15-16.

46. Van Liemt, "Economic Globalization," p.463. See also C. Palloix, "Conceptualizing the Internationalization of Capital," *Review of Radical Political Economics*, 9,1 (Summer 1977), p.24. Such "equalization" comes about as a consequence of the repeated movements of capital to benefit from whatever advantages there may be in unequal conditions.

47. See I. Alpert and A. Markusen, "Think Tanks and Capitalist Policy," in *Power Structure Research*, ed. G.W. Domhoff (Beverly Hills, Cal.: Sage Publications, 1980); and van der Pijl, "International Level," p.263. Also, "The World's Richest Countries Should Roll Back Workers' Rights, Raise Retirement Ages and 'Rationalize' Their Health-care Systems, a Confidential Report from Group of Seven Finance Ministers Will Urge Leaders at this Week's Summit," *The Guardian*, July 7, 1993.

48. Van der Pijl, *Making of an Atlantic Ruling Class*; Overbeek, ed., *Restructuring Hegemony*.

49. This is not to underestimate the importance of the United States and others of the Group of Seven countries in this transition. These representatives of the most powerful capital formations must attempt to ensure that the transition unfolds "as it should," embracing all nations, and deploying military, economic, and diplomatic sanctions when it does not. Such pressures, however, are not to be seen principally as in the "national" interest any more; rather, in the interests of a global capitalism that still wears the dress of its preceding era, reflecting the relative degrees of political, economic, and military power. In time, all forms of persuasion will be supranational in form and content.

50. That is, the philosophy of Keynesianism had been abandoned. Many of the practices remain as ways of attracting international investment, although as policies for the management of national economies they no longer have relevance. For an early set of conflicting evaluations on the end of Keynesianism, see R. Skidelsky, ed., *The End of the Keynesian Era* (London: Macmillan, 1977).

51. J.M. Buchanan and R.E. Wagner, *Democracy in Deficit* (New York: Academic Press, 1977). This critique of Keynesianism is made at the level of purported policy consequences with very little consideration of real political and economic changes taking place.

52. In this light it is no small irony to see monetarism touted as national policy, as the means to the economic recovery of national economies.

53. Not that monetarism can guarantee such stability, any more than Keynesianism could guarantee "full employment." There are many intervening variables, not the least of which are the currency markets.

54. Some of these ideas are found in P. Uusitalo, "Monetarism, Keynesianism and the Institutional Status of Central Banks," *Acta Sociologica*, 27,1 (1984).

55. "Salinas Moves to Make Bank Independent," *Financial Times*, May 18, 1993.

56. By the mid-1970s, in many industrial countries "real wage trends [showed] hardly any change between 1975 and 1981." After 1980 these trends showed "no significant improvement" in any of the OECD member countries. ILO, *World Labour Report* (Geneva), 1 (1984), p.137.

57. The increasing poverty of some Third World populations forestalls growth in consumer markets; the indebtedness of many less developed countries prevents the same rate of "development" as before; even military procurements become more difficult to finance; and political volatility would appear to be increasing. See S. George, *A Fate Worse Than Debt: The World Financial Crisis and the Poor* (New York: Grove Press, 1988); and S. Branford and B. Kucinski, *The Debt Squads: The US, the Banks, and Latin America* (Atlantic Highlands, N.J.: Zed Books, 1988); and E. Altvater et al., eds., *The Poverty of Nations* (London: Zed Books, 1991).

58. See P. Lange, G. Ross, M. Vannicelli, *Unions, Change, and Crisis: French and Italian Union Strategy and the Political Economy, 1945-1980* (London and Boston: George Allen and Unwin, 1982); P. Bassett, *Strike Free: New Industrial Relations in Britain* (London: Macmillan, 1987);

and M. Goldfield, *The Decline of Organized Labor in the United States* (Chicago: University of Chicago Press, 1987).

59. "Externalities" are nothing other than the hidden or ignored costs in modern production and distribution processes. Or, as one economist put it, an externality is a "non-priced effect on a third party arising as a by-product of the actions undertaken by another."

60. One of the early new right arguments against the welfare state pointed to an ostensible "contradiction" or "paradox" within it; namely, that while dependent on economic growth, the welfare state implied forms of "protectionism" that inhibited international economic growth. See M.B. Kraus, *The New Protectionism: The Welfare State and International Trade* (Oxford: Basil Blackwell, 1979). There is an element of superficial accuracy to such an argument, in that the KWS has been incompatible with world wages and prices, global labour and capital markets, and international trade and competition. But if the logic of the argument is to abandon the KWS in order to encourage economic growth *and so* produce social security, some of the problems of the argument are not difficult to point out. First, to the degree that the welfare state is a form of "shared" national income it has for the most part been exacted by an organized working class from capital. In other words, regardless of the rate of growth it is unlikely that capital would "share" the wealth created without legislated social reforms. Second, to make the welfare state in part responsible for the decline in economic growth is to ignore the cyclical pattern of economic growth long before it came into being. It was, after all, this cycle that made the welfare state necessary; national social reforms have been legislated to save national capitalism from itself. Third, the present evidence would suggest that relatively unregulated international economic expansion produces anything but social security for the working classes.

61. This is not to say that at the same time rivalries between trading blocs and corporate conglomerates over shares of the world market disappear; in fact, they may well intensify until a "winner" or mutual agreement ensues; but this is part of the natural course towards internationalization. See Ohmae, *Triad Power*.

V Neo-liberal Policies and Their Rationale

1. Agenda is the word often used by those promoting these policies. It denotes a coherent program of "things to be done," and these "things," it is argued, reflect the national changes necessary to remove the barriers to a world economy.

2. Capital confronts state property not only in the West but also in those countries that represent state property (such as the former U.S.S.R., China, North Korea, Libya, Cuba), and sets about to transform them (the arms race helps to bring down the U.S.S.R.; military, political, and economic pressure on Libya; threats to Korea; the economic embargo on Cuba).

3. A. Smith, "Conclusions," *Wealth of Nations*, Bk.I, Part II, London.

4. Marx, *Capital*, vol. 1, pp.280, 292, 730, 1083.

5. That is to say that capitalist private property based on the appropriation of labour and the products of that labour could not exist if the working population worked only for itself using its own means of production and exchanging the products of its own labour.

6. J.L. Campbell and L.N. Linberg, "Property Rights and the Organization of Economic Activity by the State," *American Sociological Review*, 55 (1990).

7. M. Friedman, *Capitalism and Freedom* (Chicago: University of Chicago Press, 1962), chap. 1. These theoretical positions bear little relation to a reality of large and growing social and economic inequalities, in the context of which liberal political liberties do not mean very much.

8. The opposite view is easily argued. The competitive market possesses vast inefficient duplications of economic processes; it results in periodic excess capacity with consequent enormous wastage; planned obsolescence means continuous waste of material resources; market-related social inequalities produce continuous destruction of human resources; and the unaccounted costs of production ("externalities") are now recognized to be so great as to threaten life itself on the planet.

9. Cited in C. Harris, "The State and the Market," in *Beyond Thatcherism*, ed. P. Brown and R. Sparks (Milton Keynes, Eng.: Open University Press, 1989), p.9.

The view of classical political economy is that human beings are in effect "merchants" of commodities, if only of their own labour power, and "society" merely the exchange of these commodities. This view is accurate enough on the level of appearance as the portrayal of life under capitalism, but it is ideological when taken as the essence of humankind. See K. Marx, "Economic and Philosophical Manuscripts of 1844," in *Marx-Engels: Collected Works*, vol. 3 (London: Lawrence and Wishart, 1975), p.319.

10. This was recognized early on even in the United States, the least "planned" of the capitalist economies. See M.D. Reagan, *The Managed Economy* (New York: Oxford University Press, 1963).

11. R. Murray, ed., *Multinationals beyond the Market* (New York: John Wiley and Sons, 1981). According to Murray (p.2): "A growing proportion of international trade is not really trade at all but transfers within single multinational corporations." At least one estimate places intracorporate trade at 30 per cent of all trade.

12. C.H. Goff and C.E. Reasons, *Corporate Crime in Canada: A Critical Analysis of Anti-Combines Legislation* (Scarborough, Ont.: Prentice-Hall, 1978); J.E. Conklin, *"Illegal but Not Criminal": Business Crime in America* (Englewood Cliffs, N.J.: Prentice-Hall, 1977).

13. C. Johnson, *MITI and the Japanese Miracle* (Stanford, Cal.: Stanford University Press, 1982); S. Melman, *The Permanent War Economy* (New York: Simon and Schuster, 1974). The lessons of the 1930s and more recently the crash of 1987 make it clear that regulation is needed to prevent the system from self-destructing in the short term. See J.E. Spero, "Guiding Global Finance," in *International Economics and International Economic Policy*, ed. P. King (New York: McGraw-Hill, 1990), p.441.

14. For an example of control at the international level, see R. Dale, *The Regulation of Banking* (Cambridge: Woodhead-Falkner, 1984).

15. E.H. Chamberlain, ed., *Monopoly and Competition and Their Regulation* (London: Macmillan, 1954).

16. *The Economist*, February 8, 1992, May 30, 1992.

17. *The Independent*, January 29, 1993; *The Observer*, February 3, 1993.

18. "Market criteria" is but a euphemism for criteria that improve profits and therefore is a rationale for increasing the capitalist share of wealth generated.

19. E. Butler and M. Pirie, eds., *Freeports* (The Adam Smith Institute, 1983), p.9; *World Link*, 5,2 (March/April 1992), pp.118-19. For a review of the early history of free ports, see R.S. Thomas, *Free Ports and Foreign Trade Zones* (Cambridge, Mass.: Cornell Maritime Press, 1956).

20. G.T. Crane, *The Political Economy of China's Special Economic Zones* (New York: M.E. Sharpe, 1990), p.6.

21. V.N. Morganchev, "Russia's Free Economic Zones," *World Link*, 5,2 (March/April 1992), p.124.

22. P. Hall, "Enterprise Zones: A Justification," in *International Journal of Urban and Regional Research*, 6 (1982), p.416.

23. P. Warr, "Export Processing Zones," in *Export Promotion Strategies*, ed. C. Milner (Hemel Hempstead, Eng.: Harvester/Wheatsheaf, 1990), p.137. See also K. Herbst, "The Regulatory Framework for Foreign Investment in the Special Economic Zones," in *China's Special Economic Zones*, ed. Y.C. Jao and C.K. Leung (Oxford: Oxford University Press, 1986), p.130.

24. Warr, "Export Processing Zones," p.159. On the U.S. experience, see R. Vincent and M. Rosenberg, *Foreign Trade Zones: Separating Myth from Reality* (Ottawa: Carleton University, 1984). For an early assessment of their effect in Asia, see T. Tsuchiya, "Free Trade Zones in Southeast Asia," in *International Capitalism and Industrial Restructuring*, ed. R. Peet (Boston: Allen and Unwin, 1987).

25. Crane, *Political Economy of China's Special Economic Zones*, p.10.

26. P. Mirowski and S. Helper, "Maquildoras: Mexico's Tiger by the Tail?" *Challenge*, May/June 1990. See also K. Rosa, "Strategies of Organization and Resistance: Women Workers in Sri Lankan Free Trade Zones," *Capital and Class*, 45 (Autumn 1991); and Pacific-Asia Resources Center, "Free Trade Zones and Industrialization of Asia," *AMPO Japan-Asia Quarterly Review*, Tokyo, 1977; A. Fuentes and B. Ehrenreich, *Women in the Global Factory* (Boston: South End, 1983).

27. Butler and Pirie, *Freeports*, p.16.
28. J.L Howard and W.T. Stanbury, "The Size, Scope, and Growth of Governments in Canada," in *Probing Leviathan*, ed. G. Lerner (Vancouver: The Fraser Institute, 1984), p.153.

    Public corporations come under regulation as well, but when their mandate includes a social purpose and not simply the socially irresponsible criterion to maximize profit, the regulation required is less.
29. An early review of deregulation in the United States under Reagan can be found in S.J. Tolchin and M. Tolchin, *Dismantling America: The Rush to Deregulate* (Boston: Houghton Mifflin, 1983).
30. On the S and L scandal, see P.Z. Pilzer, *Other People's Money* (New York: Simon and Schuster, 1989). On the British affairs, see "Burying BCCI," *The Economist*, November 30, 1991; and "After Maxwell," *The Economist*, November 9, 1991.
31. For many of these ideas, see P.G. Cerny, "The Limits of Deregulation: Transnational Interpenetration and Policy Change," *European Journal of Political Research*, 19 (1991).
32. Even the new right recognizes this point. See C. Veljanovski, ed., *Privatisation and Competition: A Market Prospectus* (London: IEA, 1989), in which the contributors share the view that privatization of public corporations has failed to bring about the desired competition.
33. There is a broader meaning of privatization from the perspective of property rights, mentioned earlier, which "sees privatization as a reassignment of claims to the control and use of [state] assets." In this sense, privatization is intended to undermine "the foundation of claims for public purpose and public service." P. Starr, "The Meaning of Privatization," in *Privatization and the Welfare State*, ed. Kamerman and Kahn, p.42.
34. K. Ascher, *The Politics of Privatisation: Contracting out of Public Services* (London: Macmillan, 1987). For an unabashedly positive description of the main methods for privatization and a review of developments to the late 1980s, see M. Pirie, *Privatization* (Aldershot, Eng.: Wildwood House, 1988).
35. For analyses of privatization in several countries, see Suleiman and Waterbury, *Political Economy*; and I. Harik and D.J. Sullivan, eds., *Privatization and Liberalization in the Middle East* (Bloomington: Indiana University Press, 1992). For a review of the policies in Britain, see Veljanovski, *Selling the State*. For a defence by a true believer, see O. Letwin, *Privatising the World* (London: Cassell, 1988).
36. See J.M. Buchanan and R.E. Wagner, *Democracy in Deficit* (New York: Academic Press, 1977).
37. Several commentators on privatization see the dismantling of public-sector unions and the "disciplining" of workers as key motives for privatization. These are important consequences for capital and perhaps even objectives, but they are not the main motive. Once privatized, former state-owned corporations become avenues of increasing accumulation and open to purchase by international capital.
38. For an early, less than sanguine view of privatization, see J.A. Kay and D.J. Thompson, "Privatisation: A Policy in Search of a Rationale," *The Economic Journal*, 96 (March 1986).
39. Many of the points drawn out in this section are from G.J. Ikenberry, "The International Spread of Privatization Policies," and P. Starr, "The New Life of the Liberal State," in *Political Economy*, ed. Suleiman and Waterbury.
40. An example of "people's capitalism" from the early 1980s and the unscrupulous use made of it can be found in the experiment called British Columbia Resources Investment Company (BCRIC). For a short review of how the "people" lost their shirts and a few businessmen profited, see R. Williamson, "How BCRIC Became a Black Hole," in *The Globe and Mail*, June 6, 1992. For an early detailed description of the process, see T.M. Ohashi, "Privatization in Practice," in T.M. Ohashi and T.P. Roth, eds., *Privatization: Theory and Practice* (Vancouver: The Fraser Institute, 1980).
41. R. Forrest and A. Murie, *Selling the Welfare State: The Privatization of Public Housing* (London: Routledge, 1991). This provides a good review of some issues surrounding public housing, but the authors reveal a lack of a broader comprehension when they conclude (p.252): "The sale of council houses could have formed part of an imaginative and socially just restructuring of housing opportunities."

42. Sigmund, "Chile: Privatization, Reprivatization, Hyperprivatization," p.355.

43. The new right attention to "culture" is much more involved than suggested here. See R. Keat and N. Abercrombie, eds., *Enterprise Culture* (London: Routledge, 1991); and P. Cohen, "Teaching Enterprise Culture: Individualism, Vocationalism and the New Right," in *The Social Effects of Free Market Policies*, ed. I. Taylor (Hemel Hempstead, Eng.: Harvester/ Wheatsheaf, 1990).

44. For a general discussion of pre- and post-Keynesian welfare state tax policies, see J.E. Cronin and T.G. Radtke, "The Old and New Politics of Taxation: Thatcher and Reagan in Historical Perspective," in *The Socialist Register 1987*, ed. R. Miliband et al. (London: Merlin Press). For a brief discussion of changes to U.S. policies, see T.B. Edsall, *The New Politics of Inequality* (New York: Norton, 1984). For the shift to individual over corporate taxes, see K.C. Messere and J.P. Owens, "International Comparisons of Tax Levels: Pitfalls and Insights," *OECD Economic Studies*, 8 (Spring 1987), pp. 103-4. See also R.P. Hagemann, B.R. Jones, and R.B. Montador, "Tax Reform in OECD Countries: Motives, Constraints and Practice," *OECD Economic Studies*, 10 (Spring 1988), p.213.

45. F.A. Hayek, *The Constitution of Liberty* (London: Routledge 1960), chap. 20.

46. See H. Shibata, "The Theory of Economic Unions: A Comparative Analysis of Customs Unions, Free Trade Areas and Tax Unions," in *Fiscal Harmonization in Common Markets*, ed. C.S. Shoup (New York: Columbia University Press, 1967); and P. Robson, *The Economics of International Integration* (London: George Allen and Unwin, 1980), pp.91-108.

47. H. Shibata, *Fiscal Harmonization under Freer Trade* (Toronto: University of Toronto Press, 1969), p.14. See also J.D.R. Adams and J. Whalley, *The International Taxation of Multinational Enterprises in Developed Countries* (London: IFS, 1977).

48. For a current review of the issues and status of international corporate taxation, see OECD, *Taxing Profits in a Global Economy* (Paris, 1991).

49. P. Saunders and F. Klau, *The Role of the Public Sector* (Paris: OECD, 1985).

50. See J.M. Buchanan and R.E. Wagner, *Democracy in Deficit* (New York: Academic Press, 1977). For a critical review of such views, see J. Tomlinson, "The 'Economics of Politics' and Public Expenditure: A Critique," *Economy and Society*, 10,4 (November 1981).

51. Given the earlier argument here that the working class receives less from the state than is extracted from it (that expenditures in all aspects of social security are less than the "social wage" and other taxes employed to finance them), the real beneficiaries of the debt are the corporate creditors (interest payments and policy leverage) and corporate recipients (state investment in infrastructure, school and hospital construction, loans, grants and guarantees, tax expenditures).

52. W. Keegan and R. Pennant-Rea, *Who Runs the Economy?* (London: Temple Smith, 1979), p.32, cite the view of a British senior civil servant: "If markets take the view that the policies pursued by a particular country are likely to damage assets held in that country or in that country's currency, they are likely to behave in ways which can actually enforce a policy change. Market behaviour has become a significant input in policy making."

53. According to Keegan and Pennant-Rea, *Who Runs the Economy?* p.133, the financial markets stopped buying long-term debt for several months – a "gilt strike" – in order to impose their view that the British government's borrowing and expenditures were too high.

54. The same change can be seen from a policy perspective: on the one hand, the Keynesianism associated with postwar Fordism required a substantial state sector to effect various interventions; monetarism, on the other hand, associated with post-Keynesianism, can be realized with a minimal public sector. Indeed, it brings pressure to transfer to the market many facets of the Keynesian model of government. For a popular U.S. presentation and promotion of this shift, see D. Osborne and T. Gaebler, *Reinventing Government* (New York: Penguin, 1993).

55. This possibility is more abstract than real for there is little chance of its realization. If a nation is to remain capitalist, no political party will be able to overturn neo-liberal policies. Witness the legislation of social-democratic parties in power around the world, not to mention the Communist Party of China. If a nation were to try to move to a form of socialism or state ownership of property as a policy, it is not clear that the attempt would

be allowed to succeed; the examples of Chile, Nicaragua, El Salvador, Cuba, and Libya suffice to make the point.

56. The right wing is very aware of this point; see J.M. Buchanan, *Freedom in Constitutional Contract: Perspectives of a Political Economist* (College Station: Texas A&M University Press, 1978).

57. See A. Norton, "Western European Government in Comparative Perspective," in *Local Government in Europe*, ed. R. Batley and G. Stoker (London: Macmillan, 1991).

58. L.J. Sharpe, "Is There a Fiscal Crisis in Western European Local Government? A First Appraisal," in *The Local Fiscal Crisis in Western Europe*, ed. L.J. Sharpe (London: Sage Publications, 1981).

59. M. Keating, *Comparative Urban Politics* (Aldershot, Eng.: Edward Elgar, 1991), pp.158-67. See also M. Keating and P. Hainsworth, *Decentralisation and Change in Contemporary France* (Aldershot, Eng.: Edward Elgar, 1986). For a good review of British alternative experiments, see A. Cochrane, "In and Against the Market? The Development of Socialist Economic Strategies in Britain, 1981-1986," *Policy and Politics*, 16,3 (July 1988).

60. See D. Blunkett and K. Jackson, *Democracy in Crisis: The Town Halls Respond* (London: Hogarth, 1987); and M. Mackintosh and H. Wainwright, eds., *A Taste of Power: The Politics of Local Economies* (London: Verso, 1987).

61. The degree of centralization in Britain led two academics to conclude that Britain "stands within sight of a form of government which is more highly centralized than anything this side of East Germany." K. Newton and T.J. Karran, *The Politics of Local Expenditure* (London: Macmillan, 1985), p.129. For discussion of centralization, see C. Pickvance and E. Preteceille, "Conclusion," in *State Restructuring and Local Power*, ed. Pickvance and Preteceille (London: Pinter Publishers, 1991), p.222. For a good discussion of this paradox in Sweden, see I. Elander and S. Montin, "Decentralisation and Control: Central-local Government Relations in Sweden," *Policy and Politics*, 18,3 (1990).

62. The British experience provides good examples of these developments. Concerning social policy, see H. Glennerster, A. Power, and T. Travers, "A New Era for Social Policy: A New Enlightenment or a New Leviathan?" *Journal of Social Policy*, 20,3, (1991).

63. For an overview of these questions see Keating, *Comparative Urban Politics*, especially chap. 4.

64. For a brief examination of this dismantling in several countries, see Taylor, *Social Effects of Free Market Policies*; F. Block et al., eds., *The Mean Season: The Attack on the Welfare State* (New York: Pantheon Books, 1987); Brown, *Remaking the Welfare State*; Mishra, *Welfare State in Capitalist Society*; D. Stoesz and H. Karger, "The Corporatisation of the United States Welfare State," *Journal of Social Policy*, 20,2 (1991).

65. R. and M. Friedman, *Free to Choose* (New York: Harcourt Brace Jovanovich, 1980).

66. M. O'Higgins, "Social Welfare and Privatization: The British Experience," in *Privatization and the Welfare State*, ed. Kamerman and Kahn.

67. The principles of welfare imposed on the Third World are being reintroduced to the industrial nations. See J. Midgley, "Poor Law Principles and Social Assistance in the Third World: A Study in the Perpetuation of Colonial Welfare," *International Social Work*, 27,1 (1984).

68. D. Fraser, "The English Poor Law and the Origins of the British Welfare State," in *Emergence of the Welfare State*, ed. Mommsen.

69. For a discussion of some of these changes in the context of contemporary America, see N. Fraser, "Clintonism, Welfare and the Antisocial Wage: The Emergence of a Neoliberal Political Imaginary," *Rethinking Marxism*, 6,1 (Spring 1993).

70. There are already many examples of this fate; for instance, the loss of pension funds, the illegal corporate use of pension funds, and the lowest possible benefit protection for employees.

71. Declining real wages in the industrial nations mean the gradual reduction of that portion of income deducted as taxes, premiums, and deferred payments, which in turn results in the decline of the social wage. Indeed, wages and salaries increasingly become sufficient only to reproduce labour power during periods of employment, leaving periods of unemployment, invalidity, old age, and maternity with increasingly only private or other very limited resources.

72. The most significant umbrella charity in North America is the United Way. Promoted vigorously by corporations, its annual drive for funds amounts to another tax on the working class, while corporate donations remain by comparison very limited.

73. G. Barak, *Gimme Shelter: A Social History of Homelessness in Contemporary America* (New York: Praeger, 1991); P. Burman, *Killing Time, Losing Ground* (Toronto: Wall and Thompson, 1988); G. Riches, *Food Banks and the Welfare Crisis* (Ottawa: CCSD, 1986). The dramatic proliferation of food banks in North America and the increasing numbers of homeless and unemployed around the world since 1980 are depressing testimony to the failure of the system to provide the basic necessities for increasing numbers.

74. See P. Lernoux, *Cry of the People* (New York: Doubleday, 1980); C. Brown, *With Friends Like These* (Washington, D.C.: Americas Watch on Human Rights and U.S. Policy in Latin America, 1985); G. Mower, *Human Rights and American Foreign Policy: The Carter and Reagan Experience* (London: Greenwood Press, 1987); N. Chomsky and E.S. Herman, *The Washington Connection and Third World Fascism*, vol. 1, *The Political Economy of Human Rights* (Boston: South End Press, 1979).

   From the point of view of international investors in China, the massacre in Tiananmen Square (1989) must appear in part as a demonstration that civil liberties, integral to the demand for liberal democracy but fetters to the "freedom" of capital, would not be tolerated. The bloody coup d'état in Chile in 1973 was followed by significantly renewed investor confidence.

75. I. Glasser, "The Coming Assault on Civil Liberties," in *What Reagan Is Doing to Us*, ed. A. Gartner et al. (New York: Harper and Row, 1982); M. Rankin, "Human Rights Under Restraint," in *The New Reality*, ed. W. Magnusson et al. (Vancouver: New Star Books, 1984).

76. J. Reiman, *The Rich Get Richer and the Poor Get Prison: Ideology, Class, and Criminal Justice* (New York: Wiley, 1984).

77. P. Birkinshaw, *Freedom of Information: The Law, the Practice and the Ideal* (London: Weidenfeld and Nicolson, 1988).

78. I. Galnoor, ed., *Government Secrecy in Democracies* (New York: Harper and Row, 1977).

79. K.D. Ewing and C.A. Gearty, *Freedom under Thatcher: Civil Liberties in Modern Britain* (Oxford: Clarendon Press, 1990).

80. S. Manwaring-White, *The Policing Revolution* (Brighton, Eng.: Harvester, 1983); F. Donner, *The Age of Surveillance: The Aims and Methods of America's Political Intelligence System* (New York: Vintage, 1981); R.S. Ratner and J.L. McMullan, "Social Control and the Rise of the 'Exceptional State' in Britain, the United States, and Canada," in *The New Criminologies in Canada*, ed. T. Flemming (Toronto: Oxford, 1985).

81. J.A.G. Griffith, *The Politics of the Judiciary* (London: Fontana, 1985).

82. Marx, *Capital*, vol. 1, p.730.

83. Chomsky, *Deterring Democracy*.

84. A good review can be found in A. Jones, *The New Inflation: The Politics of Prices and Incomes* (Harmondsworth, Eng.: Penguin, 1973); on Britain, see L. Panitch, *Social Democracy and Industrial Militancy* (Cambridge: Cambridge University Press, 1976).

   Wage and price controls come in various forms, and they have several purposes: to keep wages below the rate of inflation, to prevent increased wage demands spawned by increased taxation, to reduce wages over time to international levels, and to undermine the powers of trade unions or the organized working class.

85. Industrial relations legislation itself must be seen as an attempt to institutionalize and so control the relations between organized labour and capital; and the kind and degree of restrictions embedded here have a roughly inverse correspondence to the relative strength and militancy of union organization. See P. Anderson, "The Limits and Possibilities of Trade Union Action," and J.H. Goldthorpe, "Industrial Relations in Great Britain: A Critique of Reformism," in *Trade Unions under Capitalism*, ed. T. Clarke and L. Clamen (Glasgow: Fontana, 1977).

   Canada presents a model example of the introduction of restrictions, but is in no way unique. See L. Panitch and D. Swartz, *From Consent to Coercion: The Assault on Trade Union Freedoms* (Toronto: Garamond Press, 1985).

86. Van Liemt, "Economic Globalization," p.463.

87. K. Wedderburn, *Nationalism and the Multinational Enterprise* (New York: Oceana Publications, 1973), p.256.

88. H. Vernon-Wortzel, *Global Strategic Management* (New York: Wiley, 1990).

89. L.A. Hoskins, *The New International Economic Order* (Washington: University Press of America, 1982).

90. *The Guardian*, April 30, 1993. See also H.R. Northrup and R. Rowan, Multinational Collective Bargaining Attempts (Philadelphia: University of Philadelphia Press, 1979); and L. Ulman, "Multinational Unionism: Incentives, Barriers, and Alternatives," *Industrial Relations*, 14,1 (1975).

91. This is a reference to initiatives put forward by the European Trade Union Confederation in the 1970s and 1980s to establish a legal framework for European-wide collective bargaining. See T. DeVos, *Multinational Corporations in Democratic Host Countries* (Hanover, N.H.: Dartmouth Publishing Co., 1989). See also M. Rhodes, "The Social Dimension of the European Market: National Versus Transnational," *European Journal of Political Research*, 19 (March/April, 1991); and "Vredeling Plan for MNC's Gets Green Light 'in Principle,'" " *International Relations Europe*, 8,88 (April 1980). ("In practice" the light turned red.)

92. J. Stirling, "The Great Europe of Ours: Trade Unions and 1992," *Capital and Class*, 45 (Autumn 1991), p.15. For a good review of the attempts by the ETUC to influence the content of the Social Charter, see S.J. Silvia, "The Social Charter of the European Community: A Defeat for European Labor," *Industrial and Labor Relations Review*, 44,4 (July 1991).

93. For a discussion of the decline in membership, see P.B. Beaumont, *The Decline of Trade Union Organization* (London: Croom Helm, 1987); J. Fiorito and C.L. Maranto, "The Contemporary Decline of Union Strength," *Contemporary Policy Issues*, 5 (October 1987); M.W. Reder, "The Rise and Fall of Unions: The Public Sector and the Private," *Journal of Economic Perspectives*, 2,2 (Spring 1988); Goldfield, *Decline of Organized Labor*; K. Moody, *An Injury to All: The Decline of American Unionism* (London: Verso, 1988); Y. Reshef, "Union Decline: A View from Canada," *Journal of Labor Research*, (Winter 1990).

   The decline is not universal, but under the circumstances it is difficult to find reasons for an alternative trend. See E. Sussex, "The Impact of Structural Change on Trade Unions," in *Industry on the Move*, ed. G. van Liemt (Geneva: International Labour Organization, 1992), p.284.

   For discussion of the trend from a bourgeois nationalist outlook, see G.A. Dorfman, *Government versus Trade Unionism in British Politics since 1968* (London: Macmillan, 1979), pp.153-55. See also K. von Beyme, "Unions and Multinational Companies," in *International Perspectives on Organizational Democracy*, ed. B. Wilpert and A. Sorge (New York: John Wiley and Sons, 1984).

94. J. Muncie and R. Sparks, "Expansion and Contraction in European Penal Systems," in *Imprisonment: European Perspectives*, ed. J. Muncie and R. Sparks (Hemel Hempstead: Harvester/Wheatsheaf, 1991). "Between 1983 and 1988 substantial increases [in prison populations] were recorded in a majority of countries including the Netherlands, France and the United Kingdom" (p.90).

95. A. Rutherford, *Prisons and the Process of Justice* (Oxford, 1986), p.vii.

96. J.J. DiIulio, "What's Wrong with Private Prisons," *The Public Interest*, 92 (Summer 1988).

97. M. Brake and C. Hale, "Law and Order," in *Beyond Thatcherism*, ed. Brown and Sparks, p.145; see also Rutherford, *Prisons*, p.viii.

98. Rutherford, *Prisons*, p.48.

99. R. Mokhiber, *Corporate Crime and Violence: Big Business Power and the Abuse of the Public Trust* (San Francisco: Sierra Club Books, 1989); C. Reasons and C.H. Goff, "Corporate Crime: A Cross-national Analysis," in *White Collar Crime: Theory and Research*, ed. G. Geis and E. Stotland (Beverly Hills, Cal.: Sage Publications, 1980).

   For a good overview of the issue of corporate crime, see J.L. McMullan, *Beyond the Limits of the Law: Corporate Crime and Law and Order* (Halifax: Fernwood Publishing, 1992);

and for a recent review of literature on corporate crime, see M. Brake and C. Hale, *Public Order and Private Lives* (London: Routledge, 1992), chap. 6.

100. For an excellent, although now somewhat dated, review of these attempts, see J. Robinson, *Multinationals and Political Control* (Aldershot, Eng.: Gower Publishing House, 1983). See also D.H. Blake and R.S. Walters, *The Politics of Global Economic Relations* (Engelwood Cliffs, N.J.: Prentice-Hall, 1987).

101. See *The New Internationalist*, August 1993, p.15.

102. Les Samuelson, "Crime as a Social Problem: From Definition to Reality," in *Power and Resistance: Critical Thinking about Canadian Social Issues*, ed. L. Samuelson (Halifax: Fernwood Publishing, 1994), p.130.

103. S. Spitzer, "The Rationalization of Crime Control in Capitalist Society," in *Social Control and the State*, ed. S. Cohen and A. Scull (Oxford: Basil Blackwell, 1985).

104. On the relation between rates of unemployment and imprisonment, see S. Box, *Recession, Crime and Punishment* (London: Macmillan, 1987); and S. Box and C. Hale, "Unemployment, Imprisonment and the Enduring Problem of Prison Overcrowding," in *Confronting Crime*, ed. R. Matthews and J. Young (London: Sage Publications), chap. 4.

105. B. Barry, "Does Democracy Cause Inflation? Political Ideas for Some Economists," in *The Politics of Inflation and Economic Stagnation*, ed. L. Lindberg and C. Maier (Washington, D.C.: Brookings Institute, 1985), p.317.

106. That is, the idea that normative or ethical values should prevail over the effects of the market. For a discussion of the relation between these two forms of "justice," see C.B. Macpherson, "The Rise and Fall of Economic Justice" in his *The Rise and Fall of Economic Justice* (Oxford: Oxford University Press, 1985).

107. There is a vast literature spanning several decades on the undemocratic nature of modern democracy. See, for example, P. Green and S. Levinson, eds., *Power and Community: Dissenting Essays in Political Science* (New York: Random House, 1969); R. Miliband, *The State in Capitalist Society* (London: Weidenfeld and Nicolson, 1970); A. Wolfe, *The Seamy Side of Democracy* (New York: Longman, 1973); M. Parenti, *Democracy for the Few* (New York: St. Martin's Press, 1983); G.W. Domhoff and T.R. Dye, eds., *Power Elites and Organization* (Beverly Hills, Cal.: Sage, 1987); N. Chomsky, *American Power and the New Mandarins* (New York: Pantheon Books, 1969); E.S. Greenberg, *Serving the Few: Capitalism and the Bias of Government Policy* (New York: John Wiley and Co., 1974).

108. The impetus by civil society to make the form and rhetoric of democracy under capitalism a reality implicitly lies behind the historical drive for universal enfranchisement. In other words, the struggle for general suffrage represents the implicit demand by the majority in civil society (the working classes) to have direct access not to legislative power but to executive power, the power to make decisions over their own lives. General suffrage brought, at best, indirect access to legislative power.

109. T. Allen, "In GATT They Trust," *Covert Action Information Bulletin*, 40 (Spring 1992); see also M. Conklin and D. Davidson, "The IMF and Economic and Social Human Rights: A Case Study of Argentina, 1958-1985," *Human Rights Quarterly*, 8,2 (1986); F.K. Ekenchi, "Perspectives on the Human Effects of the Structural Adjustment Program in Nigeria," in *Debt and Development in the Third World*, ed. Ba-Nikongo; "Jeopardized by GATT – 100 US Environmental Laws," *The New York Times*, June 20, 1994.

Mutual funds have recently become one of the most important influences in the Third World, often overshadowing the role of the banks. For a brief review of their power over government policy, see C. Torres and T.T. Vogel, "The Long Arm of the Funds," *The Globe and Mail* (reprinted from *The Wall Street Journal*) June 17, 1994.

110. As at the national level, politics at the international level has become "democracy of the lobbies." See J. Grant, *The Commercial Lobbyists: Politics for Profit in Britain* (Aberdeen: Aberdeen University Press, 1991); and C. Miller, *Lobbying Government* (Oxford: Basil Blackwell, 1987); T. Edsall, *The New Politics of Inequality* (New York: Norton, 1984), pp.107-40; for an early analysis of the role of lobbies, see S.E. Finer, *Anonymous Empire: A Study of the Lobby in Great Britain* (London: Pall Mall, 1958).

111. M. Crozier, S.P. Huntington, and J. Watanuki, *The Crisis of Democracy: Report on the Governability of Democracies to the Trilateral Commission* (New York: New York University Press, 1975), pp.13, 163, 164.

112. K. van der Pijl, "The Sovereignty of Capital Impaired: Social Forces and Codes of Conduct for Multinational Corporations," in *Restructuring Hegemony*, ed. Overbeek.

113. See, for instance, B. Reading, *Japan: The Coming Collapse* (London: Weidenfeld and Nicolson, 1992). For an example of "corporate blackmail" see *BC Business*, April 21, 1992: " 'Treat us nice or kiss us goodbye,' warns mining mogul." "B.C. should give its mining companies a break or watch as they seek a warmer climate in countries like Chile, says Cominco Ltd. President."

114. While terrorism as political resistance is the antithesis of democratic action, it is usually the consequence of a very bureaucratic or non-democratic political system, where political expression and access to decision-making are non-existent or highly restricted for many. (Germany, Italy, Japan, Israel, and Northern Ireland are good examples of the last element.) In turn, terrorism can easily become the rationale for increased state arbitrariness and the restriction of legal opposition. It can also be invented or state-inspired and then used to abrogate civil liberties and the democratic process for particular political and/or economic ends. See E.S. Herman, "US Sponsorship of International Terrorism: An Overview," G. Shank, "Counterterrorism and Foreign Policy," M.D. Huggins, "US-Supported State Terror: A History of Police Training in Latin America," and N. Chomsky, "International Terrorism," *Crime and Social Justice*, 27-28 (1987). See also G. Barak, ed., *Crimes by the Capitalist State* (Albany, N.Y.: State University of New York, 1991).

115. M.A. Bienefeld, "Interpreting Excess Capacity," in *The International Politics of Surplus Capacity*, ed. S. Strange and R. Tooze (London: George Allen and Unwin, 1981); R.T. Naylor, *Hot Money and the Politics of Debt* (Montreal: Black Rose Books [1987], 1994).

116. There are many scenarios or models of the future and even debates surrounding them, but they are all still very speculative. For a brief review, see S. Gill and D. Law, *The Global Political Economy* (Hemel Hempstead: Harvester/Wheatsheaf, 1988), pp.360ff.

117. "The highest development of capital exists when the general conditions of the process of social production are not paid out of *deductions from the social revenue*, the state's taxes – where revenue and not capital appears as the labour fund, and where the worker, although he is a free wage worker like any other, nevertheless stands economically in a different relation – but rather out of *capital as capital*." Marx, *Grundrisse*, p.532.

VI The Era of the "Triumph of Capitalism"

1. By monolithic we refer to three situations: when dominant capitals have arrived at accommodation with themselves and government and have few major differences over shares of production, distribution, or financing (for example, Japan); when the interests of capital, albeit competitive, are seen as more important to defend against the possibility of working-class interests gaining power than to be divided by their own "internal" differences; and when the interests of international capital override any significant national interests of labour or capital. For a discussion of the type of political system becoming more common, see T.J. Pempel, ed., *Uncommon Democracies: The One-Party Democratic Regimes* (Ithaca, N.Y.: 1990).

2. W. Tabb, "Social Democracy and Authoritarianism: Two Faces of Trilateralism Toward Labor," in *Trilateralism*, ed. Sklar.

3. For a discussion of industrial pollution in the Third World, see M.C. Howard, ed., *Asia's Environmental Crisis* (Boulder, Col.: Westview Press, 1993).

4. For a review of these issues, see Government of Canada, Standing Committee on External Affairs and International Trade, *Securing Our Global Future: Canada's Stake in the Unfinished Business of Third World Debt*, Ottawa, June 1990.

5. M. O'Connor, ed., *Is Capitalism Sustainable?* (New York: The Guildford Press, 1994). For a discussion of the meaning of sustainability, see S. Lele, "Sustainable Development: A

Critical Review," *World Development*, 19,6 (1991); and P. Ekins, "Making Development Sustainable," in *Global Ecology*, ed. W. Sachs (Halifax: Fernwood Publishing, 1993).

6. J. Robinson and J. Eatwell, *An Introduction to Modern Economics* (London: McGraw-Hill, 1973), p.310.

7. *World Link*, 4,4 (July/August 1991), p.50. See also L.R. Brown, "The Illusion of Progress," in *State of the World 1990*, ed. L.R. Brown et al. (New York: W.W. Norton, 1990).

8. World Commission on Environment and Development, *Our Common Future* (The Brundtland Report) (Oxford: Oxford University Press, 1987). "There are also environmental trends that threaten to radically alter the planet, that threaten the lives of many species upon it, including the human species" (p.2). "Nature is bountiful, but it is also fragile and finely balanced. There are thresholds that cannot be crossed without endangering the basic integrity of the system. Today we are close to many of these thresholds; we must be ever mindful of the risk of endangering the survival of life on Earth" (pp.32-33).

9. One such attempt in the United States is the so-called "Superfund," a law that allows the Environmental Protection Agency to conduct searches for toxic sites, find those responsible, and press criminal charges and oblige partial payment for the clean-up. Its success has been limited. See Environmental Defense Fund et al., *Right Train, Wrong Track* (New York, 1988). The 1993 Earth Summit in Rio de Janeiro was a recent, albeit reluctant, attempt by capital to save itself from itself, now raised to the level of saving the planet from the ravages of capitalism insufficiently reformed.

10. Such an idea is far from widely accepted, but there is material now appearing outside environmental circles. See, for example, R.H. Gray, *The Greening of Accountancy* (London, 1992). Still, it is not a new argument: "At the beginning of the century, Pigou pointed out that it is a serious defect in the system of laissez-faire that producers bear only the costs that they pay for. The production of commodities throws costs upon society that are not paid for and do not enter into prices." Robinson and Eatwell, *Introduction to Modern Economics*, pp.309-10.

11. A. Gedicks, *The New Resource Wars: Native and Environmental Struggles against Multinational Corporations* (Montreal: Black Rose, 1994).

12. J. Ward and J. Blumenfeld, "GATT and the Global Environment: The Road Ahead," Natural Resources Defense Council, Washington, D.C., 1994, p.1.

13. D.C. Esty, "GATTing the Greens: Not Just Greening the GATT," *Foreign Affairs*, 72,5 (1993), p.32.

14. *Economics* is the study of the production and exchange of goods and services as capitalist private property or alienated social wealth. Community or social welfare, it follows, lies outside its scope. The measurement standard or indicators employed in economics, then, are intended to measure growth as capital accumulation, as the monetary value of goods and services; for example, the GNP as the measure of a nation's economic "health" or asset accumulation for "standard of living." It is increasingly the case that a growth in GNP, rather than resulting in a certain general distribution of new wealth, is accompanied by an absolute increase in poverty, unemployment, human misery, and wholesale degradation of the environment.

   There is now a large and growing body of literature on the bias of economic indicators; see, for instance, F. Block and G.A. Burns, "Productivity as a Social Problem: The Uses and Misuses of Social Indicators," *American Sociological Review*, 51 (December 1986); P. Ekins, ed., *The Living Economy: New Economics in the Making* (London: Routledge, 1986); M. Waring, *If Women Counted* (San Francisco: Harper and Row, 1988); H. Henderson, *Paradigms in Progress: Life beyond Economics* (Indianapolis: Knowledge Systems Inc.); *Redefining Wealth and Progress: New Ways to Measure Economic, Social and Environmental Change: The Caracas Report on Alternative Development Indicators* (Indianapolis: Knowledge Systems Inc.); and R. Constanza, ed., *Ecological Economics: The Science and Management of Sustainability* (New York: Columbia University Press, 1991).

15. "Development" sponsored by the World Bank has produced just such results. Although its principal mandate is the alleviation of poverty, its projects have for the most part failed in

this goal and instead exacerbated the level of poverty, and the destruction of the environment accompanying its projects is the subject of considerable criticism. See B. Rich, "The Emperor's New Clothes: The World Bank and Environmental Reform," *World Policy Journal*, 7,2 (1990).

16. It is possible, then, at the end of the twentieth century, to see that there are approaching limits to continuous economic expansion. The limits referred to here, however, are not the physical "limits to growth" asserted by the Club of Rome in 1972. Such quasi-Malthusian arguments, while drawing attention to increasing global disparities of wealth, found the cause in a growing divide between increasing levels of consumption and the future supply of resources. See D.H. Meadows et al., *The Limits to Growth* (New York: Signet Books, 1972); and D.H. Meadows et al., *Beyond the Limits* (Toronto: McClelland and Stewart, 1992).

 The limits, furthermore, are not those suggested by Fred Hirsch in his *Social Limits to Growth*. His argument, which would appear to be a variation on an aspect of "Wagner's Law," and which rests on the idea that economic growth is limited by its inability to satisfy the increasing wants resulting from affluence, has not stood up well in the era of internationalized capital, neo-liberalism, and growing relative poverty. See F. Hirsch, *Social Limits to Growth* (London: Routledge and Kegan Paul, 1978). For a set of commentaries and criticisms, see A. Ellis and K. Kumar, eds., *Dilemmas of Liberal Democracies* (London: Tavistock Publications, 1983).

 In essence the argument concerning the "continued expansion of capital" is Marx's "general law of capitalist accumulation" with the added variables of ecological deterioration and the role of the welfare state in the reproduction of the working class. See Marx, *Capital*, vol. 1, p.798.

17. L.R. Brown has stated that the world "has not succeeded in turning around a single major trend in environmental degradation" since the 1972 UN Conference on the Human Environment in Stockholm. L.R. Brown et al., *State of the World, 1991* (New York: W.W. Norton, 1991). The reason might well be found in this statement by Milton Friedman: "Few trends could so thoroughly undermine the very foundations of our free society as the acceptance by corporate officials of a social responsibility other than to make as much money for their stockholders as possible. This ["social responsibility"] is a fundamentally subversive doctrine." M. Friedman, *Capitalism and Freedom* (Chicago: University of Chicago Press, 1962), p.133.

18. At present in certain countries, such as Chile, there is rapid economic growth (or capital accumulation) because the trade unions have been weakened, the welfare state dismantled, new technology introduced, and the political representation of the working class undermined or denied. Here is a striking example of economic growth producing increased overall poverty because the struggle for surplus at the point of production is severely biased in favour of capital.

19. For a survey of the effects on several countries, see I. Taylor, ed., *The Social Effects of Free Market Policies* (Hemel Hempstead, Eng.: Harvester/Wheatsheaf, 1990).

20. "Postmodernist relativism" refers to the works of M. Foucault and E. Laclau and C. Mouffe, J. Derrida, and J. Boudrillard, among others. For those who support a revitalized liberal-democratic politics, see S. Hall, *The Hard Road to Renewal: Thatcherism and the Crisis of the Left* (London: Verso, 1988), p.243; B. Hindess, *Parliamentary Democracy and Socialist Politics* (London: Routledge and Kegan Paul, 1983), p.56; S. Bowles, D. Gordon, and T. Weiskopf, *Beyond the Wasteland: A Democratic Alternative to Economic Decline* (New York: Anchor Press, 1984); and S. Bowles and H. Gintis, "Rethinking Marxism and Liberalism from a Radical Democratic Perspective," *Rethinking Marxism*, 3,3-4 (Fall-Winter 1990).

 Even the intellectuals of the Communist Parties of Europe saw the future lying in liberal democracy. See Armen Antonian, *Toward a Theory of Eurocommunism* (New York: Greenwood Press, 1987): "Eurocommunism has disavowed any pretense at a minority seizure of power both theoretically and practically. Bourgeois democracy is no longer seen as 'bourgeois' but merely as democracy. Eurocommunism implies the withering away of Leninism and a transition, in theory, to a union of an economically, and socially radical, pluralistic parliamentary democracy" (p.9). Such a notion, however, had a short life. "Little was left of Eurocommunism . . . as a movement in Western Europe after 1982" (p.8). The concept of "Euroleft" took its place for a while in the 1980s, but by that time there was little left to distinguish the left from much of the mainstream.

For those who see a future in linking socialism to markets, see the debate around A. Nove's *The Economics of Feasible Socialism* (London: George Allen and Unwin, 1983). See also T. Bottomore, "Problems and Prospects of a Socialist Economy in Europe," *Rethinking Marxism*, 4,33 (Fall 1991).

See L. Panitch and R. Miliband, "The New World Order and The Socialist Agenda," in *The Socialist Register 1992: New World Order*, ed. R. Miliband and L. Panitch (London: Merlin Press, 1992), pp.22-23, for an argument favouring Keynesian economic reform. The lessons of Chile should have put paid to such a strategy; see Stallings, *Class Conflict*.

21. See B. Larschan and B.C. Brennan, "The Common Heritage of Mankind Principle in International Law," *Columbia Journal of International Law*, 21,2 (1983). This legal concept and the attempts to realize it are very significant for the future, but to date have been largely ignored by the left. For exceptions, see R. Bahro, *Building the Green Movement* (Worcester, Eng.: Billing and Sons, 1986); and D. Pepper, *Eco-Socialism: From Deep Ecology to Social Justice* (London: Routledge, 1993).

22. See Sara Parkin, *Green Parties: An International Guide* (London: Heretic Books, 1989).

23. L. Cheles, R. Ferguson, and M. Vaughan, eds., *Neo-Fascism in Europe* (London: Longman, 1991); S. Gunn, *Revolution of the Right: Europe's New Conservatives* (London: Pluto Press, 1989).

24. The issues central to many of these "new social movements" are usually limited to civil liberties or the particular interests of a subgroup or strata of society; where the implications of the issues are confined to a narrow group and/or solutions are feasible within the confines of the existing system, these movements meet with less counter-resistance.

25. See A. Escobar, *The Making of Social Movements in Latin America: Identity, Strategy and Democracy* (Boulder, Col.: Westview Press, 1992); P. Berryman, *Liberation Theology* (New York: Pantheon, 1987); B. Carr and S. Ellner, eds., *The Latin American Left: From the Fall of Allende to Perestroika* (Boulder, Col.: Westview Press, 1993); V. Shiva, "Ecology Movements in India," *Alternatives*, 11,2 (1986). On the democratization of these alternatives, see M. Albert and R. Hahnel, *The Political Economy of Participatory Economics* (Princeton, N.J.: Princeton University Press, 1991).

26. C. Deal, *The Greenpeace Guide to Anti-Environmental Organizations* (Berkeley, Cal.: Odian Press, 1993); C. Berlet, "Activists Face Increased Harassment," *The Humanist*, July/August 1991. See also Susan Faludi, *Backlash: The Undeclared War against Women* (New York: Vintage, 1992); M. French, *The War against Women* (New York: Summit Books, 1992); Gedicks, *New Resource Wars*; B. Glick, *War at Home: Covert Action against U.S. Activists and What We Can Do about It* (Boston: South End Press, 1989).

27. For a discussion of some of these alternatives, see G. McRobie, *Small Is Possible* (London: Sphere Books [1981], 1990); D.C. Korten, *Getting to the 21st Century: Voluntary Action and the Global Agenda* (West Hartford, Conn.: Kumarian Press, 1990); Paul Ekins, *A New World Order: Grassroots Movements for Global Change* (London: Routledge, 1992); M.H. Marchand, "Latin American Voices of Resistance: Women's Movements and Development Debates," in *The Global Economy as Political Space*, ed. S.J. Rosow, N. Inayatullah, and M. Rupert (Boulder, Col.: Lynne Rienne, 1994).

28. R. Heilbroner, "The Triumph of Capitalism," in *The New Yorker*, January 23, 1989. See also F. Fukuyama, "The End of History," *National Interest*, Summer 1989.

29. Hayek, *Road to Serfdom*, pp.92, 229.

VII Globalization as the Second Bourgeois Revolution

1. The principal source for this idea derives from the insightful article by B. Supple, "The State and the Industrial Revolution, 1700-1914," in *The Industrial Revolution*, ed. C.M. Cipolla (London: Collins/Fontana, 1973). Several more recent articles allude to Karl

Polanyi, *The Great Transformation: The Political and Economic Origins of Our Time* (Boston: Beacon Press, 1957), and discuss globalization as the "second great transformation." There is much merit in such an analogy, but none to my knowledge systematically draws out the parallel developments.

2. S. Pollard, *European Economic Integration 1815-1970* (London: Thames and Hudson, 1974), p.118.

3. Herman and Brodhead, *Demonstration Elections*. See also P. McSherry, "The Emergence of 'Guardian Democracy,' " *NACLA Report on the Americas*, 32,3 (November/December 1998).

4. C. Tilly, "The Emergence of Citizenship in France and Elsewhere," *International Review of Social History*, 40, Supplement 3 (1995).

5. M.B.E. Clarkson, ed., *The Corporations and Its Stakeholders* (Toronto: University of Toronto Press, 1998). There are many questions not dealt with in the literature concerning the stakeholder theory. For instance, who defines the stakeholder? Who determines the degree of participation? Who decides the agenda? Who chooses the stakeholder? What are the responsibilities to the stakeholder's constituency? This model of political expression contains enormous possibilities for arbitrary actions, decisions, and policies under the guise of "democracy" or "consultation."

6. The idea of society as a collectivity greater than the sum of individuals is not part of these models. There are only greater or lesser or "non"-stakeholders. It follows that in such models there is a circumscribed sense of social responsibility for the state or the corporation. With the KWS there were social rights and state social responsibility; now increasingly there is charity.

7. The demand for "liberal democracy" by the Chinese (Tiananmen Square, 1989) and other nations suffering dictatorship should be seen as a demand for the essence of democracy and not the reality of liberal democracy.

8. This was the lesson that the United States learned in Vietnam; the objectives in that war were too abstract and too obviously against the will of the Vietnamese to serve as convincing motives for a conscript armed forces, resulting by the end of the war in mutinies, revolts, and dissension among U.S. troops, not to mention the broader delegitimation of the U.S. political process.

9. S. Sheppard, "Foot Soldiers of the New World Order: The Rise of the Corporate Military," *New Left Review*, 228 (March/April 1998); D. Burton-Rose and W. Madsen, "Corporate Soldiers: The U.S. Government Privatizes the Use of Force," *Multinational Monitor*, March 1999.

10. J.U. Nef, *The Conquest of the Material World* (Cleveland: Meridian, 1967), p.349.

11. See *Business Week*, April 27, 1998.

12. Paradoxically, in this transitional stage nationalism can be both a barrier and means to the end of the nation-state. It is a barrier insofar as it functions to resist the encroachments of globalization; but it is a means when it is employed to dismantle or dismember nations that are not fully integrated. The dismemberment of the former Yugoslavia is an example of the use of petty nationalisms not only to destroy the nation-state but also to demolish its extensive collective property and to accommodate Western, in particular U.S., TNCs. Given globalization, not a single case of recent ethno-nationalist revival has the remotest chance of repeating the past growth of national integrity of the nation-state.

VIII A Critique of the Sceptics

1. D. Harvey, "Globalization in Question," *Rethinking Marxism*, 8,4 (Winter 1995), p.10.

2. Jim Davis, "Rethinking Globalisation," *Race and Class*, 40,2/3 (1998), p.45.

3. James Petras, "Globalization: A Socialist Perspective," *Canadian Dimension*, February 1999, pp.12-13. According to Petras:

"The globalization idea itself is suspect. In its most widely expressed usage, it argues for a universal incorporation to the world marketplace and the spread of benefits throughout the world. The empirical reality is neither universal incorporation nor the spread of benefits

. . . the globalist concept of interdependence is far less useful in understanding the world than the Marxist concept of imperialism. . . .

The rise of 'globalist ideology' is found originally in the business journals of the late 1960s and early 1970s. The major expansion and conquest of markets by the multi-nationals was described as globalization by business journalists searching for an alternative to the existing Marxist vocabulary, since they sought to present the process in a favorable light. . . . What emerged from the academic recycling of the concept was 'globaloney': the embellishment of the concept by linking it to what was called the third technological revolution and imputing to it a historical inevitability and degree of interdependence that was remote from reality. . . .

The ascendancy of imperialism is directly related to the circulation of the globaloney discourse and the eclipse of the revolutionary paradigm."

4. M. Wolf, "Global Opportunities," *Financial Times*, May 6, 1997. He writes: "Rather than damaging wages and throwing people out of work in advanced countries, globalization has been a force for prosperity in much of the world."

5. K.S. Kim, "Global Economic Integration: Issues and Challenges," in *Economic Effects of Globalization*, ed. J-R. Chen (Aldershot, Eng.: Ashgate, 1998), p.133. A recent report from the World Bank makes the same point: "World Bank Says Poverty Is Increasing," *The New York Times*, June 3, 1999.

6. P. Hirst and G. Thompson, *Globalization in Question* (Cambridge: Polity Press, 1997).

7. D. Gordon, "The Global Economy: New Edifice or Crumbling Foundations?" *New Left Review*, 168 (1988).

8. Harvey, "Globalization in Question," p.2; Paul Sweezy, "More (or Less) on Globalization," *Monthly Review*, September 1997, pp.1, 4.

9. E.M. Wood, "Capitalist Change and Generational Shifts," *Monthly Review*, October 1998, p.8, and (the earlier reference) *Monthly Review*, July/August, 1996, p.38; W.K. Tabb, "Progressive Globalism: Challenging the Audacity of Capital," *Monthly Review*, February 1999, p.1.

Such statements seem to be repeated everywhere: see B. Kagarlitsky, "The Challenge for the Left: Reclaiming the State," in *The Socialist Register 1999: Global Capitalism vs. Democracy*, ed. L. Panitch and C. Leys (Halifax: Fernwood Publishing, 1999). He writes (p.296): "Globalisation is nothing qualitatively new in the history of bourgeois society. Capitalism was born and grew to maturity as a world system."

10. K. Marx, *Capital*, vol. 3 (New York: International Publishers, 1967), p.333.

11. I. Wallerstein, "Theoretical Reprise," in *The Modern World-System: Capitalist Agriculture and the Origins of the European World-Economy in the Sixteenth Century* (New York: Academic Press, 1976). For another clear statement of his argument, see I. Wallerstein, "Three Instances of Hegemony in the History of the Capitalist World Economy," *International Journal of Comparative Sociology*, 24 (1983).

12. If we must make the case with Marx: "It is otherwise on the world market, whose integral parts are the individual countries." Marx, *Capital*, vol. 1, p.702.

13. C. Palloix, "The Self-Expansion of Capital on a World-Scale," *Review of Radical Political Economics*, 9,2 (Summer 1977).

14. E. Wood, "Modernity, Postmodernity, or Capitalism?" *Monthly Review*, July/August 1996, p.35.

15. Marx, *Capital*, vol. 1, pp.504ff.

16. The postwar expansion of the social sciences was primarily concerned with these changes; and the rapid growth of university training in science and technology reflected corporate demands.

17. For a good review of these issues, see J. Davis, T. Hirschl, and M. Stack, eds., *Cutting Edge: Technology, Information Capitalism and Social Revolution* (London: Verso, 1997).

18. A cautionary note on "technological determinism" should be introduced here. These scientific and technological changes take place in the context of the capitalist mode of production; they are changes whose impulse is the extraction of greater surplus value by

increasing the subordination of knowledge and skill and labour power, not to mention the forces of nature itself, to capital.

19. H. Overbeek and K. van der Pijl, "Restructuring Capital and Restructuring Hegemony," in *Restructuring Hegemony*, ed. Overbeek. This article does not make the case as broadly as made here, but it goes part of the way.

20. Some debate has taken place on these issues. See T. Morris-Suzuki, "Robots and Capitalism," *New Left Review*, 147 (September/October, 1984); I. Steedman, "Robots and Capitalism: A Clarification, *New Left Review*, 151 (May/June 1985); and T. Morris-Suzuki, "Capitalism in the Computer Age," in Davis, Hirschl, and Stack, *Cutting Edge*.

21. Y.-S. Hu, "Global or Stateless Corporations Are National Firms with International Operations," *California Management Review*, 34 (1992). This critical review of the definition of the TNC misses the point in that there is no alternative to the national legal delimitation of the corporation at the present time, but this does not mean that its operations and interests are any less transnational.

In a more quantitative way, the TNC may be defined by means of "the index of transnationality," as employed by UNCTAD, which is "calculated as the average of three ratios: foreign assets to total assets, foreign sales to total sales, and foreign employment to total employment." There are many shortcomings to the index, but it does provide a certain measure of "transnationality," and a means to follow trends and make comparisons. UNCTAD, *World Investment Report 1998: Trends and Determinants* (Geneva, 1999), p.4.

22. The Gulf War in 1991 and the war in Serbia in 1999 are good examples of the end of diplomacy or the end of war between nations (no more "formal declaration") and the rise of "police actions" at the global level. They amount to the assertion of the right of the prevailing property relations at the global level, just as previously the formation of the nation-state required such assertion across "national" territory.

23. Hirst and Thompson, *Globalization in Question*; L. Weiss, *The Myth of the Powerless State* (Cambridge: Polity Press, 1998).

24. See Weiss, *Myth of the Powerless State*, p.185. "While laying claim to being 'global' is seen as a mark of respectability for the modern firm, the number of genuinely transnational companies is rather small." Hirst and Thompson, *Globalization in Question*, p.195, write that "truly global TNCs are relatively few and that most successful multinational corporations continue to operate from distinct national bases."

25. Report of the Commission on Global Governance, *Our Global Neighborhood* (New York: Oxford University Press, 1995), p.172.

26. R. Kozul-Wright, "Transnational Corporations and the Nation State," in *Managing the Global Economy*, ed. J. Michie and J. Grieve-Smith (Oxford: Oxford University Press, 1995), p.146.

27. UNCTAD, *World Investment Report 1998*, p.1.

28. This case is best argued by R. Wade, "Globalization and Its Limits: Reports of the Death of the National Economy Are Greatly Exaggerated," in *National Diversity and Global Capitalism*, ed. S. Berger and R. Dore (Ithaca, N.Y.: Cornell University Press, 1996), pp.78-82. See also L. Weiss, "Globalization and the Myth of the Powerful State," *New Left Review*, 225 (September/October 1997), p.10; the same point is made in her book *Myth of the Powerless State*, p.185.

29. Davidow and Malone, *Virtual Corporation*; European Commission, "The Need for Strengthened International Coordination," 1998. This document outlines the current stage of development of a regulatory framework for a "global electronic marketplace." See also International Finance Corporation, "The Net Effect on the Nation State," Winter 1999, a short paper on how the "electronic economy will force change within the nation state."

30. UNCTAD, *World Investment Report 1998*, p.3; emphasis added.

31. Weiss, "Globalization and the Myth of the Powerful State," p.10.

32. UNCTAD, *World Investment Report 1998*, p.10.

33. Alliances of many sorts but especially on technology are far advanced. See P. Gugler and J. Dunning, "Technology-Based Cross-Border Alliances," in *Multinational Strategic Alliances*, ed. C. Relik (New York: International Business Press, 1993); and J. Howells, "The

Internationalization of R&D and the Development of Global Research Networks," *Regional Studies*, 24 (1990).

34. P. McMichael and D. Myhre, "Global Regulation versus the Nation-State: Agro-Food Systems and the New Politics of Capital," *Capital and Class*, 43,2 (1991); and P. McMichael and L. Raynolds, "Capitalism, Agriculture, and World Economy," in *Capitalism and Development*, ed. L. Sklair (London: Routledge, 1994).

35. OECD, *Globalization of Industry*, Overview and Sector Reports (Paris, 1996).

36. Report of the Commission on Global Governance, *Our Global Neighborhood*, pp.136ff.

37. A. Glyn and B. Sutcliffe, "Global but Leaderless? The New Capitalist Order," in *Socialist Register 1992*, ed. Miliband and Panitch, p.93.

38. M. Hoefnagels, "Growth of International Organizations since 1945," in *The Future of International Organization*, ed. R. Jutte and A. Grosse-Jutte (London: Frances Pinter, 1981).

39. C.F. Bergesten and C.R. Henning, *Global Economic Leadership and the Group of Seven* (Washington, D.C.: Institute for International Economics, 1996); and N. Bayne, "The G7 Summit and the Reform of Global Institutions," *Government and Opposition*, 3,4 (1995).

40. S. Sassen, "Towards a Feminist Analytics of the Global Economy," in S. Sassen, *Globalization and Its Discontents* (New York: The New Press, 1998), pp.96-97. The partisan use of international law on human rights abuse or crimes against humanity by the U.S. and U.K. governments in Yugoslavia does not obviate the point made here: increasingly individuals and groups are challenging the sovereign rights of states on grounds of international law. The charges against General Pinochet in the late 1990s are a case in point.

41. Prior to that war, the only significant example of world government was the League of Nations. Despite being a multinational organization, it retained the principle of the primacy of national sovereignty. This contrasts with the United Nations, which was intended to be a supranational body whose principle was the primacy of certain "universals" superior to the sovereignty of national states. Similarly, the other bodies and agencies mentioned, in principle or in operation, assert a primacy over their members or "clients."

42. J.N. Rosenau, "Governance, Order and Change in World Politics," in *Governance without Government: Order and Change in World Politics*, ed. J.N. Rosenau and E-O. Czempiel (New York: Cambridge University Press, 1992).

43. The 1999 U.S./NATO offensive in Yugoslavia goes far to reveal the nature of police actions in securing a world open to capital penetration. See M.T. Klare, "U.S. Aims to Win on All Fronts," *Le Monde Diplomatique*, May 1999.

44. The general thrust of the argument by Hirst and Thompson, *Globalization in Question*, suggests such possibilities. See the critical review by Hugo Radice, "The Question of Globalization," *Competition and Change*, 2 (1997).

45. C. Rude, "The End of the G-7 and Rising Imperialist Rivalry," *Monthly Review*, June 1997, p.51. Also (p.52): "Far from being powerless or irrelevant, the capitalist nation state, or more precisely, the conflict between the major capitalist nation states, is the reason for so much of the world economy's current instability."

46. For a good review of the "convergence" position, see R. Boyer, "The Convergence Hypothesis Revisited: Globalization but Still the Century of Nations?" in *National Diversity and Global Capitalism*, ed. Berger and Dore.

47. L. Panitch, " 'The State in a Changing World': Social-Democratic Global Capitalism?" in *Monthly Review*, October 1998. He writes (p.14): "States are the actual authors of globalization in so far as it is the changes they made in the rules governing capital movements, investment, currency exchange, and trade that permitted a new stage of global accumulation to come about."

Making the rules of governance does not necessarily make one the "author" of those changes in the sense of being the independent actor, which is the implication here. National states do not willingly introduce neo-liberal reforms. Some are obliged to introduce them on pain of loss of credit, confidence, trade, and commerce, and some do so because they are acting in the interests of "their" TNCs.

48. Much is made of the "competition state," referring to state strategies as a means of encouraging transnational investment or seeking advantages for national capital in the

global economy; but neither of these actions is to be confused with policies intended to maintain national integrity in the face of TNCs.

49. Weiss, "Globalization and the Myth of the Powerless State." She writes (p.23): "As the advantages of the coordinated market economies continue to be highlighted, potential adapters of the Asian model are more likely to emerge – at least in the Asian region – than blind followers of the neoliberal model of capitalism." No sooner was this published than the "Asian crisis" engulfed the region, bringing an end, among other things, to the so-called "Asian model," the "development state." What the author failed to see was the role of the global market, now visible in the "reconstruction" of these states, including the "reorganization" of Japan. The success of Japan was based on early initiatives in revamping mass production, access to the U.S. consumer market, export-driven production, protectionist policies and state assistance in capital accumulation, and reciprocal corporate shareholding. By the early 1990s all of this had begun to unravel. See C. Wood, *The End of Japan Inc.* (New York: Simon and Schuster, 1994).

50. E. Helleiner, "Post-Globalization: Is the Financial Liberalization Trend Likely to Be Reversed?" in *States against Markets: The Limits of Globalization*, ed. R. Boyer and D. Drache (London: Routledge, 1996), p.204.

51. Among dozens of writers from the early 1980s, see J.E. Spero, "Guiding Global Finance," in *International Economics and International Economic Policy*, ed. P. King (New York: McGraw-Hill, 1990).

52. Weiss, *Myth of the Powerless State*, p.11: "Globalization, which I argue is more appropriately termed 'internationalization.'"

53. Weiss, "Globalization and the Myth," p.23.

54. R. Palen, J. Abbot, and P. Deans, *State Strategies in the Global Political Economy* (London: Pinter, 1996), p.5.

55. Weiss, "Globalization and the Myth of the Powerless State," p.11.

56. Hirst and Thompson, *Globalization in Question*, p.2.

57. Numerous books and articles discuss the Third World debt crisis. See, for instance, C. Payer, *Lent and Lost: Foreign Credit and Third World Development* (London: Zed Books, 1991); S.B. MacDonald, M. Lindsay, and D.L. Crum, eds., *The Global Debt Crisis* (London: Pinter, 1990); and J. Schatan, *World Debt: Who Is to Pay?* (London: Zed Books, 1987).

58. F.H. Cardoso, "North-South Relations in the Present Context: A New Dependency?" in *The New Global Economy in the Information Age: Reflections on Our Changing World*, ed. M. Carnoy et al. (University Park: Pennsylvania State University Press, 1996), p.157; emphasis in original.

59. A. Hoogvelt, *Globalization and the Postcolonial World* (Baltimore: Johns Hopkins University Press, 1997), p.241.

60. Wm. Robinson, "Latin America and Global Capitalism," *Race and Class*, 40,2/3 (1998-99), p.116.

61. P. Belli, "Globalizing the Rest of the World," *Harvard Business Review*, July-August 1991.

62. R. Wade and F. Veneroso, "The Asian Crisis: The High Debt Model versus the Wall Street-Treasury-IMF Complex," *New Left Review*, 228 (March/April 1998). For another view of the end of the "Asian model," see M. Bernard, "East Asia's Tumbling Dominoes: Financial Crises and the Myth of The Regional Model," in *Socialist Register 1999*, ed. Panitch and Leys.

63. K. Lehman and A. Krebs, "Control of the World's Food Supply," in *The Case against the Global Economy*, ed. J. Mander and E. Goldsmith (San Francisco: Sierra Club Books, 1996).

64. A. Kimbrell, "Biocolonization," in *The Case against the Global Economy*, ed. Mander and Goldsmith, p.143. See also S. Biggs, "The Biodiversity Convention and Global Sustainable Development," in *Globalisation and the Third World*, ed. R. Kiely and P. Marfleet (London: Routledge, 1998).

IX The Question of Resistance and Alternatives

1. K. Marx and F. Engels, *The Communist Manifesto*, 1848. "Though not in substance, yet in

form, the struggle of the proletariat with the bourgeoisie is at first a national struggle. The proletariat of each country must . . . first of all settle matters with its own bourgeoisie."

2. Panitch, "State in a Changing World," p.14. He writes: "The contradictions of globalization are such today that the political and ideological leadership of the neoliberal right is increasingly vulnerable to challenge, as is evidenced in the fact that in fourteen of the fifteen European Union countries, social democrats now occupy governmental office." The point is difficult to understand given that national sovereignty in Europe is being systematically usurped by the EU and that most social-democratic parties around the world have abandoned the promotion of social reform and become advocates of neo-liberalism.

3. M. Bienefeld, "Capitalism and the Nation State in the Dog Days of the Twentieth Century," in *The Socialist Register 1994: Between Globalism and Nationalism*, ed. R. Miliband and L. Panitch (London: Merlin Press, 1994), p.122. He holds out a hope for something the national KWS promised: "What are the prospects for a restoration of national sovereignty? And, what are the prospects for a restoration of a positive humane nationalism?" It is not clear that such a nationalism ever existed and even less clear that it could be "restored" under the present circumstances.

4. Kim Moody, "Towards an International Social-Movement Unionism," *New Left Review*, 225 (September/October 1997).

5. B. Harrison, *Lean and Mean: The Changing Landscape of Corporate Power in the Age of Flexibility* (New York: Basic Books, 1994); see also various articles in M. Simai, *Global Unemployment* (Helsinki: United Nations University, 1995).

6. N. Harris, *The New Untouchables: Immigration and the New World Worker* (London: Penguin, 1995).

7. ILO, *World of Work*, 22 (1997). On p.24: "According to a recent ILO study, some 250 million children aged five to fourteen are working. About half, or 120 million, work full-time, while the remaining children struggle to combine work with schooling or other non-economic activities. The figure of 250 million working children is considered to be an underestimate."

8. M. Mies, *Patriarchy and Accumulation on a World Scale* (London: Zed Books, 1998).

9. There really is no alternative at present to the coming of the global market, just as there was no alternative to the bourgeois revolutions and the making of the integrated national markets in the eighteenth and nineteenth centuries (except in the form of reaction by precapitalist forces or the theoretical possibility of moving from precapitalist co-operative property to postcapitalist socialized property). Resistance to it must include global demands and can only succeed by understanding the contradictions at that level.

10. See K. Kumar, "Civil Society: An Enquiry into the Usefulness of an Historical Term," *British Journal of Sociology*, 44,3 (1993). Here is a good review of the "career" of the concept, but the article fails to address the point that civil society can only be understood in relation to the state.

11. On the MAI, see A. Jackson and M. Sanger, eds., *Dismantling Democracy: The Multilateral Agreement on Investment (MAI) and Its Impact* (Ottawa: Canadian Centre for Policy Alternatives, 1998).

12. The struggle in Chiapas is different insofar as it has been framed as a conflict between countervailing peoples rights and corporate rights as advanced by NAFTA-inspired neo-liberal policies.

13. To assume that the liberal democracy of the industrial nation-state is actually democracy and not a political structure of compromise resting on certain historical conditions is an idea that moves much of the left to defend national political systems as genuine but perhaps flawed democracy or to suggest that the same political structures should be instituted at the global level.

14. There is a growing body of literature attempting to address these issues. See A. Breitenfellner, "Global Unionism: A Potential Player," *International Labour Review*, 136 (1997); Kim Moody, *Workers in a Lean World: Unions in the International Economy* (London: Verso, 1997); J. Smith, C. Chatfield, and R. Pagnucco, eds., *Transnational Social Movements and Global Politics* (Syracuse, N.Y.: Syracuse University Press, 1997).

Index

AGMV
MARQUIS
Québec, Canada
2000